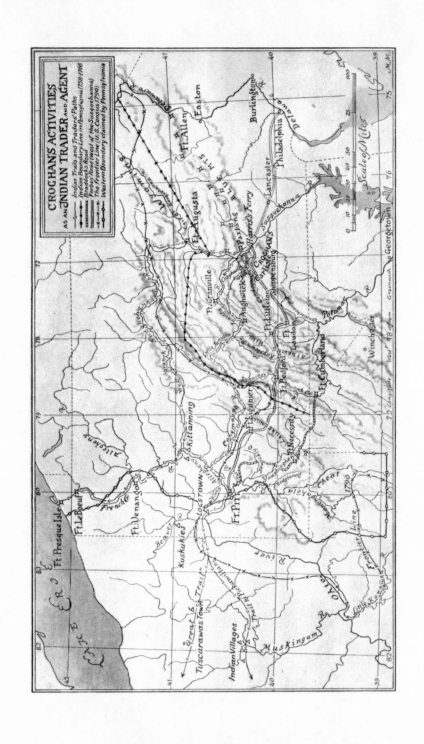

CROGHAN'S ACTIVITIES
AS AN INDIAN TRADER AND AGENT

Indian Trails and Traders' Paths
Indian Boundary Line in Pennsylvania 1758-1768
Braddock's Road
Forbes Road (West of the Susquehanna)
The Frontier Line (U.S. Census 1790)
Western Boundary claimed by Pennsylvania

Scale of Miles
10 20 30 40 50   75   100

George Croghan
and
the Westward Movement
1741-1782

by

Albert T. Volwiler

with maps

AMS PRESS
NEW YORK

Reprinted from the edition of 1926, Cleveland
First AMS EDITION published 1971
Manufactured in the United States of America

International Standard Book Number: 0-404-06779-4

Library of Congress Catalog Number: 77-137274

AMS PRESS INC.
NEW YORK, N.Y. 10003

TO THE MEMORY OF
MY MOTHER AND FATHER

Contents

Illustrations

Preface

George Croghan was the leading exponent of the expansion of the Anglo-Saxon race into the Ohio region during the generation before 1775. He was preëminent as an Indian trader, an Indian agent, a land speculator, and a projector of inland colonies. His trading houses were scattered throughout the upper Ohio region and the activities which radiated from them constituted one of the chief causes of the French aggression in the Ohio valley from 1749 to 1754. To help stem this aggression, Croghan was employed as an Indian agent, first by his colony, Pennsylvania, and then by the British Empire. His immediate superior, Sir William Johnson, relied upon him to conduct the most important and delicate negotiations with the Indians. The westward advance of the English settler's frontier during Croghan's generation is graphically illustrated by the shifting of his place of residence. In the 1740's this was located near Carlisle, Pennsylvania; during the next decade he moved westward forty miles to Aughwick; and after 1758, he made his home at Pittsburg.

Croghan was one of the first Englishmen to grasp a clear vision of the future greatness of the forest-clad kingdom beyond the Appalachians. This vision came to dominate all of his later activities and it exerted great influence upon other colonial leaders and upon imperial officials. He was one of the leaders of that group which, during the period from 1763 to 1775,

organized great land companies to develop the newly
won territory and which planned to establish the colony
of Vandalia.   These interests exerted an important influence upon constitutional development during the
period from 1775 to 1789.   From one point of view,
the history of the United States until the twentieth
century is the story of a long struggle for the possession
of a continent.   In this struggle, George Croghan was
one of the leaders of the vanguard of that mighty host
which made the great march across the continent and
carved an empire out of an uncharted wilderness.
His place in American history can be more correctly
estimated if in studying Indian affairs, the emphasis
is placed upon normal trade conditions and land relations, rather than upon local wars with their lurid and
heroic episodes.   The latter point of view pervades
too much of American historiography.

In the preparation of this work I am especially indebted to the courtesy and stimulating helpfulness of
Professor St. George L. Sioussat of the University of
Pennsylvania.   For helpful suggestions I am indebted
to Professors Clarence W. Alvord, of the University
of Minnesota, Clarence E. Carter, of Miami University, William V. Pooley, of Northwestern University,
Albert E. McKinley, of the University of Pennsylvania, and to Dean Herman V. Ames of the University
of Pennsylvania.   Courteous assistance was given by
Dr. Thomas L. Montgomery and Miss Jennie C. Wylie
of the Historical Society of Pennsylvania; Mr. H. H.
Shenk, Custodian of the Public Records, Pennsylvania
State Library; Mr. Victor H. Paltsits of the Division
of Manuscripts, New York Public Library; Mr. Peter
Nelson of the New York State Library; Dr. Richard

E. Day and Dr. James Sullivan, of the New York State Historian's office; Mr. Francis J. Audet of the Public Archives of Canada at Ottawa; Misses Louise P. Kellogg and Alice Nunns of the Wisconsin Historical Society; Mr. John C. Fitzpatrick of the Division of Manuscripts, Library of Congress; and Mr. William V. Byars of St. Louis. Mr. Simon Gratz of Philadelphia and Mr. Anderson Gratz of St. Louis very generously placed at my disposal materials from their private libraries. It is impossible to express adequately the debt I owe to my wife, Ada White Volwiler, for the encouragement and untiring aid which she rendered at all stages of the work. As Harrison Fellow in History, 1921-1922, and as Harrison Research Fellow, 1922-1923, I was materially assisted by the generosity of Dr. Charles C. Harrison, former Provost of the University of Pennsylvania, who established the George Leib Harrison Foundation to encourage scientific study and research.

ALBERT T. VOLWILER

University of Pennsylvania

The Indian Trader, 1741-1754

The mainspring which kept the Indian trade in North America in operation during the eighteenth century was the demand for furs and skins in western Europe. The customs and styles of dress among European nobles and courtiers, ecclesiastical and university officials, and wealthy burghers created the demand for furs; the demand for skins rested chiefly upon the needs of the more humble classes of society. A second great market for furs and skins was in China. Until towards the close of the period under consideration this market only indirectly affected the Indian trade by absorbing the cheaper grade of Russian furs and skins and thus decreasing the supply available for western Europe. By the time of the American Revolution, however, a considerable number of American furs and skins were sent from London to China, either through Russia or in the ships of the East India Company, thus fore-shadowing the trading ventures of John Jacob Astor and Stephen Girard.[1]

From the earliest days of the Greeks and Romans until the sixteenth century the people of central Asia and western Europe were supplied with furs and skins from the great northern plains of Eurasia. Here the Russian trader's frontier was gradually pushed eastward until in the latter part of the eighteenth century it was moving rapidly down the western coast of North

---

[1] Papers relating to Canada, 1692-1792, George Chalmers Coll.

America.[2]   The furs and skins from the second great region of supply — northern North America — had to compete with those from Russia and Siberia in the markets of Europe.   So successfully was this done that the great fur marts were shifted from Vienna, Danzig, and Lübeck to London, Amsterdam, and Paris.   The quest for, furs took the place of the quest for gold, silver, and precious stones in luring the white man to penetrate into the vast unknown regions north of Mexico.

If the trade in furs and skins is looked at from the point of view of the uncivilized native who could furnish peltry and hides, one finds equally strong economic forces influencing his conduct.   In his estimation of values, based upon the laws of supply and demand, the exchange of a fine beaver pelt for a single sharp knife was a great bargain.   The mutual immense profits of the trade in furs and skins and other irresistible economic forces involved, led both savages and civilized men to desire to establish and maintain trading relations in spite of the heavy risks to life and property to all concerned in such trade.

The desire to control the lucrative trade in furs and skins with the natives in North America was one of the numerous causes for the great rivalry of England and France during the seventeenth and eighteenth centuries.   Towards the close of the former century they entered upon an important trade war in North America for the control of this traffic which, unlike their military conflicts, never ceased until after 1763.   In it the native tribes were mere tools and pawns which both sides exploited.

---

[2] The following quotation is suggestive for the colonization of North America: "Der Zobel [sable] hat die Erschliessung und Eroberung Sib-

The trader's frontier in this conflict was long, wide, and constantly shifting. During the second quarter of the eighteenth century French and English traders met in the region between Lake Superior and Hudson's Bay, but here there were such vast regions to exploit that for a long time their rivalry was only serious to those immediately involved. Similar competition took place in the wilderness between New England and Canada, but here also the rivalry was not serious, for there were no longer rich fur fields to exploit in this region nor were there strategic lines of communication to threaten. The Indian country between New York and New France controlled great arteries of commerce; here, however, the English forces of expansion, which in earlier decades had begun to penetrate the region around Lake Michigan, soon lost vitality. Trading relations were established whereby Albany traders gave up their dreams of trading directly with the far West in return for the opportunity of exchanging English manufactured goods for French furs near at home. In contrast to the Indian traders of Pennsylvania, those of New York generally did not penetrate far into the interior to seek furs and skins at each Indian village, but utilized the Iroquois as middlemen to bring furs and skins to them at such posts as Albany and Oswego. In the extreme south, Carolina traders had once planned to develop the distant trans-Mississippi country and even the Ohio and Illinois regions. By about 1725, the French had limited the activities of the English until their trade with tribes which bor-

iriens veranlasst; er hat auch einen grossen Teil der Kosten mit seiner Haut bezahlt." – Klein, Joseph: *Der Sibirische Pelzhandel und seine Bedeutung für die Eroberung Sibiriens,* i. Cf. Golder, Frank A.: *Russian Expansion on the Pacific, 1641-1850.*

dered the Gulf of Mexico or the Mississippi had almost ceased.[3]

During the generation preceding 1754, the most
dynamic and significant phase of the Anglo-French
rivalry in the Indian trade was in the central and upper
Ohio valley and in the region south of Lake Erie.   In
preceding decades a few Carolina, New York, and perhaps Virginia, traders had reached this region, but
their visits were sporadic and not consistently followed
up.   Later, Pennsylvania traders began to develop consistently its rich trading possibilities.   The expansion
of the field of their activities was based upon a sufficient
supply of low-priced merchandise and it was the result
of their own initiative and resourcefulness; not until
their influence had about reached its height did their
government aid them.   Meanwhile, the French had
been moving eastward into this region.   They shifted
their main line of communication between the Great
Lakes and the Mississippi from the Fox-Wisconsin
route to the Chicago-Illinois route and then to the
Maumee-Wabash route.   To control the latter, Fort
Ouiatenon was erected by New France, about 1720, at
the head of navigation for large canoes on the Wabash,
and Fort Vincennes by Louisiana, in 1731, on the lower
Wabash.   At times, a small fort on the Maumee was
maintained which, with Detroit, completed this line of
defense against English penetration.   The region east
of this line was left open to the English.   The first
"Winning of the West" by the Anglo-Saxon followed;
in almost every important Indian village in this region
one or more Pennsylvania traders were to be found.

    [3] Cf. Verner W. Crane: "The Tennessee River as the Road to Carolina",
in *Miss. Valley Hist. Rev.*, III, 3ff., and Crane: "The Southern Frontier in
Queen Anne's War", in *Am. Hist. Rev.*, XXIV, 379ff.

The growth of their influence is well shown by the following incidents. In 1707, Governor Evans of Pennsylvania feared the influence of French traders even east of the lower Susquehanna; he personally led a party thither to capture Nicole Godin, a trader of French birth, who was suspected of aiding the enemy. The governor reported to the provincial council that after he had captured Nicole, "having mounted Nicole upon a horse, and tied his legs under the Belly," he "brought him a Prisoner to Philadia, in the Common Gaol of which he now lies." [4] Less than half a century later, in the early fifties, Paul Pierce, a Pennsylvania trader, had "4,000 Weight of summer skins taken at another town on Wabasha. . . " [5]

These incidents illustrate the fact that the Pennsylvania traders had assumed the aggressive and, in spite of the Appalachian barrier, had pushed the trader's frontier 500 miles westward in less than a half century; in 1750, this line was near the Wabash and Maumee rivers, nearly 500 miles in advance of the settler's frontier in Pennsylvania, which was just starting to move up the Juniata valley and to cross the Blue Mountains. Nor had the expansive force of this movement been exhausted when it reached the Wabash and Maumee; it began to cross this line – a weak barrier at best – and move on towards the Mississippi, bringing anxiety into the hearts of the best French officials, who felt the potential power of English influence even in the distant Illinois country. [6] A con-

---

[4] Gov. Evans' journal and report, in *Pa. Col. Rec.*, ii, 385, 390.

[5] Pierce's affidavit of losses, in Ohio Co. MSS., i, 32.

[6] In 1742, Bienville reported home that the Illinois tribes were restless and that some of them had gone east to meet English traders. – C 13A, 27: 81-84. (Archives Nationales, Paris.) Vaudreuil reported in 1744 and in 1745 recommending the establishment of a fort on the lower Ohio to limit

temporary map legend described the attitude of the Indians in Illinois as follows: "Illinois mostly inclined to the French at the Treaty of Utrecht and to the English at that of Aix-la-Chapelle." [7]

Thus by 1750, the English were ready to take control of the Wabash-Maumee route, the best line of communication between New France and Louisiana, and they threatened French dominion in the West. When, during King George's War, the highest French officials considered the danger of this quiet penetration of English power, they determined at any cost to secure sole and absolute control of the entire Ohio country. The Pennsylvania Indian traders were thus chiefly responsible for the immediate opening of the French and Indian War.

Their aggressive westward push during the period of 1730-1775, was aided by the moral and financial support of the wealthy merchants and colonial officials in Philadelphia. During this period Philadelphia had become the largest town in all America. Its virile energy and the many-sidedness of its interests were typified in the life of its greatest citizen, Benjamin Franklin. Its large and profitable commerce, firmly buttressed upon a prosperous and rich agricultural region resulted in the accumulation of surplus capital, part of which was available for projects to exploit and

the activities of the English traders and to keep control of the Kickapoo and Mascoutens. – c 13A, 28: 245-250 and c 13A, 29: 69. An official of Louisiana reported in 1750 that the influence of an English establishment on the Rivière de la Roche (Great Miami) extended even to the Illinois country and that it should be broken up. – c 13A, 34: 321-323. In 1751, thirty-three Piankashaw Indians (an important tribe living west of the Wabash whose friendship was to play an important part in Croghan's activities) appeared among the French settlements in Illinois to start an Indian uprising. – Alvord, Clarence W.: *Centennial History of Illinois*, I, 234.

[7] Gibson, John: Map of the Middle British Colonies in America, 1758.

develop the vast wilderness beyond the settler's frontier.

The man who played the most prominent part in this highly important and significant phase of the westward movement of Anglo-Saxon civilization was George Croghan. Of his early life and the more personal side of his career we know but little. No portrait of him has been discovered [8] and in the course of this investigation, not a single reference to his wife was found; the date and exact place of his birth are also unknown. We know that his early life was spent in Dublin, Ireland.[9] The education which he there received was so meager that he was pronounced illiterate by Bouquet.[10] One finds the spelling in Croghan's letters amusing, provided it is not necessary to decipher many of them.[11] He migrated to America in 1741.[12]

Because he came from Dublin he was charged during the French and Indian War with being a Roman

---

[8] In Joseph S. Walton's *Conrad Weiser and the Indian Policy of Pennsylvania* there is a picture of Colonel George Croghan, famous in the War of 1812, taken in a U.S. Army uniform, which is erroneously ascribed to the earlier George Croghan.

[9] Gov. Morris to Gov. Sharpe, Jan. 7, 1754, in *Pa. Arch.*, II, 114.

[10] Bouquet to Gen. Gage, Dec. 22, 1764, in Bouquet Coll., A 23-2: 464. No evidence has been found to prove the statement that Croghan was educated at Dublin University, made by C. R. Williams in an article on George Croghan in the *Ohio Arch. and Hist. Pub.*, XII, 381, and by L. E. Keeler in an article on the Croghan Celebration in the same publication, XVI, 8.

[11] The legibility of Croghan's letters varies greatly. The following postscript to a letter to Peters, dated Sept. 26, 1758, suggests one cause of such variation: "You 'l Excuse boath Writing and peper, and guess at my Maining, fer I have this Minnitt 20 Drunken Indians about me . . ." – *Pa. Arch.*, III, 544. Croghan's own name was spelled in the following ways by his contemporaries: Croane, Croghan, Croughan, Cremche, Crohan, Crogan, Croughean, Grahoon, and Grochan.

[12] Various dates from 1740 to 1747 are given by writers on Pennsylvania history. The date 1741 is established by an affidavit which Croghan made before the Board of Trade in London on July 27, 1764, to aid the Penns in their case against Connecticut's land claims. – Wyoming Controversy, V, 71-75, Penn MSS. A copy of this affidavit, not corrected by Croghan, is found in Penn Land Grants, 1681-1806, pages 205-209.

Catholic.[13] We know, however, that he was an Episcopalian. His signature, along with those of Robert
Callender and Thomas Smallman, his close associates
in the Indian trade, was attached to a petition in 1765
from the handful of Episcopalians in the frontier town
of Carlisle, Pennsylvania, to their provincial assembly.
It asked for the authorization of a lottery for the benefit
of ten Episcopal churches; the one at Carlisle was to
receive £200 to aid its building fund.[14] In 1769, Croghan wrote to Sir William Johnson to recommend an
Episcopal rector for an appointment, modestly adding,
"for tho I love ye Church very well I know I ought
Nott to Medle with Church Matters." [15] When Croghan died his funeral was held in St. Peter's Episcopal
Church in Philadelphia.[16]

These facts are significant. Evidently Croghan was
not a typical Scotch-Irishman, for he had the religion
of the English Pale. The fact that he was interested
in a church at once puts him on a higher plane than
most Indian traders who cared nothing for either
church or religion. Being a member of the Church of
England helped him to establish closer relations with
the Penns and with many British officials. In the
normal conduct of his business and in his official duties
Croghan was not often near any minister or church.
Even at Fort Pitt, where he usually had his headquarters from 1758 to 1777, there was no organized
church till after his death.[17] Army chaplains were
sometimes stationed there and missionaries came to

---

[13] Gov. Sharpe to Gov. Morris, Dec. 27, 1754, In *Md. Arch., 1888*, 153.

[14] *Pa. Stat. at Large*, VI, 382.

[15] Croghan to Johnson, Nov. 16, 1769, in *Doc. Hist. of N.Y.*, IV, 419.

[16] William Powell's account with the Croghan Estate, 1804, MSS., Register
of Wills, Philadelphia.

[17] Dahlinger, Charles W.: *Pittsburgh: A Sketch of its Early Social
Life*, 9-10.

tarry a few days. The latter were usually welcomed by Croghan, at whose home they frequently dined. One of these in describing his visit to Croghan in 1772, writes that the latter presented him with "a bear's skin to sleep on, a belt of wampum to present to the Indians, and 60 pounds of biscuit to supply me on my journey."[18] Croghan's religion was reflected in his daily conduct in business and in office to about the same extent as is religion in the life of the average business man or office-holder of today.[19]

Croghan had a number of relatives in America who had a common interest in developing the great West of their day and to whom he was a guide and leader. William Trent was his brother-in-law, Edward Ward his half brother, Thomas Smallman his cousin, John Connolly his nephew, and William Powell and Daniel Clark his kinsmen.[20] Clark emigrated from Ireland and became a clerk to Croghan; after the Revolution he became the most prominent American in New Orleans. A Mohawk Indian daughter of Croghan became the wife of the famous Mohawk chief, Joseph Brant.[21] His only white child, Susannah, for whom he had a tender regard which was reciprocated by her,[22]

[18] Jones, Rev. David: *Diary,* 21; McClure, Rev. David: *Diary,* 46, 101.

[19] This statement is based upon a study of Croghan's entire life. E. W. Hassler's statement in *Old Westmoreland: a history of Western Pennsylvania during the Revolution,* 10, that "He was an Irishman by birth and an Episcopalian by religion, when he permitted religion to trouble him," is probably an incorrect deduction from the general characterization of Indian traders.

[20] Croghan's will, Register of Wills, Philadelphia.

[21] Brant MSS., 1G2, 1F24, 13F103; Thomson, Charles: *Alienation of the Delaware and Shawanese, etc.,* 178. Croghan, like so many English traders and agents and like the French but unlike the English settlers, was willing to cross his blood with the Indians. The consequent effects upon Indian relations offer interesting opportunities for sociological reflections.

[22] Croghan's will; Trent to Mrs. Prevost, Aug. 21, 1775, in Hist. Soc. of Pa., Coll.

was born in 1750 at Carlisle and died in 1790. At the age of fifteen she was married to Lieutenant Augustine Prevost, son of the British general of the same name, with whom he is sometimes confused. To them twelve children were born at various places from Quebec to Jamaica inclusive, six of whom survived infancy and became the chief heirs of Croghan.[23] Aaron Burr was related to Prevost by marriage and served as his attorney; Burr's interest in the West may therefore have emanated from Croghan.

The immigrant who went west from Philadelphia during the decade 1740 to 1750, as did Croghan, would find that soon after he had left the Quaker city behind, the German element became predominant and that as he approached the frontier the hardy Scotch-Irish in turn composed the majority of the population. The road which he followed would take him through Lancaster, the largest inland town in the British colonies; from it one important road led through Paxtang Township, which bordered the eastern bank of the Susquehanna in the vicinity of the present city of Harrisburg. At this place the river is not deep, but is a mile wide. John Harris had settled here and was operating one of the most important ferries which crossed it; Harris's Ferry is shown on all contemporary maps of Pennsylvania.

The newcomer was now close to the settler's frontier

---

[23] Brant MSS., 16F65, 16F66, 16F72; Draper MSS., 16F76. Dennis Crohan was an intimate friend but no relation to Croghan. – Etting Coll., Misc. MSS., I, 110. General William Croghan of the Revolution, who married a sister to George Rogers Clark and helped develop the state of Kentucky, was an intimate personal friend of George Croghan. – Byars, William V.: *Barnard and Michael Gratz*, 175, 183, 185, 194. Colonel George Croghan, son of William Croghan and hero of the War of 1812, is often confused with the elder George Croghan. Some of the descendants of the Kentucky Croghans recognize a relationship to the elder Croghan while others deny it.

line. The region across the river towards Maryland
had been purchased from the Iroquois in 1736, though
squatters in this region were legally recognized since
January 14, 1734, when the first "Blunston License"
was issued to allow settlement before the Indian claims
had been purchased.[24] The Juniata valley with the
region south of it extending to the Maryland border
was not purchased till 1754. In the preceding decade
the most distant lands open to settlement in the province were in the level and fertile Cumberland valley.
This lay beyond Harris's Ferry, on either side of the
winding Condogwinet River, which empties into the
Susquehanna, and of the Conococheague River, which
flows in the opposite direction and empties into the
Potomac. South Mountain, later made famous by
Robert E. Lee, forms a wall on the southeast for this
physiographic unit. From its crest one can see on a
clear day the opposite rampart, North Mountain, also
known as the Kittatinny or the Blue Mountains. Beyond them in the primeval forest lay the Indian country, but to get to its most attractive regions it was necessary to cross range after range of the mountain barrier.
This was done by the venturesome Indian traders of the
province. When the fur fields east of the mountains
had been exhausted, with no enticing possibilities to
the north or south, the traders were presented with the
alternative of either settling down to a more prosaic
life, or of somehow getting across the barrier to the
far western country. A contemporary describes the
result of their decision as follows: "Between 4 and 10

[24] Samuel Blunston was granted a special commission on January 11,
1734, authorizing him to issue special licenses upon which patents could
be obtained after the Indian claims had been purchased. The original list
of licenses granted, ending on October 31, 1737, has been recently found
in the Pennsylvania State Library.

degrees of Longitude west from Philadelphia there is
a spacious country which we call Allegenny from the
name of a River which runs thro' it and is the main
branch of the Mississippi. . . In this country all
our Indian trade centers . . . the most of our return is Deer Skins. The Indian traders have had
great credit with the merchants." [25]

Various routes across the mountains had been prepared for the traders by nature, by the buffalo, and by
the Indian; they have since become great arteries of
commerce followed by trunk line railroads. The least
important and most difficult of these followed the West
branch of the Susquehanna. Another route passed
through Shippensburg and Bedford, utilizing the
Raystown branch of the Juniata; from 1758, when
Forbes constructed the road which bore his name, until
after 1830, when the railroad and canal became important, this was one of the most important routes to the
West; as a turnpike it was the great rival of the Cumberland Road. The oldest and most important route
to the West during the decade, 1740 to 1750, followed
the Juniata and Conemaugh (Kishkimentas) rivers.[26]
It was almost always followed by the traders before
1754 in going to the West and somewhat less frequently
on their return. Shortly before 1754, Pennsylvania
traders in returning from the West were beginning to
follow the fourth great route across the mountains,
which utilized the Monongahela, Will's Creek, Water
Gap, and the Potomac.[27] When they had once reached

---

[25] Evans, Lewis: A Brief Account of Pennsylvania, 1753, in Papers
relating to Pa., Car., etc., Du Simitiere Coll.

[26] In 1855, the traces left by thousands upon thousands of warriors and
packhorses which had traveled this trail for years were still plainly visible.
— Jones, U. J.: History of Juniata Valley, 135.

[27] Washington to Bouquet, Aug. 2, 1758, in Writings of George Washington, II, 62; Pa. Col. Rec., V, 607.

the latter near the end of Cumberland valley they found available a "great road" recently finished, leading through the valley and connecting at Harris's Ferry with the great highway to Philadelphia.[28]

To traverse one of the great routes from the Susquehanna to the Ohio required about fourteen days. Until after the French and Indian War transportation by wagon stopped at the mountains; from there on only Indian trails were available. These passed up and down rugged mountains. He who traveled over them was shut in between impervious walls of trunks, boughs, and matted thickets and passed under a canopy of leaves and branches. At times, glimpses could be had of forest-covered mountain ridges stretching far away in all directions to a misty horizon. To the Pennsylvania trader the packhorse therefore took the place which the canoe occupied among the *coureurs de bois*; even after he was across the mountains and beyond the Ohio he preferred it to the canoe. Usually two or more men went with a packhorse train, which seldom consisted of more than twenty horses, each carrying about one hundred and fifty pounds on their pack saddles. They followed the trail in single file with one man in front and one in the rear. At night the horses were turned loose to secure their forage as best they could. Bells were fastened to them to aid in finding them again. A packhorse equipped with saddle, surcingles, and bells was valued at from £7 to £25. From twenty to thirty per cent was normally added to Philadelphia prices for the cost of transporting goods by wagon and packhorse to the Ohio.[29]

[28] *Pa. Col. Rec.*, VI, 302; Evans: Map of the Middle British Colonies, in *Pa. Arch., 3rd ser., Appendix to Volumes* I-X; Instructions of Gov. Hamilton to N. Scull and T. Cookson, surveyors, in *Early Hist. of Carlisle*, (1841), I, 6.

[29] Ohio Co. MSS., I, 7; *Md. Arch., 1889*, 126; *Pa. Col. Rec.*, V, 294, 295,

The chief Indian tribes with whom the Pennsylvanians traded were the Six Nations, who claimed
dominion over the entire Ohio region and several hundred of whose representatives were scattered along
the Ohio and known as Mingoes; the Delawares, living around the upper Ohio; the Shawnee, dwelling
along the Ohio and Scioto; the Wyandots or Hurons,
inhabiting the territory south of Lake Erie; and the
Miami or Twightwee, living on the Big Miami and
beyond.

To them were brought rum; guns, gunpowder, lead,
flints, tomahawks and vermilion; strouds, especially
those of a "Deep Blue or Lively Red," blanketing,
matchcoating, linen and calicoes "of the brightest and
flourishing collours"; wampum; lace, thread, gartering, ribbons; women's stockings, "red, yellow, and
green" preferred, and all kinds of ready-made clothing; knives of all kinds, brass and tin kettles, traps,
axes, hoes, brass wire, files, awls, needles, buttons, and
combs; jewsharps, bells, whistles, looking glasses, rings,
and silver jewelry of all kinds.[30]

These goods, with the exception of rum, came principally from England. For them were bartered deer,
elk, buffalo, and bear skins; beaver, raccoon, fox, cat,
muskrat, mink, fisher, and other furs; food supplies
and sometimes personal services. The annual value
of this trade was about £40,000.[31]

This trade involved a connected chain of credits
based in the end upon English capital. The English

490, 498; *idem,* IX, 495; Evans, Lewis: *Analysis of a Map of the Middle
British Colonies,* 25.

[30] Lists prepared under Croghan's supervision are found in Ohio Co.
MSS., I, 37 and in C. O., 5: 61. Cf. *Wis. Hist. Coll.,* XVIII, 245; Byars; *B. and
M. Gratz,* 114.

[31] *Pa. Gazette,* Sept. 26, and Apr. 25, 1754.

manufacturer or merchant sold to the Philadelphia merchant on credit; he in turn advanced the goods to the larger traders and they to their employees; finally, it also became more and more customary to trust the Indians with goods in order that they could hunt successfully. If, therefore, something should happen to the Indian so that he failed to bring in skins and pelts, bankruptcy and financial stringency would follow all along the line.[32] Certain merchants in London, Bristol, Philadelphia, and Lancaster specialized in this trade. The firm of Shippen and Lawrence and the Jewish firm of Levy, Franks, and Simon, with whom the Gratzs were later connected, are examples of those groups of Pennsylvania merchants that served as factors in the Indian trade. They were usually composed of one or more residents in Philadelphia and a western representative in Lancaster. The former often had his own ships and imported suitable goods from England; under his management the skins and furs for export were sorted, examined for moth, and finally packed for shipment; the representative in Lancaster usually had charge of warehouses where trader's supplies were kept and where furs and skins were temporarily stored. Frequently these groups were "concerned" with a prominent Indian trader in active charge of a number of ordinary traders. Aside from these regular partnerships and joint-stock companies these men were often "concerned" together in an "adventure;" i. e., when a particular business opportunity presented itself they would pool a part of their capital, goods, or personal services, sometimes without even signing articles of agreement, and then divide the profits or losses in pro-

---

[32] Cf. Gov. Wright to Board of Trade, Dec. 29, 1754, in Bd. of Tr. Pap., Plantations General, XXII, 163.

portion.   Such a business system was especially favorable to the young man or the newcomer with little more than his personal services to contribute.   Such groups, especially when united, were an important factor in trade, land speculation, and politics, particularly in relation to the West.

It was into such an environment that Croghan entered soon after coming to America.   Shortly after 1741 we find him on the frontier in the lower Condogwinet valley, then organized as Pennsborough Township of Lancaster County.   Here he soon acquired over 1,200 acres of land.   It was on a 354 acre tract, located but five miles from Harris's Ferry, Pennsylvania's gateway to the West, that Croghan established his home.[33]   This he made his headquarters during approximately his first ten years in America.   It was strategically located with reference to all of the routes across the mountains; the newly-discovered and best approach to the Juniata route passed by his home and crossed the Blue Mountains through the best gap in the vicinity.   This soon appeared on all contemporary maps as "Croghan's Gap." [34]   His home, "Croghan's," likewise appeared on these maps along with Carlisle and Shippensburg, as being one of the three landmarks on the important road through Cumberland valley. It soon became one of the places where traders and emissaries stopped on their way to and from the western country.   It also served as a convenient meeting-place for whites and Indians.

Croghan made this place the eastern terminus for his operations as an Indian trader.   It served as his home for a few weeks in each year and provided food and

---

[33] *Pa. Arch.,* II, 135; *Pa. Arch., 3d ser., Appendix to Volumes* I-X.

[34] Today it is called Sterret's Gap and is still important, being utilized by a state highway.

shelter for employees and for his packhorses. Here they could recuperate after their fatiguing journeys over the mountains. Log warehouses provided storage for skins, furs, and Indian goods. On an adjacent tract of 171 acres he had an extensive tanyard where an additional value could be given to the deerskins which he brought out of the West.[35]

Croghan was probably able to acquire and develop these properties through his profits from the Indian trade. In all likelihood he came to America with little or no capital, but fortunately for him, business methods did not require much for the Indian trade. This trade appealed to his restless spirit and adventurous nature. He entered into it almost immediately upon his arrival in 1741.[36] In 1744, 1747, and probably in other years, he was licensed as an Indian trader.[37] His success is graphically shown by the fact that only five years after he had left his European environment he was trading on the distant borders of Lake Erie aided by servants and employees.[38]

In carrying on this trade beyond the mountains, Croghan's packhorse trains usually passed through Croghan's Gap and followed the Juniata-Conemaugh route to the Ohio. Near its forks, he soon established secondary bases of operations. About three miles from the forks on the northwestern side of the Allegheny at the mouth of Pine Creek, Croghan and his partner had a storehouse, some log houses, numbers of batteaux and canoes, ten acres of Indian corn, and extensive fields cleared and fenced. The latter were probably used as

---

[35] Peters MSS., VI, 87; Weiser to Peters, July 10, 1748, in *Pa. Arch.*, II, 8.

[36] Gov. Morris to Gov. Hardy, July 5, 1756, in *Pa. Arch.*, II, 689.

[37] *Pa. Arch.*, II, 14; *Pa. Arch., 2nd ser.*, II, 619. This is the earliest contemporary reference to Croghan that was found in the course of this study.

[38] Minutes of the provincial council, June 8, 1741, in *Pa. Col. Rec.*, V, 72.

pastures. In 1754 the total estimated value of his property was £380. At Oswegle Bottom, which was located on the Youghiogheny, twenty-five miles from the forks of the Ohio, he had another establishment similar to the one at Pine Creek and which was valued at £300.[39] Another storehouse valued at £150 he had located at the important Indian village of Logstown, about eighteen miles below the forks. This was used as living quarters by Croghan when at Logstown, by his employees, and by Englishmen who happened to be in Logstown for a short time. Farther down the Ohio at the mouth of Beaver Creek, in another important Indian village, Croghan also had a "trading house."[40] Wherever Croghan had a storehouse he probably had at least one person stationed to take care of it and to carry on local trading operations.

From these bases near the forks of the Ohio trading routes spread out like the sticks of a fan. These routes were followed by Croghan, often accompanied by some employees, by men sent out by him, and by rival traders. One route led up the Allegheny past the present site of Venango. At this place Croghan competed with another Pennsylvania trader, John Fraser, who had here established a trading house and gunsmith's shop. The favorite route of Croghan himself, during his early years, followed the excellent "Great Trail," which led towards Detroit. It passed through the Wyandot village of one hundred families near the forks of the Muskingum, where Croghan had a prominent trading house valued at £150.[41] This, however, he regarded chiefly as a post on his trade route to Lake Erie. To the exasperation of the French, he and his

---

[39] Croghan's affidavit of losses in 1754, in Ohio Co., MSS., I, 7.
[40] Weiser's Journal to Ohio, 1748, in *Pa. Col. Rec.*, V, 349.
[41] Darlington, William M.: *Christopher Gist's Journals*, 37.

men pressed on until Governor Jonquière of Canada complained to Governor Clinton of New York that the English were trading under the very guns of Fort Miami and even proceeding to within sight of Detroit. Four English traders, two of whom were Croghan's men, were captured here by the French in 1751, taken to Detroit, Quebec, and then to France and were not released until the British ambassador at Paris demanded it.[42]

In 1747, Croghan is spoken of as "The Trader to the Indians seated on Lake Erie," where he had a number of storehouses.[43]   He was especially fond of the region around Sandusky Bay during this period, because of several reasons.   ". . .   the Northern Indians cross the Lake here from Island to Island, . . " wrote Evans in 1755,[44] and Croghan himself wrote: "We sold them goods on much better terms than the French, which drew many Indians over the Lakes to trade with us."[45]   Thus Croghan tapped the great eastward flowing streams of furs which went to Quebec.   He made close friends among the Ottawas, allies of the French,[46] and probably had much to do with the Indian

[42] Jonquière to Clinton, Aug. 10, 1751, in *N.Y. Col. Docs.*, VI, 731-733; *Pa. Arch.*, 2nd ser., VI, 126; *Wis. Hist. Coll.*, XVII, 474 and XVIII, 112; John Patten's account, in Papers relating to Pa., Car., etc., Du Simitiere Coll.; Vaudreuil to Minister, Dec. 30, 1745, C 13A 29: 89-92; Moreau, Jacob N.; *Mémoire contenant le précis des faits, avec leurs pièces justificatives, pour servir de réponse aux Observations envoyées par les ministres d'Angleterre, dans les cours de l'Europe*, App. V, 89ff.

[43] Peters to Weiser, Sept., 1747 (?), in Prov. Pap., X, 17; cf. *idem*, IX, 64.

[44] Evans: *Analysis of a Map of the Middle British Colonies*, 30; cf. Hutchins, Thomas: *Topographical Description of Va., Pa., Md., and N.C.*, 96.

[45] Croghan's transactions, etc., in *N.Y. Col. Docs.*, VII, 267.

[46] Croghan states in his journal that while he was traveling along Lake Erie to Detroit in 1760, he met several Ottawas "who received us very kindly, they being old Acquaintances of mine." – *Mass. Hist. Coll., 4th ser.*, IX, 365.

plot of 1747. Its timely discovery by the French prevented an uprising somewhat similar to that of Pontiac. The failure of this plot, together with the coming of peace in 1748, and the more aggressive hostility of the French, seem to have caused Croghan to shift his major attention to the Miami tribes.

The route to the Miami left the Great Trail at the forks of the Muskingum and led west towards Pickawillani, located on the upper Great Miami a little below the mouth of Loramie Creek near the present site of Piqua. Gist visited Pickawillani in 1751 and wrote in his Journal: "This Town . . . consists of about 400 Families, and daily encreasing, it is accounted one of the strongest Indian Towns upon this Part of the Continent." [47] A contemporary identifies it by writing, "This is the Village where George Croghan generally Trades, all the Indians of which are firmly attached to the English . . ." [48] Here a stockade was erected inside of which were storehouses and log houses. One-fourth of the white men, who were captured when the French attacked this village in 1752, were Croghan's associates. [49] At the time of its destruction, Croghan was making it a new center for his trading operations towards the Wabash.

Croghan also followed the Ohio below the forks for several hundred miles. In 1750, we find him trading at the large Shawnee village, Lower Shawnee Town, near the mouth of the Scioto, where he had a storehouse valued at £200. [50] His trading ventures

[47] Darlington: *Gist's Journals*, 47.

[48] B. Stoddert to Sir William Johnson, July 19, 1751, in *N.Y. Col. Docs.*, VI, 730.

[49] Goodman, Alfred T.: *Journal of Captain William Trent from Logstown to Pickawillani*, 86-88; Ohio Co. MSS., I, 7.

[50] Croghan's deposition in 1777, in Palmer, William P.: *Calendar of Va. State Papers*, I, 276.

probably did not go beyond the falls of the Ohio. For this region he used water transportation to some extent.

From Pine Creek and Lower Shawnee Town as bases, his traders worked the region south of the Ohio in what is today known as West Virginia and eastern Kentucky. Here the curtain is lifted but once to show us a highly significant and interesting incident and we are left to surmise from this what took place during the years before 1754. In January, 1753, a party of seven Pennsylvania traders and one Virginia trader were attacked by seventy French and Indians at a place about one hundred and fifty miles below Lower Shawnee Town on the Kentucky River. All their goods were lost. Two of the traders escaped and six were taken prisoners to Montreal; two of these were sent to France, and later made their return home after many hardships. All except one had been associated with Croghan in business; their loss was stated to have been £267, 18s, of which about forty-five per cent represented the cost of transportation.[51]

It is in the report of this incident that there occurs one of the earliest uses of the word "Kentucky;" it being spelled "Kantucqui" and "Cantucky." [52] Lewis Evans utilized information secured from members of this party for his maps. These traders were trading with the Cherokees in Kentucky and, according to one statement, they had been even in Carolina trading with the Catawbas. The friendly Indian, who was with the

[51] O'Callaghan, Edmund B.: *Calendar of Historical Manuscripts in the Office of the Secretary of State of New York*, 603; *Pa. Col. Rec.*, v, 627; Trent to Gov. Hamilton, Apr. 10, 1753, in Darlington: *Gist's Journals*, 192; Ohio Co. MSS., I, 7.

[52] *Pa. Gazette*, July 30, 1754; Deposition of one of the prisoners, in *Pa. Col. Rec.*, v, 663.

party, may have guided them along Warrior's Path
into Carolina.   No reasonable doubt exists, however,
that Croghan's traders frequented Kentucky twenty
years before Daniel Boone made his famous excursions
into this region.

In a summary of Indian affairs, probably prepared
in 1754 for the new governor of Pennsylvania, there
occurs the following unique description of Croghan's
field of activities: "Croghan and others had Stores on
the Lake Erie, all along the Ohio   . . ., all along the
Miami River, and up and down all that fine country
watered by the Branches of the Miamis, Sioto and
Muskingham Rivers, and upon the Ohio from   . . .
near its head, to below the Mouth of thee Miami
River, an Extent of 500 miles, on one of the most
beautiful Rivers in the world   . . ."[53]   With great
daring and boldness Croghan pushed out to the peri-
phery of the English sphere of influence where danger
was greater, but prizes richer, than in less remote
regions.   He did not, however, neglect the latter.   His
active and unceasing efforts to push and develop his
trade probably did more than any other one factor to
increase English influence west of the mountains.   The
export of furs and skins from Philadelphia showed a
marked increase during the decades before 1754.   The
French came to regard Croghan and his associates as
poachers upon their private beaver warrens.

Of the number of men and packhorses employed by
Croghan we can but make an estimate.   In his affidavit of losses due to attacks by the French during the
period 1749 to 1754, the names of about twenty-five
employees occur and more than one hundred pack-

---

[53] Detail of Indian affairs, 1752-4, in *Pa. Arch.*, II, 238; the use of the
phrase "Croghan and others", instead of "the Pennsylvania traders", or "the
English traders" is excellent evidence of Croghan's preëminence.

horses are mentioned as having been captured. In all probability at least a like number escaped attack. It is also probable that on an average at least two men were stationed at each of the half dozen or more posts maintained by Croghan. Those of his traders who were paid a wage received about £2 per month.

About half of his trading activities Croghan conducted solely on his own responsibility; about one-third were carried on in association with William Trent, who was Croghan's partner from 1749 to 1754 and perhaps even longer; in the remaining portion Croghan was "concerned" with William Trent, Robert Callender (Callendar) and Michael Teaffe (Taffe). These four men were associated in trade from about 1749 to 1754.[54]

Croghan's chief competitors were the five Lowrey brothers, who were closely associated with the Jewish merchants, Joseph Simon and Levi Andrew Levy at Lancaster; Callender and Teaffe; James Young and John Fraser; the three Mitchells; Paul Pierce, John Finley and William Bryan; and the individual traders, Thomas McKee, Hugh Crawford, John Galbreath, John Owen, and Joseph Neilson.[55] The field available was large enough, however, so that coöperation rather than competition was the rule among Pennsylvania traders. • The competition which they met from New York and Maryland was slight and for a long time Virginia Indian traders had a tendency to drift southwest instead of across the mountains. Probably a few entered the Ohio country before 1754.[56] However, one

---

[54] Ohio Co. MSS., I, 7.

[55] Ohio Co. MSS., I, 85-86.

[56] No mention of such traders was encountered in this study. The various memorials sent to the Crown between 1756 and 1775 by the Indian traders, asking restitution for their losses in the Ohio country from 1749 to

of the motives in the formation of the Ohio Company in 1749 was to secure a share of the profitable trade which was monopolized by the Pennsylvania traders and had it not been for the coming of the French, in all likelihood a bitter cut-throat competition between the Virginians and the Pennsylvanians would have ensued.[57]

Croghan's eastern factors included Quakers, Episcopalians, and Jews. Probably his chief factor was the firm of Shippen and Lawrence; the following quotation from Croghan's letter to Lawrence, dated "Pensborrow, Sept. 18, 1747," is illustrative: "I will Send you down the thousand weight of Sumer Skins Directly, by first waggon I Send Down, I have Gott 200 pisterns and som beeswax To Send down to you, as you and I was talking of, To Send To Medera." [58]   In September, 1748, Croghan shipped "1800 weight of fall deer skins" to Philadelphia.[59]   He also had business relations with Jeremiah Warder and Co., S. Burge and Co., Abraham Mitchel and Co., and probably with others.[60]

It is significant to note that even the most prominent Pennsylvania trader after he had developed a prosperous business, did not furnish much of the capital he needed, but secured it in Philadelphia and Lancaster. By far the largest amount was supplied by Richard Hockley, Receiver-General of Quit-rents.[61]   Richard

---

1754, include no Virginia or Maryland traders; had there been any they probably would have pooled their claims in spite of their great rivalry.

[57] Croghan to ———, July 3, 1749, in Prov. Pap., x, 62.

[58] Prov. Pap., x, 17; cf. Croghan to Barnard Gratz, Mar. 15, 1779, in McAllister Coll.

[59] George Gibson to Edward Shippen, Sept. 28, 1748, in Shippen Corresp., I, 75.

[60] Original accounts, Ohio Co. MSS., I, 12, 14, and 68; Peters MSS., III, 46; Etting Coll., Misc. MSS.; Votes of the Assembly, IV, 524-525.

[61] Shippen Corresp., I, 159; Pa. Col. Rec., V, 743; Ohio Co. MSS., I, 15.

Peters, Secretary to the Council, also invested some capital with Croghan,[62] as did other easterners.

Croghan had probably the largest trade of all the Pennsylvania Indian traders in an age when they were most enterprising. He is spoken of in 1747 in the minutes of the provincial council, as a "considerable Indian Trader" and in 1750, as "the most considerable Indian trader."[63] In 1756, Governor Morris wrote that "For many years he has been very largely concerned in the Ohio trade. . ."[64] The lawsuits in the Common Pleas Court of Cumberland County in which Croghan was involved give a side-light on his business status. From 1751 to 1753, eleven cases involving more than £2,500 came up.[65] The long list of Croghan's eastern creditors and the private moratorium for ten years which they had succeeded in securing for him and his partner, Trent, is one measure of the size and importance of his activities. The best concrete evidence which we have of the relative size of his business is contained in the list of losses, due to the coming of the French, of thirty-two individuals or partnerships engaged in the Pennsylvania Indian trade. The total losses were approximately £48,000; Croghan's individual losses were stated to be over £8,000, or twice as large as the loss of any other individual; Croghan and Trent's losses were placed at more than £6,500, or twice as large as the loss of any other partnership or individual; Croghan, Trent, Cal-

---

[62] Deed Bk., A, 1: 19, Register of Deeds, Carlisle, Pa. We have a long list of Croghan's creditors in 1754, but whether they had furnished him capital or goods, or both, is not evident.

[63] *Pa. Col. Rec.*, V, 72, 461.

[64] Gov. Morris to Gov. Hardy, July 5, 1756, in *Pa. Arch.*, II, 689.

[65] Ohio Co. MSS., II, 114. George Ross, who was later to become chairman of the United Illinois and Wabash Land Co., and Joseph Galloway, later interested in the Indiana Co., served as Croghan's attorneys.

lender and Teaffe's losses were placed at almost £2,500, and were among the larger losses. Thus Croghan's losses were about one-fourth of the total losses.[66] This probably indicates the relative size of his trade.[67]

That Croghan had so quickly reached such a position of preëminence was due to several factors. In 1741, the Pennsylvania traders had opened up, but not yet exhausted, the rich resources of the upper Ohio country. The French left it unoccupied for another decade and for almost half that time war practically eliminated them as competitors. During King George's War the operations of the British navy made it so difficult for the French to secure goods for the Indian trade that prices advanced as much as one hundred and fifty per cent. The effect of these conditions on Indian relations is suggested in the following unusual episode reported by Weiser in 1747. A French trader in the Ohio country offered but one charge of powder and one bullet to an Indian in exchange for a beaver skin. Thereupon "The Indian took up his Hatchet, and knock'd him on the head, and killed him upon the Spot." Several factors made it also easy in time of peace for Croghan and his fellow English traders to meet French competition. The English practically had a monopoly of rum and strouds, two of the most important articles that entered into the Indian trade; other articles for this trade could be manufactured more advantageously

---

[66] Ohio. Co. MSS., I, 85-86; cf. *idem*, I, 7. In a letter to Sir William Johnson, May 15, 1765, Croghan estimates both his own and Trent's losses at between £5,000 and £6,000, or about half their government claim. – Johnson MSS., I, 168. This would not affect the relativity of his losses, however. Cf. *Pa. Col. Rec.*, V, 663; Darlington: *Gist's Journals*, 192.

[67] A modern French historian writes of the "fameux traitant George Croghan l'adversaire acharné des Francais." – Villières du Terrage: *Les Dernières Années de la Louisiane Française*, 87; cf. Moreau: *Mémoire contenant le précis des faits, etc.*, App. V, 89ff.

by the English than by the French. Though the English traders were not directly supported by their government, neither were they handicapped by minute regulations. The northern winter closed up the St. Lawrence for nine months out of the year. Because of the rapids in this river it took the French from twenty to forty days to go from Montreal to the Niagara portage, whereas Pennsylvania traders could go from the Susquehanna to the Ohio in less than twenty days.[68]

Moreover, the character of most of the English traders was such that it was not difficult for an able man to surpass them. Governor Dinwiddie wrote to Governor Hamilton of Pennsylvania on May 21, 1753: "The Indian traders, in general, appear to me to be a set of abandoned wretches," and the Assembly of Pennsylvania, in a message to the Governor, February 27, 1754, said: ". . . our Indian trade [is] carried on (some few excepted) by the vilest of our own Inhabitants and Convicts imported from Great Britain and Ireland. . . These trade without Controul either beyond the Limits or at least beyond the Power of our Laws, debauching the Indians and themselves with spirituous Liquors. . ."[69] Croghan, like James Adair and Alexander Henry, was one of the few men of ability who personally embarked in the Indian trade. The malicious envy of his fellow traders, however, was seldom aroused by his success. Christopher Gist, the agent of the jealous Ohio Com-

---

[68] Vaudreuil to Minister, Apr. 12, 1746, C 13A, 30: 57, 245; same to same, Apr. 8, 1747, C 13A, 31: 52-55; Instructions to La Galissonière, etc., Feb. 23, 1748, B 87: 31; C 13A, 36: 309; La Galissonière and Hocquart to Minister, Oct. 7, 1747, in *Wis. Hist. Coll.*, XVII, 470, 503; Beauharnais to Minister, Sept. 22, 1746, *idem*, XVII, 450; Cèloron's Journal, *idem*, XVIII, 43, 57; Weiser's Report in *Pa. Col. Rec.*, V, 86.

[69] *Pa. Col. Rec.*, V, 630, 749.

pany, described him as "a meer Idol among his Countrymen, the Irish traders." However, when Gist was
traveling in the interests of the Ohio Company through
what is now Ohio and encountered the hostility of the
Indians, he used Croghan's name to protect himself and
was glad to avail himself of Croghan's company and
influence during the journey.[70]

Neither did Croghan arouse the enmity of the
natives, as did so many traders, but instead, he fur-
thered his trading operations by making intimate
friends among the Indians, particularly of their chiefs;
these friends were to stand him in good stead at critical
times in later years.[71]   At Logstown, in 1752, when the
treaty was being made between Virginia and the Ohio
Indians, the leading Iroquois chief, Half King, spoke
of Croghan as "our brother, the Buck" who "is approved of by our Council at Onondago, for we sent to
them to let them know how he has helped us in our
Councils here: and to let you and him know that he is
one of our People and shall help us still and be one of
our Council." [72]

The friendship of the Indians for Croghan was due
to various factors. He learned the Delaware and
Iroquois languages and could express himself in the
figurative speech so dear to the Indian.[73]   He had an
intimate knowledge of their customs and traits of
character.   Most important of all, however, was the

---

[70] Darlington: *Gist's Journals*, 35.

[71] Croghan's journals and letters, in Thwaites, Reuben Gold: *Early
Western Travels*, I, 82, 107, 142, 150.

[72] "Journal of the Virginia Commissioners," in *Va. Mag. of Hist. and
Biog.*, XIII, 165; this report was made by rivals of Croghan. Thomson states
that Croghan, when in council, sometimes claimed he was an Indian. –
Alienation of the Delawares and Shawanese, 173.

[73] Croghan's deposition in 1764, in Wyoming Controversy, V, 71, Penn
MSS.; *N.Y. Col. Docs.*, VII, 295.

fact that he regarded the Indian, not as a dog, but as a human being. The Indian was ready to befriend the trader who was reliable and fair in his dealings and who was willing to render services to the red man when sick or in need. Not once do the records examined for this study tell us that Croghan personally killed an Indian or that he gloried in their destruction. He labored to maintain peace between the Indians and the English, knowing well that an Indian war might mean death to many traders and would almost certainly mean bankruptcy to him, since almost the whole of his fortune was represented in packs of skins and furs several hundred miles from the nearest white settlements across the mountains. That Croghan was fearless is self-evident; every Indian trader accepted danger as a matter of his daily routine. The average trader's life must have been short. If a trader survived crisis after crisis when others were ruthlessly struck down, it was usually due to his Indian friends and his own superior intelligence. The material weapons of the white man were of but little value as a means of defense in the heart of the Indian country.[74] Other personal qualities which helped to make Croghan successful were his habit of early rising and of putting in long hours of work, his vigor, and his shrewd tactfulness in barter.[75]

While a number of factors were responsible for Croghan's success, but one factor, over which he had no control, was responsible for his bankruptcy, viz., the aggression of the French in the Ohio country from 1749 to 1754. The Pennsylvania traders in a memorial ask-

[74] Byars: "The Fur Trade, the Beginning of Transcontinental Highways as Trails followed by Fur Traders," in Gratz Pap., 1st ser., VI, 1-35; cf. idem, VI, 44-50.

[75] Ill. Hist. Coll., XI, 316.

ing restitution stated that the French forces and their Indian allies "most barberously and unexpectedly attacked" them in time of profound peace in Europe.[76] Croghan summarized the effect on himself as follows: "Capt Trent and myself were deeply engaged in the Indian Trade. We had trusted out great quantities of Goods to the Traders; the chief of them were ruined by Robberies committed on them by the French and their Indians and those which were not quite ruined when the French army came down as well as ours for what the French and Indians had not robed us of, we lost by the Indians being prevented from hunting, by which means we lost all our debts. After this Coll. Washington pressed our Horses by which means a parcell of Goods and Horses we had left fell into the Enemy's hands, our whole losses amounts to between five and Six Thousand Pounds." [77]

This estimate included goods and horses taken at Venango in 1749, and valued at approximately £1,255; goods valued at £329 taken with two traders on the upper Scioto in 1749; seven horse loads of skins and two men taken west of Muskingum in 1750; and three men and their goods taken in the Miami country in 1751. At the capture of Pickawillani, assuming that Croghan had an equal share in those goods which belonged to Croghan and Trent and to Croghan, Trent, Callender, and Teaffe, Croghan lost approximately £1,000, or one-third of the total loss. In 1753, goods valued at £267, 18s. were captured on the Kentucky River. The news of other attacks by the French early in 1753, sent Croghan and some of his traders hurrying back through the woods or up the Ohio and caused

---

[76] Ohio Co. MSS., I, 5.
[77] Croghan to Sir William Johnson, May 15, 1765, in Johnson MSS., I, 168; Croghan's affidavit of losses, in Ohio Co. MSS., I, 7-8.

Trent to leave Virginia with provisions for them. No longer was it safe for an English trader to venture far beyond the forks of the Ohio. John Fraser, who had left Venango and established himself fourteen miles south of the forks, wrote on August 27, 1753: "I have not got any Skins this Summer, for there has not been an Indian between Weningo and the Pict Country hunting this Summer, by reason of the French." [78] In the fall of 1753, the French occupied Venango. Callender and Teaffe, Croghan's associates, wrote home describing conditions and added, "Pray, Sir, keep the News from our wives, but let Mr. Peters know of it, . . ." [79] Croghan's men and packhorses were near the Ohio in 1754, awaiting developments, when Washington commandeered the horses to help carry his cannon and stores on his retreat to Fort Necessity, leaving to the French goods of Croghan and Trent, valued at £369.

Croghan's losses included, besides movable goods and horses, boats, buildings, and improvements on lands; debts of the Indians, which made up one-half of the total losses; and most serious of all, the entire field of his activities, where all of his customers lived, was now wholly closed to him. The business which he had built up through years of activity was ruined and he himself was so deeply involved in debt that if he returned to his home in the east he would be imprisoned for debt.

To a man who for years had known the freedom of the western wilderness and to whom the sky had served as a roof, night after night, death was preferable to immurement in a cell of an eighteenth century

---

[78] Trent to Gov. Hamilton, Apr. 10, 1753, in Darlington: *Gist's Journals*, 192; *idem*, 37; *Pa. Col. Rec.*, v, 222, 660.

[79] Letter to William Buchanan, Sept. 2, 1753, in *Pa. Col. Rec.*, v, 684.

debtor's jail. Croghan therefore kept out of the immediate reach of the law and established a new home
near the path which he had traveled for many years.
This he located on Aughwick Creek near its confluence
with the Juniata, at the site of the present town of
Shirleysburg. Here, surrounded by mountains on all
sides, was a small fertile valley which still belonged to
the Indians in 1753. Croghan had erected a house
here as early as September, 1753, and his whereabouts
was well known to the authorities of Pennsylvania.[80]
"I Live 30 Miles back of all Inhabitance on ye fronteers . . ." wrote Croghan to Sir William Johnson,
on September 10, 1755,[81] while to Governor Hamilton
he wrote on November 12, 1755: "From ye Misfor-
tunes I have had in Tread, which oblidges me to keep
at a Greatt distance, I have itt nott in my power to
forward Intelegence as soon as I could wish. . ."[82]
After Braddock's defeat, the oncoming tide of fire and
slaughter threatened to envelop Croghan in his exposed
position; friendly Indians came with intelligence of
raids by the French and their Indian allies and desired
that Croghan be given "speedy Notice to remove or he
would certainly be killed," and several times rumors
came to Philadelphia that he had been cut off.[83]

Life at Aughwick was not so difficult, nor was
Croghan so destitute, as might be supposed. He still
had at least fifty packhorses, and like the typical frontiersman, he had some cattle. He also had some negro
slaves and some servants; the latter were probably indentured servants. His brother stayed with him and
doubtless some of his employees remained with him.

[80] *Pa. Col. Rec.*, v, 675, 707; *Pa. Arch.*, ii, 689.
[81] Johnson MSS., ii, 212.
[82] *Pa. Arch.* ii, 484.
[83] *Pa. Arch.*, ii, 452, 454.

Conrad Weiser, who visited him, reported to the governor that Croghan had butter and milk, squashes and pumpkins, and between "twenty-five and thirty Acres of the best Indian Corn I ever saw;" Croghan made his home at Aughwick from 1753 to about July, 1756. To protect themselves, he and his men erected a stockade around their log buildings. It is self-evident that this was not an ordinary squatter's improvement. After the French and Indian War Croghan secured legal title to the lands which he had improved and to other nearby tracts.[84] Under the circumstances, imprisonment would be unjust. Croghan's services as Indian agent to Pennsylvania deserved consideration. If, imprisoned, he could not reëngage in business and thus pay his numerous creditors. But most important was the need by the government for his great knowledge of Indian affairs and for his influence with the Indians during the critical times which followed Braddock's defeat.

In other similar cases where only a few small creditors were concerned, the usual method of a general letter of license was employed,[85] but Croghan's creditors were so numerous and scattered that this method was not feasible in his case. As early as December 2, 1754, he had written Peters asking if the assembly could not pass an act of bankruptcy for himself and Trent, and if so, how he should proceed. Some of his friends evidently interested themselves in his cause, for on November 26, 1755, a petition was introduced into the assembly, signed by fifteen of his creditors, asking leave to bring in a bill granting Croghan and Trent

[84] James Burd to ——, Mar. 11, 1755, in Shippen Corresp. I, 173; Croghan to Gov. Morris, May 20, 1755, in *Pa. Col. Rec.,* VI, 399; Weiser to Gov. Hamilton, Sept. 13, 1754, in *idem,* 149.

[85] *Votes of the Assembly,* IV, 524; Byars: *B. and M. Gratz,* 31.

freedom for ten years from all legal procedure to collect debts contracted before the passage of the act. This was granted and the bill became law on December 2, 1755.[86]

The charter of Pennsylvania required that all acts be submitted to the crown for approval or disapproval within five years of their passage. The act passed on December 2, 1755, was not delivered by the agent of the Penns to the clerk of the Privy Council till January 20, 1758. This body referred it to the Board of Trade for examination. The Board of Trade referred it to the attorney-general, who reported that the act was legal. The Board then discussed the merits of the act, granting the Penns an opportunity to state their attitude. On May 12, 1758, the Board in a representation to the Privy Council recommended that the act be disallowed. On June 16, an order in council was issued in almost the exact words of the representation, disallowing the act. A copy of this order was not sent to the Board of Trade till May 21, 1760, nor read there till July 8. The Board then informed the governor and colonial agent of Pennsylvania of the action taken.

The order in council expressed surprise at the delay in delivering the act, that such an extraordinary indulgence should be granted on the petition of only a portion of the creditors, and that the bill should be introduced one morning, read twice during the same morning, never committed, and passed on the afternoon of the same day; it annulled the act as being contrary to the rules of justice in all cases affecting private property and a dangerous precedent.   By the time,

---

[86] *Votes of the Assembly*, IV, 524-527; *Pa. Stat. at Large*, V, 212-216; *Pa. Col. Rec.*, VI, 211, 214, 743-745; Gov. Morris to Gov. Hardy, July 5, 1756, in *idem*, 689; James Burd to ———, Sept. 25, 1754, in Shippen Corresp., I, 159.

however, that this order reached America and came to the notice of the various creditors, Croghan had enjoyed the benefits of the act during about five of the ten years provided by it. He had made some arrangements to meet his obligations and, was now an imperial official performing much-needed war services, and hence imprisonment for debt no longer troubled him.[87]

The traders who suffered losses as a result of the French aggression, together with the eastern merchants who were their creditors, soon began an active, well-planned campaign to secure restitution. Efforts were made by Croghan and Trent to collect, first from Virginia and then from Braddock, the losses incurred when Washington impressed their horses. After these efforts failed, Croghan, Trent, a number of their employees, and nine other traders gathered at Carlisle, Pennsylvania, and made numerous detailed affidavits of their losses. Croghan himself made five affidavits. Governor Morris signed the complete document, which listed about half of all claims made. A number of traders also gathered at Lancaster and at Philadelphia and took similar action.[88]

These thirty-two traders then authorized William Trent to draw up a memorial to be presented to George II in Council. It asked for reimbursement out of the money received from the sale of French prizes taken before the declaration of war in retaliation for French aggression. These prizes were sold for £650,000; the total trader's claims amounted to £48,572, 4d. The critical situation during the war caused this memorial

---

[87] *Acts of the Privy Council, Colonial ser., 1745-1766,* 341; Bd. of Tr. Pap., Proprieties, xx, w14, w20, w49; Bd. of Tr. Journal, LXVIII, 189; *Pa. Stat. at Large,* IV; 576, 577, 582, 584, 585, 592; *Pa. Col. Rec.,* VIII, 320. This is a good illustration of the way in which royal disallowance of Pennsylvania laws actually worked.

[88] Ohio Co. MSS., I, *passim,* particularly 5-7, 85-86.

to be neglected. When peace negotiations began, another memorial was sent to the crown asking that the French be required to indemnify the traders and merchants. Its failure ended the attempts to secure restitution in money from the French. Thereafter, all efforts were directed towards securing restitution in the form of a large grant of land from the Indian allies of the French; this promised greater speculative opportunities. After 1763, the project became associated with the more promising one of the "Suff'ring Traders" of Pontiac's uprising.[89]   Both groups of claims were still pending when the Revolution ended all hopes of securing restitution from England.

Some of the traders who had lost so heavily in 1754 maintained that they were not bound to pay their debts to the merchants unless they received restitution. "I will pay them when I am reimbursed and surely that is all they can ask of me or anybody else," wrote one of them.[90]   Croghan, however, tried to free himself of his liabilities. As early as 1754 he had conveyed some lands in the Cumberland valley to Richard Peters. In 1761, Croghan and Trent paid £1,000 to their creditors, transferred to them several tracts of lands on Aughwick Creek, and assigned to them a prior lien on all financial reimbursement which might be received from the crown, sufficient to pay the debts without interest. In return Croghan and Trent received a full legal discharge from all their debts. The debts which Croghan did not pay in full remained to trouble him to his last days. He felt morally bound to pay the principal, but not the interest. On March 15, 1779, he wrote to Barnard Gratz: ". . . itt was of my own free will

---

[89] See Chapter VII for developments after 1763.
[90] Hugh Crawford to Trent, Dec. 10, 1768, in Ohio Co. MSS., I, 54.

I promised to pay all those old Debts which was Nott Commonly Done by people that failed in Trade." Some of his creditors insisted on being paid both principal and interest and also asked for payment in coin which during the Revolution was very difficult to obtain; consequently, they failed to secure a settlement.[91]

Never again after 1754, did Croghan devote his major attention to the Indian trade. At intervals he made a few shipments of furs and skins to London or Philadelphia, and in the early seventies he was associated with Thomas Smallman in the Indian trade. He also assisted such friends as the Gratzs to make good connections with the Indians. His chief attention after 1754, however, was devoted to his work as an Indian agent and later on to land speculation and western colonizing projects.[92] Even before the inroads of the French into the Ohio region became serious, his interest was being transferred to furthering the official relations between the Ohio Indians and Pennsylvania. Private as well as public interests caused such men as Croghan to enter into the service of the government to aid in saving English rule in the West.

Croghan's wide experience for over a decade in the actual field work as an Indian trader was the foundation upon which his later career was built. During

[91] Peters MSS., VI, 87; Deed of Franks and Warder to Croghan and Trent, July 19, 1761, in Deed Bk. M, 1; 402, Register of Deeds, Huntingdon Co., Pa.; Croghan to Warder and Franks, Dec. 21, 1768, in Gratz Pap. 1st ser., VIII, 105; Croghan to B. Gratz, March 15, 1779, in McAllister Coll.

[92] These statements are based on the lack of any evidence in the records examined to show large and consistent trading activities. For the exceptions see, Pa. Col. Rec., IX, 495; Pa. Mag. of Hist. and Biog., XXXVII, 13, 194; Ohio Co. MSS., II, 24; Croghan to M. Gratz, July 29, 1773, and to B. and M. Gratz, Aug. 26, 1772, in Simon Gratz Coll. A striking exception is a consignment of furs valued at £1,200 sterling and shipped via Detroit and Quebec to London. – Croghan to Richard Neave and Son, June 24, 1767, in Dreer Coll.

these years he secured an intimate first hand knowledge
of the Indian, learning how to manage the red man and
making personal friends with some of the chiefs.   He
also learned to know the frontiersman and the friends
he made among his more able white associates coöperated with him in later years.   And finally, he became
well known to the wealthy merchants and highest
officials in Lancaster and Philadelphia; these were the
men who gave him his first opportunities to show his
value as an Indian agent and to whom Croghan was
to bring a new interest in the great West beyond the
mountains.

During the period 1741 to 1754, Croghan left behind
him the life of Dublin and was transformed into a
typical American frontiersman.   He followed the roads
that led west from Philadelphia, and traveled practically every path and trail which began where the roads
left off, crossed the mountain barrier, and then spread
out over the region bounded by Lake Erie, the Maumee
and Wabash rivers, and the Cumberland Mountains.
He crossed and recrossed the mountains.   His journeys
enabled him to spy out the finest lands strategically
located.   As he lived day after day in the fertile valley
of the Ohio and on the Lake Plain in the primeval
forests, he unconsciously imbibed a deep-seated appreciation of the vast possibilities of the region, which was
later to develop into a vision of the future greatness of
the trans-Allegheny region.   His deep love for the
western wilderness and his outlook towards the west
were to have a dynamic influence during the next two
decades upon the leaders who lived in the Delaware
valley and whose outlook was towards the ocean.   His
influence was also to be felt in Virginia, New York,
New Jersey, and in London itself.

Indian Agent: The French Advance on the Ohio, 1747-1756

Before 1755, Indian affairs in Pennsylvania were controlled by the Penns and by the local provincial government. The former negotiated treaties for the purchase of Indian land claims and paid all costs thereof. All other Indian affairs were controlled by the governor, council, and assembly of Pennsylvania. The large amount of space given to Indian affairs in the official records shows what an important part they played in the life of the people.

For the regulation of the Indian trade, the assembly passed laws to secure justice for the Indian. These required traders to be licensed and forbade them to carry large quantities of liquor to the Indians. These laws could not, however, be enforced. Generally speaking, policies were initiated and carried out by the governor and council; the expenses thereof were met by the assembly. After 1750, when such expenses were becoming very great, the assembly unsuccessfully tried to persuade the proprietors to bear a fixed ratio of Indian expenses. It argued that their interests and the interests of the province were constantly being intermixed at many Indian treaties and that cordial relations with the Indians aided the proprietors in the sale of their lands.[93] Pennsylvania never delegated its powers over Indian affairs to an Indian agent as did

[93] *Pa. Col. Rec.*, V, 235, 487, 616, 749; *Pa. Arch.*, II, 112; *Votes of the Assembly*, IV, 104, 194-195; Acrelius, Israel: *History of New Sweden*, 132.

New York and South Carolina. Instead, the governor
and council, for each particular task to be done,
usually employed a man capable of carrying on negotiations with the Indians and paid him his expenses
and for his time. Conrad Weiser practically had a
monopoly of this work before 1748; after 1748, when
there was more work than one man could perform,
William Trent, Andrew Montour, and Croghan were
often employed. These four men were also employed
at times by Virginia and Maryland. Weiser recommended Croghan as an available man and when Weiser
became fully occupied with the affairs of the Six
Nations, Croghan was relied upon to conduct negotiations with the Ohio Indians.

The rapidly increasing importance of Pennsylvania's
Indian affairs, which gave rise to the need for Croghan's services, is clearly reflected in her Indian expenditures. The cost to Pennsylvania of her Indian
affairs for the years 1748 to 1752 equaled the cost for
the preceding thirty years. Evidently, King George's
War had developed a new Indian policy. Before
1747, the government of Pennsylvania had never taken
cognizance of the interests of its citizens on the Ohio;
most of its officials in Philadelphia were ignorant of
conditions beyond the mountains. A few French leaders had realized before 1744 the serious menace to them
of having the trade of the Ohio region controlled
by the English. The latter instigated the Huron conspiracy of 1747, which had threatened to shake the
foundations of French power in the West. The
French were now convinced that if they wished to
maintain their western Indian trade and to keep open
the best lines of communication between Canada and
Louisiana, they must give to the Indians better service

May ye 26 1747

FACSIMILE OF LETTER FROM CROGHAN TO RICHARD PETERS
[Reduced to about one-third size of original]

This letter is the earliest known document written by Croghan. It is preserved among the Provincial papers in the Pennsylvania State Library at Harrisburg

and prices in trade and use force to drive out the
English traders.[94]

The "walking purchase" of 1737 and the purchase
of 1754 made by the Penns, the advent of the Ohio
Company of Virginia and the encroachment of squatters on the Indians' land all helped to cause the Ohio
Indians to desert the English; but the chief cause was
the aggressive policy of the French. So successful was
this policy that while the conflict in the West during
King George's War took place in the Maumee valley
near Detroit, during the French and Indian War it
took place east of the forks of the Ohio. During the
years 1748 to 1754 both the English and French, time
after time, met the Ohio Indians in council and gave
them large presents. The French and English councils
frequently alternated. Croghan participated in at least
ten such councils. The struggle for the Ohio valley
instead of beginning in 1754, as is usually stated, really
began in 1747 and the first phase ended in 1754 with
the French policy completely successful.

While the French were developing their policy Croghan had begun to interest the colonial officials in
Philadelphia in an aggressive Indian policy in the far
West. He forwarded to Richard Peters, secretary to
the provincial council, a letter dated May 16, 1747,
purporting to come from three Iroquois chiefs near
Lake Erie. It stated that they had "killed five of the
french hard by this fortt which is Call^d Detroat and

---

[94] Vaudreuil to Minister, Mar. 20, 1748 in c 13A, 32:28, 120 (Archives
Nationales, Paris); Alvord, *The Illinois Country, 1673-1818*, 184-189.
Croghan wrote on July 3, 1749, "I make no Doubt butt the french will make
use of all unfair Methods they can to bring over all the Indians they can to
there Interest Butt I am of opinion that the Indians are So well grafted
in the English Interest that they will nott be Easy Deceaved."–Prov. Pap.,
x, 62. The difficulties of the French are graphically portrayed in the journals
of Céloron de Blainville's expedition.

wee hope in a Litle Time To have this fortt in our posision." [95] This letter is in Croghan's handwriting and on the same kind of paper that he used at this time, indicating that he instigated this attack while trading along Lake Erie. On May 26 he wrote to Peters: "I am Just return[d] from the Woods and has brought a Letter a french Scalp and some Wompom for the Governer from a part of the Six Nations Ingans That has thire Dweling on the borders of Lake Arey. . . ." [96] He added that these Indians had just turned against the French and joined the English and that it was a fine opportunity to gain further allies by means of a small present of powder and lead. This he offered to transport and deliver with the aid of his men.

These letters were read before the council and on June 18, Governor Thomas sought an appropriation from the assembly for a present. He succeeded, but the council took no action. [97] Croghan, tiring of the summer's delay, wrote to Thomas Lawrence, his eastern representative and a member of the council, requesting him to ascertain whether a present was to be sent; should it not be sent, he did not wish to send out his men with goods because the new English allies would probably turn to the French again. [98] Lawrence laid this letter before the council which then authorized Shippen and Lawrence to furnish a present valued at £200. Croghan was to be paid for transporting and delivering it. Peters was directed to prepare speeches and to procure wampum to accompany the present, but

[95] Prov. Pap., IX, 63.

[96] Prov. Pap., IX, 64; Pa. Col. Rec., V, 138.

[97] Pa. Col. Rec., V, 72, 97, 102, 119, 120, 137, 189; Votes of the Assembly, IV, 58.

[98] Croghan to Lawrence, Sept. 18, 1747, in Prov. Pap., X, 17.

before any action was taken Weiser was to be consulted.
Croghan's business relations with Peters and Lawrence
doubtless aided his project which was favorable to the
large business interests.

This action was taken by the council with many misgivings. Up to this time gifts to the Indians had been
delivered in or near Philadelphia and Lancaster, often
in the presence of members of the council. It realized
its absolute dependence upon Indian traders for the
delivery of presents in the distant West. There was
nothing to prevent the traders selling a portion of the
goods or distributing them to favor their own private
interests. Weiser, however, wrote reassuringly:
". . . I think George Coughon is fit to perform it.
I always took him for an honest man, and have as yet
no Reason to think otherwys of him." [99] The Penns
and the aged Quaker, James Logan, who had advocated establishing a fort on Lake Erie as early as 1718,
supported Croghan's policy of opening official relations with the western Indians. Finally about £40 was
spent for powder and lead to be sent with Croghan, but
when they learned that he could not deliver it in person
further delays ensued.[100]

A new factor appeared, perhaps a shrewd move due
to Croghan, when on November 12, 1747, ten Iroquois
from the Ohio representing five hundred warriors
arrived unexpectedly in Philadelphia.[101] It was the
first official visit that any Ohio Indians had ever made
to Pennsylvania. Before meeting them in conference,

---

[99] Weiser to Peters, July 20, 1747, in *Pa. Arch.*, I, 762; *Pa. Col. Rec.*,
v, 122; Henderson, Archibald: *Conquest of the Old Southwest*, 35.

[100] Logan documents, in Hazard, Samuel: *Register of Pa.*, III, 210-213;
Proprietors to the President and Council, Oct. 16, 1747, in *Pa. Col. Rec.*, v,
217; *idem*, 121, 139, 149; Peters to Weiser, Sept. 25, 1747, in Prov. Pap. x, 13.

[101] *Pa. Gazette*, Nov. 12 and 19, 1747. Franklin's *Gazette* seldom gave
news from beyond the mountains before 1754.

the council consulted Weiser and sought the advice of James Logan. The Indians were informed that Weiser would return with them as far as John Harris's and there present them with goods valued at £148, 7s. 6d.; that gifts would be sent to the Lake Erie Indians with Croghan; and that in the spring, Weiser would be sent to the Ohio with a large present for all the Indian tribes.[102] Palmer's message to the assembly on November 26, 1747, said of the visit: "This is an extraordinary Event in our favour which ought to be improv'd to the greatest Advantage. From the Situation of these People . . . they are capable of doing or preventing the greatest Mischiefs . . ." The assembly promised the necessary funds, but urged that the goods presented ought not to be such as would encourage war. Croghan furnished men and horses to transport the presents to the Ohio.

Meanwhile, Lawrence and Logan supervised the expenditure of more than £800 in Philadelphia and New York for the larger present which Weiser was to deliver the following spring; they also arranged for its transportation to Croghan's.[103] During the spring of 1748, Croghan kept twenty packhorses and several men waiting for Weiser's coming. Several factors, how-

---

[102] *Votes of the Assembly,* IV, 58; *Pa. Col. Rec.,* V, 145-156, 166, 184; the present made to the Lake Erie Indians by the Quaker province consisted of the following:

	£	s	d
4 cwt. Barr Lead @ 45s	9	0	0
3 half Barrells and 2 Quarter caskes of Gunpowder	24	0	0
2 doz. best Knives @ 10s. 6d.	1	1	0
4 Guns @ 55s.	11	0	0
1000 Flints	1	5	0
Cash paid John Smith, Waggoner	11	2	6
	47	18	6

[103] *Pa. Col. Rec.,* V, 188, 197, 224; 18 bbl. of gunpowder, 20 cwt. of bar lead, and 40 guns were included in the present.

ever, delayed Weiser. Shikelemy, the Iroquois chief who looked after the Susquehanna tribes and who was the friend of Weiser, refused to go with him to the Ohio. He was jealous of any direct negotiations with the Ohio Indians. Weiser was also delayed because some Iroquois chiefs were coming to Philadelphia for a conference.[104] The chief reason for the delay, however, was the desire to await the action of Maryland and Virginia. Because their interests were also involved, expresses had been sent to their governors with the request that they also send representatives and presents with Weiser and Croghan. The assembly of Maryland declined to participate, but Virginia appropriated £200 for a present. This was transported to the Ohio by Croghan. He found it difficult to collect for this service.[105]

To explain the delay and to transport the goods valued at £200 which in 1747 had been promised to the Indians, Croghan was dispatched to the Ohio in April, 1748. He met the Indians in conference and told them that in answer to their complaints the governor had issued a proclamation strictly forbidding under severe penalties all traders to carry any liquor into the Indian country. It authorized the Indians to report any traders bringing in liquor and to stave the casks they brought. This seemed to please the Indians, but they requested that their new brothers who had not yet tasted English rum and who would be very glad to taste it, be given some by the traders. When Croghan began to distribute the present, he soon found that it

104 Peters to Croghan, Mar. 31, 1748, in *Pa. Col. Rec.*, v, 13; Weiser to Peters, Nov. 28, 1747, in *idem*, 167; *idem*, 212, 223-224; Weiser to Peters, July 10, 1748, in *Pa. Arch.*, II, 8.

105 Weiser to Peters, Mar. 10, 1749, in Peters MSS., II, 116; *Pa. Col. Rec.*, V, 188, 202, 209, 230, 235, 258, 290.

was not large enough to satisfy the fifteen hundred Indians and so added goods valued at £119 from his own private stock.   To this sum he added £50 for transporting them and £55, 5s. for transporting the provincial present and then sent a bill to the council for £224, 5s.   His mission in the end cost the province £424, 5s. instead of a little over £200.[106]   Croghan in later years did not hesitate to exceed in a similar manner his instructions and powers.   He had the initiative characteristic of the frontier: when he saw a need for action, he proceeded to meet it.   Because of this trait he was more efficient but less trusted as an Indian agent.

Croghan was probably responsible for the departure of a delegation of Shawnee and Miami (Twightwee) Indians from the Ohio for Lancaster within a few weeks after he had distributed the present.   He, himself, returned home about the same time and then proceeded to Lancaster where he announced the coming of the Indians and stated their desires.   Weiser, Montour, Peters, four members of the council, the magistrates of Lancaster County, Croghan, and some other local inhabitants met with the fifty-five Indians of various tribes at the courthouse in Lancaster from July 19 to July 23, 1748.   At this treaty the Shawnee

---

106 Croghan's Journal, in *Pa. Col. Rec.*, v, 287-289; *idem,* v, 294-295. Croghan's official journals were usually written up in good form by a clerk, especially during later years.   None of the original copies which the writer has seen are in Croghan's handwriting.   Speeches reported to have been made to the Indians were often prepared beforehand.   The official journals were frequently written up from rough notes and as a result we have different versions of some journals.   It is almost impossible to determine whether the Indian speeches are accurately reported in the journals of an Indian agent, for there is seldom any other evidence available.   The accuracy of Croghan's journals was questioned on several occasions. – Cf. *N.Y. Col. Docs.*, VII, 268, 775; *Pa. Mag. of Hist. and Biog.*, XXXVII, 26; Thwaites: *Early Western Travels*, I, 283-285.

who had robbed some English traders were again received as allies. The Six Nations then introduced the Miami who were received as English allies. They were located four hundred miles further west than the delegation which had visited Philadelphia the preceding November. They hoped to influence twelve neighboring tribes to make a treaty with the English. Croghan was one of the signers of this treaty.[107] After it was signed, Weiser accompanied the Indians to Croghan's home where they remained for some days. Here they were given some of the provincial goods stored there and some goods which Weiser purchased from Croghan for £62. On August 8, 1748, Croghan wrote to Peters: ". . . the Ohio Ingans Sett off from my hous Last week very well Satisfy[d] with the reception they received, only the Sick Man remains still att my house till his back is well." [108] This treaty helped to widen the horizon of the colonial leaders living in Philadelphia and increased their interest in the far West.[109]

[107] Minutes of the Conference, in *Pa. Col. Rec.*, V, 307-319; *Votes of the Assembly*, IV, 13; *Pa. Gazette*, July 28, 1748; Depuy, Henry F.: *Bibliography of English Colonial Treaties, etc.*, 27.

[108] *Pa. Col. Rec.*, V, 327; *Pa. Arch.*, II, 9-13.

[109] The following extract from the minutes of the conference is illuminating: "The Commissioners gave a handsome Entertainment to the Deputies of the Twightwees and the Indians who conducted them from Ohio, and after Dinner enter'd into a free Conversation with them . . . by their Informations it appears that the River Ouabache takes its rise from a Lake at a small distance from the West end of Lake Erie, from which it runs South-Westerly 4 or 500 Miles, and falls into the Ohio about 300 Miles from the Mississippi; that on this River and another River called the Hatchet, the Twightwees and their Allies have Twenty Towns, and that they count one thousand fighting Men; that it is a plain Country and of a rich Soil abounding with Game. The principal Deputy of the Twightwees laid down with Chalk the Courses of the Mississippi, of Ouabache, and of Ohio, marking the Situation of their own Towns, of Lake Erie, and of two Forts that the French have on the Mississippi, whereby it is Manifest that if these Indians and their Allies prove faithful to the English,

Shortly after this treaty Weiser, Croghan, and Montour left Croghan's on their mission to the Ohio Indians. The council had instructed Weiser to study conditions among the Ohio Indians and to secure intelligence of the French. Croghan served as a guide and furnished twenty packhorses with drivers to transport the Pennsylvania and Virginia presents valued at £500 and £200 respectively. The mission reached the Ohio on August 27, 1748, and made Croghan's trading house at Logstown their headquarters. During the next few weeks Weiser visited the surrounding villages. Soon twenty English traders and a large number of Delaware, Shawnee, Iroquois, and Wyandot Indians gathered at Logstown. Weiser met each tribe separately and then in a general council he announced that the war had ended. He sought closer relations between the English and the Indians, especially in regard to trade. After the presents had been carefully distributed, Weiser returned to Croghan's where he rested and awaited his baggage.[110]

It was a significant incident of this mission that Benjamin Franklin's son, William, then a youth of nineteen, accompanied Croghan and Weiser. This journey was probably arranged by his father as a part of William's education. During the long hours spent on the trail while crossing the mountains and while

the French will be deprived of the most convenient and nearest communication with their Forts on the Mississippi, the ready Road lying thro' their Nations, and that there will be nothing to interrupt an Intercourse between this Province and that great River." – *Pa. Col. Rec.*, v, 315; President and Council to the Proprietors, July 30, 1748, in *idem*, 322; Palmer's Message to the Assembly, Aug. 24, 1748, in *idem*, 330.

[110] Instructions to Weiser, June 23, 1748, in *Pa. Col. Rec.*, v, 290-293; Weiser's Journal, in *Pa. Col. Rec.*, v, 348-358. Another version of this journal is found in volume one of the *Collections* of the Hist. Soc. of Pa. Both versions are used for the journal as printed in Thwaites: *Early Western Travels*, I.

sitting before the camp fires in the evening, Croghan doubtless told of his experiences and described the country to the youth. William Franklin kept a journal of his trip which Lewis Evans used in making his map. William's father sent to a member of the Royal Society in England information which he secured from his son's and Weiser's journals. William's journey was an important factor in arousing in both the Franklins a keen and vital interest in the future greatness of the West. In later years this led to their active association with Croghan in projects to establish new colonies beyond the mountains.[111]

The events of the year 1747-1748 clearly presented to the colonial officials of Pennsylvania the possibilities of developing a rich Indian trade in the far West. This appealed to the Quaker as well as to the Episcopalian and the Scotch-Irish Presbyterian. A marked increase in the export of furs and skins from Philadelphia followed. The expansion of the Indian trade was closely associated with the policy of an aggressive defense against a possible attack by the French and Indians. The treaty of Logstown in 1748 represents the zenith of English influence in the Ohio region until after 1763. In 1749 came Céloron's expedition and thereafter the English were on the defensive. The unlicensed English traders became more numerous and carried increasing quantities of rum to the Indians. Croghan probably felt the tide turning when he wrote on July 3, 1749: ". . . No people Carries on the Indians Trade in So Regular a manner as the French. I wish with all My hart the Government of this Prov-

[111] Weiser to Peters, July 17, 1748, in *Pa. Arch.*, II, 10; *idem*, 15; Franklin to Collinson, Oct. 18, 1748, in *Writings* (ed. Smyth), II, 365; Evans: *Analysis of a General Map*, etc., 10. A search was made for Franklin's Journal, but in vain. It would be a valuable document could it be found.

ince wol'd Take Some Method to Regulate the Indian Trade. . ." [112]

The English were further handicapped by the bitter rivalry which arose at this time between the traders from Pennsylvania and those from Virginia and Maryland. The latter, supported by the powerful Ohio Company, promised the Indians cheaper goods and threatened to take away much of the trade which the former had long monopolized. The Pennsylvanians told the Indians that the roads which the Virginians were building would lay them open to attack by the Catawbas and that the Virginians intended to take all their lands. Croghan and his partner, William Trent, however, frequently served Virginia officially during the years 1752 to 1754. These leaders were too shrewd to become openly hostile to the Ohio Company. The plans of this company made it easier for the French to win over the Ohio Indians, for as Croghan wrote: ". . . the Indians Dos nott Like to hear of there Lands being Setled over Allegany Mountain . . ." Meanwhile, Weiser was suggesting that the lands beyond the Kittatinny Mountains be purchased from the Indians, settlements made upon them, and a wagon road opened to the Ohio in order to meet the prospective advantages of the Virginia traders. The western boundary dispute between Pennsylvania and Virginia began at this time.[113]

[112] Minutes of the treaty of Logstown, in *Va. Mag. of Hist. and Biog.*, XIII, 166; Croghan to Peters, July 3, 1749, in *Pa. Arch.*, II, 31; Croghan's Transactions with the Indians, 1748-1756, in Indian Affairs, I, 51-52, Penn MSS. A copy of this document is also found in the Du Simitiere Coll. It is printed in the *N.Y. Col. Docs.*, VII, 267ff., in the *Pa. Arch.*, 2nd ser., VI, 516ff., and in Thwaites: *Early Western Travels*, I, 88ff.

[113] *Pa. Col. Rec.*, V, 423, 424, 440; Dinwiddie to Hamilton, May 21, 1753, *idem*, 631; Croghan to ——, July 3, 1749, Prov. Pap., X, 62; Weiser to Peters, May 8, 1749, in Weiser's Corresp., I, 19.

From now on, rumors and intelligence of the preparation of the French became frequent: magazines and stores were being replenished at Detroit, boats were plying on Lakes Erie and Ontario, and several hundred soldiers and Indian allies were being collected. Soon Céloron de Blainville's well-known expedition was on its way down the Ohio to warn the English traders to depart. Céloron dispatched official letters to the governors of Pennsylvania and Carolina. So hostile were the Indians, even to his large force, that he frequently feared an attack. When Governor Hamilton was informed that Céloron's army, a thousand strong, was headed for the Ohio, he asked Croghan to proceed immediately to the Ohio and to send out scouts to secure intelligence and to warn the traders. Croghan sent one of his men to Lake Erie with instructions for Montour to investigate and then meet him at Logstown. Croghan, himself, started for the Ohio and planned to remain if necessary to aid in keeping the Indians steady. He arrived at Logstown immediately after Céloron had left and did much to undo what harm had been done.[114]

These warnings of danger made it desirable for Pennsylvania to cultivate the friendship of her own Indians. Their chief cause of complaint was the pressure on their lands. Settlers had crossed the Susquehanna in such numbers that Cumberland County had been organized in 1750. Croghan was appointed one of the justices of the peace and of the common pleas of the new county.[115] His chief service as a justice was

---

[114] Céloron's Journal, in *Wis. Hist. Coll.*, XVIII, 36ff.; Parkman, Francis: *Montcalm and Wolfe*, I, 36-63; *Pa. Col. Rec.*, V, 387, 425; *Pa. Arch.*, II, 45; Croghan to Peters, July 3, 1749, in Prov. Pap. x, 62. Reports exaggerated the size of Céleron's force, it consisted of less than 200 men.

[115] *Stat. at Large of Pa.*, V, 87-94; *Pa. Col. Rec.*, V, 408, 436, 529.

in connection with the removal of squatters from the Indian lands beyond the Blue Mountains and in the Juniata valley concerning which complaints had frequently been made by the Iroquois. They stated that the magistrates, who had been sent in 1742 to remove the squatters, instead of doing so had made surveys for themselves.[116]   In 1750 decisive action was felt to be necessary. Secretary Peters, Weiser, a deputy sheriff, and six justices of the new county attempted to remove the squatters; Croghan participated in all the proceedings. Two trying conferences were held at his home with the incensed Indians.[117]

The officials made trips to various fertile spots north and west of Croghan's. Croghan furnished men and horses to carry provisions and supplies for which he was paid £30 by the proprietors.[118]   About sixty squatters were found. The original intentions were to arrest, convict, fine, and imprison them, but two of the first five arrested fled calling back: "You may take our Land and Houses and do what you please with them, . . . but we will not be carried to Gaol." A third squatter met the officials with a loaded gun. To prevent the squatters from fleeing further into the Indian country or uniting to resist by force, a new method of procedure was adopted. Practically all the squatters confessed to being trespassers and gave one bond to appear in court and another bond, five times as large, to remove their families, cattle and goods. Peters gave money to some of the poorer squatters with large families. Those who removed were never prosecuted. Not even were the better cabins burned.

---

116 *Pa. Col. Rec.*, IV, 570, 648; *idem*, V, 389, 394, 399, 401; *Pa. Arch.*, II, 15.
117 The minutes are found in the *Pa. Col. Rec.*, V, 431-438.
118 Accounts, I, 84, Penn. MSS.; Penn-Physick MSS., I, 25. Croghan was also asked to stop the building of a house on a proprietary manor. – *idem*, V, 10.

Such a destruction of the capital of frontier society would have aroused the enmity of the frontiersmen. They felt that the land would shortly be purchased from the Indians and in that case a cabin with a plot of cleared ground would give the squatter a prior lien to the choicest lands. Still, an outward visible sign had to be given to appease the Indians. After great deliberation it was decided to burn some cabins after the occupant had carried out his goods. Peters reported that "the Cabbins or Log Houses which we burnt were of no considerable Value, being such as the Country People erect in a Day or two . . ." As a result, the westward movement of settlers was checked and this served to diminish temporarily the danger of Indian hostilities. Four years later, the Penns bought at Albany the claims of the Iroquois to the lands in question.[119]

During the summer of 1750, Sir William Johnson had sent word to Governor Hamilton that the French were planning a second expedition to the Ohio. Hamilton immediately asked Croghan and Montour to proceed to the Ohio and invite all the tribes to come the following spring to a treaty and receive a large present. Croghan wrote Hamilton from the Ohio on November 16, 1750, that Joncaire, the French leader, was at the head-waters of the Ohio giving out presents and preparing to build a fort; that traders and Indians were being robbed, taken prisoners, or killed by both sides; that war was expected by the English traders; and that there was general alarm among all the Indian tribes

---

[119] Official report of Peters to Gov. Hamilton, July 2, 1750, in *Pa. Col. Rec.*, v, 440-449; Thomson: *Alienation of the Delaware and Shawanese, etc.*, 65ff. The official report enables one to locate exactly the settler's frontier in 1750. The notorious renegade, Simon Girty, was one of the squatters removed by Croghan. The present town of Burnt Cabins in Fulton County secured its name as a result of these events.

who felt the need of an English fort on the Ohio. This letter Hamilton sent to the assembly saying that "it contains several matters worthy of your greatest Attention." [120]

Croghan had also been entrusted with a small present for the Miami, who had been bribed and threatened by Céloron and whose exposed position caused them to desire closer relations with the English. Croghan, therefore, continued his journey westward during the midwinter. Christopher Gist, who had been to Logstown to invite the Indians to a treaty with Virginia, was glad to accompany Croghan part of the way for safety. Croghan's acknowledged leadership in the West was strikingly shown on this journey. At the Indian villages he received reports from traders and Indians; sometimes they told of the capture of some of his own men. When reports of the capture of several English traders came to him at the Muskingum villages, he sent out Indian runners to summon the neighboring traders and chiefs for a council. English traders sent to him three French deserters to save them from the Indians. After Croghan had arrived at Pickawillani and delivered the goods to the Miami, four French emissaries came with presents to urge the Miami to trade with the French. The French and English colors were both raised in the council chamber and both sides were given a hearing, but Croghan had the pleasure of seeing the French colors lowered.[121]

While the Philadelphia officials were beginning to establish friendly relations with Indian tribes as far

[120] Message to the assembly, Oct. 16, 1750, in *Pa. Col. Rec.*, v, 485; *idem*, 462, 481, 496, 498 (on page 496, the date of Croghan's letter is incorrectly given as December; cf. p. 498 and Darlington: *Gist's Journals*, 34); Croghan to Hamilton, Apr. 11, 1751, in Offic. Corresp., v, 133, Penn MSS.

[121] *Pa. Col. Rec.*, v, 437, 455, 460; Darlington: *Gist's Journals*, 37-53, *passim*.

west as the Wabash, Croghan was cultivating relations with tribes beyond the Wabash towards the Mississippi. However, he could not carry official support with him into this distant region. In February, 1751, while he was at Pickawillani, chiefs of the Piankashaw and Wea (Wawioughtanes) Indians, two tribes living west of the Wabash River, came to him and requested to be received as English allies. A treaty was drawn up and signed by Croghan, Montour, Gist, and three other traders. Croghan assumed the authority to present these Indians with goods to the amount of £100. These probably came out of his private storehouse at Pickawillani, but he presented them in the name of Pennsylvania and upon his return he presented his bill for them to the council. Governor Hamilton sent the treaty, Croghan's reports and his bill to the assembly, but the assembly repudiated the treaty and requested the governor to be careful to select Indian agents who could be trusted not to exceed their instructions.[122] The treaty was not without effect, however, nor did Croghan lose on his investment. During the next year, the Piankashaw killed five Frenchmen near Lake Erie, and two Frenchmen and two slaves near Vincennes; thirty-three of their warriors appeared at Kaskaskia in a conspiracy with the Illinois to destroy the French villages on the Mississippi. Vaudreuil reported home that the Piankashaw favored the English and helped to seduce other tribes from the French. The French finally imprisoned their chief. Croghan was probably reimbursed by his profits from the in-

---

[122] Gibson: A General Map of the Middle British Colonies, etc., 1758; Croghan's report, the treaty, and the messages of the governor and assembly are found in the *Pa. Col. Rec.*, v, 521-527. In Hodge, Frederick W.: *Handbook of American Indians*, II, 925 and 926, this treaty is erroneously dated 1757 and associated with Virginia.

creased trade. In 1765, during the critical days after
Croghan had been attacked, tomahawked, and then
taken prisoner to the Piankashaw country, his old acquaintances among that tribe befriended him.[123]

When Croghan returned to Philadelphia about May
1, 1751, he found Hamilton exerting all his influence
to induce the assembly to follow an aggressive Indian
policy and to induce New York, Maryland, and Virginia to participate in sending a gift to the Ohio
Indians. The governors of these provinces desired to
coöperate, but their assemblies declined to act. Virginia finally did provide a present, but it was to be
delivered separately and in the interests of the Ohio
Company. The assembly of Pennsylvania provided a
present valued at £700. Weiser was to take charge of it,
but when it became necessary to send him to Albany to
meet the Iroquois, he recommended that Croghan and
Montour be given charge of the Ohio mission, stating
that "If Mr. Croghan's Integrity is questioned some
of the Traders at Ohio might be required to be present
and see the Goods delivered Article for Article. . .
I believe he will do all in his Power to Act According to your Honour's Commands and leave no room
of Suspicion. . ."[124]

His recommendation was followed and on May 18,
1751, Croghan, Montour, and ten other English traders
arrived at Logstown where a large number of Indians
had assembled. They welcomed Croghan's party by
firing their guns and hoisting the English colors. Two

[123] Longueil to Rouille, Apr. 21, 1752, in *Pa. Arch., 2nd ser.*, VI, 133;
Alvord: *The Illinois Country, 1673-1818*, 234; C 13A, 38:88-93; Makarty
to ———, June 15, 1752, C 13A, 36: 309; *Wis. Hist. Coll.*, XVIII, 58-61, 85-94,
112-114; Croghan's Journal, 1765, in Thwaites: *Early Western Travels*, I,
141-143.
[124] Weiser to Hamilton, Apr. 22, 1751, in *Pa. Col. Rec.*, V, 518; *idem*,
486-522, *passim*.

days later Joncaire and a French party including forty
Iroquois also arrived at Logstown.   Joncaire asked for
a reply to Céloron's demand that the Indians send the
English traders away.   Croghan faced him in open
council with the Indians and adroitly outmaneuvered
the astute Frenchman.   He left with Croghan a letter
for Governor Hamilton which stated the French claims
and demands; Croghan received it and brought it to
Hamilton for which he was severely criticized by the
assembly.   Croghan delivered separate speeches to the
Delawares, Shawnee, Wyandots, Miami, and Six
Nations.   The domination of the Six Nations over the
Ohio tribes is well shown in this council.   It was an
Iroquois chief who answered Joncaire.   Croghan conferred privately with their chiefs before he acted and
he mentioned them in every speech.   They also helped
him to distribute the presents.[125]

The most significant phase of Croghan's mission
concerned the erection of a fort at the forks of the
Ohio.   When the Penns in England heard of the
French aggression they became alarmed lest they lose
their western lands and at once consulted the Duke
of Bedford and Lord Halifax.   They wrote Hamilton
offering to contribute £400 towards the erection of a
fort and £100 annually for its upkeep and suggested
that the "command of this might be given to the principal Indian Trader, and be obliged to keep Four or
Six Men at it who might serve him in it; and the House
be his Magazine for Goods."   Croghan was doubtless
enthused by the possibility of attaining a position sim-

125 Croghan to Hamilton June 10, 1751, in *Pa. Col. Rec.*, V, 539.   Croghan's
journal for this mission is found in Indian Affairs, I, 72-74, Penn MSS. and
in the *Pa. Col. Rec.*, V, 530-540.   It has been reprinted several times.   In
Thwaites: *Early Western Travels*, I, 58ff., the minutes for May 29 are
omitted.   In reading the above account it must be borne in mind that it is
based on Croghan's own journal which is our only source for these events.

ilar to that of Byrd and Wood in Virginia, Johnson in
New York, or of a French seigneur. Because the
Quaker leaders of the assembly were extremely adverse
to the erection of a fort, Hamilton instructed Croghan
to take it up privately with the Indian chiefs only.
They, however, replied in open council: "We expect
that you our Brother will build a strong House on the
River Ohio, that if we should be obliged to engage in
a War that we should have a Place to secure our Wives
and Children, likewise to secure our Brothers that
come to trade with us, for without our Brothers supply
us with Goods we cannot live." After Croghan's
return Hamilton placed the Quaker assembly in an
uncomfortable position by recommending to it the
erection of such a fort. The assembly took testimony
to prove that the forks of the Ohio were outside the
limits of Pennsylvania and it proceeded to investigate
the nature of Croghan's instructions and his conduct.
Weiser denied any knowledge of instructions relating
to a fort and Hamilton denied giving any, though both
were concerned therewith. The assembly finally paid
Croghan's bills, but its message to the governor insin-
uated that Croghan had inserted the Indian's request
for a fort in his journal and stated that he either mis-
understood or misrepresented both the request of the
Indians and the danger from the French. In spite of
this, Croghan continued to use every means in his
power to strengthen the Indians in their friendship for
the English.[126]

The neglect of Pennsylvania to erect a fort on the
Ohio helped to alienate the Delaware and Shawnee
Indians, for though they now turned to Virginia and

---

[126] *Pa. Arch.*, II, 632; *Pa. Col. Rec.*, V, 514, 515, 522, 529, 547; Croghan's
Transactions, etc., in *N.Y. Col. Docs.*, VII, 268.

repeated their request at the treaty at Logstown in 1752 and again at Winchester in 1753, by the time Virginia acted it was too late. After 1751, the leading rôle in the English defensive against the French aggression passed from Pennsylvania to Virginia. Had the assembly been in harmony with Hamilton, Croghan, not Washington, would probably have been sent to warn the French to leave Venango and Le Boeuf. Though these forts were on Pennsylvania soil, Hamilton did not act, for he knew that his Quaker assembly would not support him with force if necessary. Instead he could only encourage Virginia to act and ask that she respect the Penns' title to the land east and southeast of the forks. To Governor Clinton he wrote prophetically: ". . . I have little reason to expect they will ever act a proper part in Indian affairs, untill either some notable calamity befall our back inhabitants, or till they have such injunctions laid upon them from home as they will not venture to disobey." [127]

Virginia took advantage of her opportunity. Gist and Nemacolin blazed a path to the Ohio for the Ohio Company and presents were provided for a treaty with the Ohio Indians at Logstown in June, 1752. Croghan was present and aided the Virginians. Their task was a difficult one because the Pennsylvania traders had prejudiced the Indians against them and because they asked the Indians to give up their claims to the land desired by the Ohio Company. Permission to erect two forts and to make some settlements was finally granted and the Indians agreed to coöperate in developing trade. After the treaty the Virginia com-

[127] Message to the assembly, Mar. 2, 1754, in *Pa. Col. Rec.*, v, 751-756; Hamilton to Dinwiddie, May 6, 1753, in *idem*, 629; Hamilton to Clinton, June 6, 1751, in *N.Y. Col. Docs.*, VI, 710.

missioners sent Trent to Pickawillani with gifts for the Piankashaw.[128]

Jonquière, who until this time had been governor of Canada, had carefully refrained from using force to secure the Ohio country and had thereby incurred the displeasure of the home government. The new governor, DuQuesne, was under instructions to drive out the English traders, seize their goods and destroy their posts.[129] The French regarded Croghan in particular as an obstacle to their plans. They spoke of him as "sieur George Crocqueu Négociant", "grand-interprète Anglois pour les Sauvages", and "interprète-général." They offered one thousand dollars for the scalps of Croghan and James Lowrey "imagining if they were taken off as they had great Influence with the Ohio Indians they Could easily gain over those Indians to them." So safe did Croghan feel among the Indians that when he met the Shawnee in council at Lower Shawnee Town on January 30, 1750, he boldly told them of the French offer.[130]

The first important open attack by the French was made on Pickawillani on June 21, 1752, and caused great excitement in the Ohio region. News of their intentions had been secured by Johnson and sent to Hamilton as early as August, 1751. Charles Langlade

---

[128] Instructions to the Commissioners and Minutes of the Treaty, in *Va. Mag. of Hist. and Biog.*, XIII, 143-177; *Dinwiddie Pap.*, I, 6; Va. Commissioners to Trent., June 14, 1752, in Revolutionary Pap., 90, Etting Coll.

[129] Instructions to Jonquière, Aug. 27, 1751, in B 93: 30-31 (Archives Nationales, Paris); Instructions to DuQuesne, May 15, 1752, in *Wis. Hist. Coll.*, XVIII, 121.

[130] Moreau: *Mémoire contenant le précis des faits, avec leurs pièces justificatives, pour servir de réponse aux Observations envoyées, par les ministres d'Angleterre, dans les cours de l'Europe*, App. I, 92-99, *passim*; Johnson to Gov. Clinton, Sept. 25, 1750, in *N.Y. Col. Docs.*, VI, 600; *Pa. Col. Rec.*, V, 483; Darlington: *Gist's Journals*, 44; Croghan to Hamilton, Sept. 27, 1754, in *Pa. Arch.*, II, 173.

with two hundred and forty French and Indians marched from Detroit and surprised Pickawillani. About thirty, including one English trader, were killed in the attack. Five traders were taken prisoners and their goods valued at £3,000 were taken. Of these goods about one-third belonged to Croghan. La Demoiselle, the chief of the village who from his great friendship for the English was called "Old Briton," was boiled and eaten. News of the attack was hurried to Philadelphia by special express, but Pennsylvania and Virginia were not ready to aid the Indians in a reprisal. Virginia, however, did send Trent to the Ohio in the summer of 1753 with a present of powder, lead, guns and blankets. DuQuesne wrote home: "I trust that this blow, added to the complete pillage suffered by the English on this occasion, will discourage them from trading on our lands." [181]

From this time forth, Croghan and his associates were compelled to cease trading in the more distant regions. He must have viewed with growing dismay the rapid crumbling away, as the French advanced eastwards, of the business which it had taken ten years of his life to build up. His partner, Trent, wrote to Governor Hamilton: "I am much surprised at the several Governments to suffer us dryly to be robed and Murdered without putting it in our power to do ourselves Justice since they don't think us worthy [of] their protection." [132]

In May, 1753, Johnson was again sending intelli-

---

[181] *Md. Gazette,* Nov. 9 and Dec. 7, 1752; Goodman: *Journal of Capt. William Trent, etc.,* 86-88; Gibson; A General Map of Middle British Colonies; Callender to Hamilton, Aug. 30, 1752, in *Pa. Col. Rec.,* V, 599; *idem,* 549, 568-572; Trent's Journal for 1753, in Darlington, Mary C.: *History of Col. Henry Bouquet,* 17-40, *passim*; *Wis. Hist. Coll.,* XVIII, 129.

[132] Trent to William Logan, May 8, 1753, in Shippen Corresp., I, 147.

gence to Hamilton of a large French expedition headed
for the Ohio for the purpose of erecting forts and ex-
pelling the English. Expresses were at once sent by
Hamilton to the governors of Maryland and Virginia
and the traders on the Ohio were warned by two messengers. These brought to Croghan copies of all the
papers sent by Johnson. Before this message was received, Trent had written to Hamilton that the French
attacks on traders near Lake Erie, along the Great
Miami, and in Kentucky had caused Croghan to return
through the woods with some Indians and whites and
that the rest of the traders were coming up the Ohio in
a body. Trent was preparing to go to the Ohio with
provisions for their aid. He added: "the Indians are
in such confusion that there is no knowing who to trust.
I expect they will all join the French except the Delawares, as they expect no assistance from the English." [133]

On May 7, 1753, while these refugees were gathered
at Croghan and Trent's storehouse at the mouth of
Pine Creek, the Indians were thrown into consterna-
tion by a message sent down from Venango by the
trader John Fraser. It stated that the French were
coming with eight brass cannon, ammunition, and
stores. On May 8, two Iroquois runners from Onondago brought similar intelligence. On May 12, John
Harris arrived with Hamilton's warning. In this
crisis the entire party looked to Croghan as a leader.
The Indians were called into council and asked what
their attitude was going to be. The distracted red men
after anxious deliberation announced that they would
receive the French as friends or as enemies depending
upon their attitude, but that the English would be safe

[133] Gov. Hamilton to Gov. Clinton, May 10, 1753, in C. O., 5: 1065; *Pa.
Col. Rec.*, v, 607-609, 622ff.; Trent to Hamilton, Apr. 10, 1753, in Darlington: *Gist's Journals*, 192.

as long as they themselves were safe. Croghan's partners, Teaffe and Callender, with the two messengers that had been sent out by Hamilton, returned to Philadelphia on May 30 to report in person. The next day the assembly appropriated £200 for a condolence present to the Twightwees and £600 for "the Necessities of Life" (guns and ammunition) for the other Ohio Indians.[134]

Virginia also provided gifts for the Ohio tribes. A deputation of about one hundred Indians came to Winchester in September, 1753, to confer with Virginia. Croghan was present to assist the Virginia commissioner, William Fairfax. The Virginians were placed in a dilemma when it came to giving out the goods which consisted chiefly of guns and ammunition: they feared to give it out liberally lest the Indians use it later to attack the Virginia frontier; but if they did not do so, the Indians could make no defense and moreover would be offended and turn to the French. The Indians finally were given a small portion of the goods and informed that the rest would be distributed later by Trent, Gist, and Montour.

The Indians then went to Carlisle to receive the present which Pennsylvania had provided for them. Benjamin Franklin, Peters, and Isaac Norris, the speaker of the assembly, had been appointed commissioners to meet them and Croghan was present to give advice. The Indians requested that no settlements be made beyond the mountains, that all trade in the Ohio region be confined to three posts, that prices be reduced, that less liquor be brought by the traders, and that future councils be held at Croghan's house at

134 Message to the Governor, May 31, 1753, in *Pa. Col. Rec.*, v, 616; Dinwiddie to Hamilton, Sept. 3, 1753 in *idem*, 687; *idem*, 614ff., 657ff.

Aughwick. The commissioners, facing the same dilemma as had confronted the Virginians, informed the Indians that the goods for the present would be kept at their good friend George Croghan's who would give them out on the governor's orders. Such a policy did not send the Indians home well satisfied.[135]

Meanwhile, the French had established forts at Presque Isle, Le Boeuf, and Venango. In a message to the assembly, February 1, 1754, Governor Hamilton said: ". . . so alarming an Occasion has not occurred since the first Settlement of the Province, nor any one thing happen'd that so much deserves your serious Attention." Finally all the governors, after months of waiting, received instructions from England to protest formally and then, if necessary, take military action should the French invade English territory. Governor Dinwiddie now sent Washington on his famous mission to Le Boeuf and prepared for active military operations.[136]

The Ohio Company materially aided his plans. It had employed Trent to engage laborers and erect a strong storehouse on the Monongahela and another at the forks of the Ohio. In January, 1754, Dinwiddie gave Trent a captain's commission. John Fraser, the Indian trader, was made lieutenant and Edward Ward, Croghan's half-brother, was made ensign; Colonel Fry and Major Washington were their superior officers. Enlistment was encouraged by promising each soldier a land grant near the forks of the Ohio. Trent was handicapped by the lack of provisions and when his men had no food left except Indian corn, he, himself,

---

[135] Instructions and Report of the Commissioners and Minutes of the Conference, in *Pa. Col. Rec.*, v, 658-659, 665-687; *idem*, 693, 703, 708.

[136] Dinwiddie to Hamilton, Sept. 3, 1753, in *Pa. Col. Rec.*, v, 687; Instructions to Gov. Hamilton, Aug. 28, 1753, in *idem*, 689; *idem*, 660,722.

started east to secure supplies. Croghan had anticipated this demand and found employment for his idle
packhorses and men by contracting with the Ohio
Company to furnish provisions valued at £500 from the
back country of Pennsylvania. Half of these were on
the way to the Ohio when on April 17, 1754, Contre-
coeur with a force of five hundred men appeared
before the half-finished fort and demanded its surrender. The fort at the time had but forty-one men,
no cannon, and but few provisions and was commanded
by Ward. He was permitted to march off with the
honors of war carrying with him even his tools.[137]

Croghan had been on the Ohio early in the year with
these old associates of his. He wrote Hamilton on
February 3, 1754, that Trent had just arrived with
Indian presents and with tools and workmen to begin
a fort. Croghan tarried to help deliver the presents
because Trent could not speak the Indian language.
The building of the fort pleased the Indians and put
them in high spirits.[138] Croghan happened to be on the
Ohio at this time because Hamilton had sent Croghan,
Andrew Montour, and John Patten, to hold a council
at Logstown and encourage the Indians. Croghan
arrived at the Ohio shortly after Washington had
passed by on his return from Le Boeuf. Croghan included a concise summary of this mission in his report
to Hamilton. He also reported that the Miami had

---

[137] Ward's affidavit, 1756, in Ohio Co. MSS., I, 10; Croghan to Hamilton,
May 14, 1754, in *Pa. Arch.*, II, 144. Washington accused Trent of great
timidity and of being absent from his post and Dinwiddie ordered Trent
and Fraser to be tried by court martial. After Fort Necessity was surrendered the eastern gentry were more appreciative of the services of the
Indian traders. In 1760, Trent sued Dinwiddie at Williamsburg for
malicious attacks on his character and was awarded £800 with costs. —
Washington to Dinwiddie, June 10, 1754, in *Writings*, I, 96-99; Mercer to
Trent, Nov. 8, 1760, in Ohio Co. MSS., I, 34.

[138] Official Corresp., VI, 21., Penn MSS.; *Pa. Arch.*, II, 119, 144.

become allies of the French and that a large party of
French and Indians was coming up the Ohio to coöperate with the force which was moving south from Lake
Erie; that when he had asked the Indians about the
clause in Lewis Montour's treaty by which they ceded
all their lands east of the Ohio to the traders in return
for cancelling their debts, they replied that this clause
must have been added by the traders who wrote the
treaty, for they knew nothing of it.

This council at Logstown was one of the most difficult which Croghan had conducted. When Croghan,
Montour, and Patten arrived they found that the
greater number of the Indians were drunk and the
drinking continued so that ten days elapsed before
they could open a council. Moreover, the attitude of
the Indians had so changed that they saluted Croghan
and his party by informing them that they were prisoners. They saved themselves by announcing that they
had come to restore two Shawnee prisoners. The day
after Croghan had arrived, five French canoes with
two officers, fifteen soldiers, and some Iroquois arrived
from Venango. When Patten walked by their tents
he was taken prisoner and released only after Croghan
and Montour had gone to the French officers and
demanded it. The threats of the Ohio Indians caused
the French to go down the Ohio, but they returned and
on January 26, they met the Indians in council, asked
them to drive out the English, and gave them a present.
The next day Croghan met the same Indians and also
made them a gift.[189]

The English were losing the support of the Indians

    [189] Croghan's Journal, Jan. 12-Feb. 3, 1754, is found in Indian Affairs, II,
1ff., Penn MSS., in *Pa. Col. Rec.*, V, 731-735, and in Thwaites: *Early Western
Travels*, I, 72-82; Hamilton sent a copy to Dinwiddie. Cf. Prov. Pap., XII,
49; *Pa. Col. Rec.*, V, 591-700, 707, 757.

principally because they did not erect forts and prepare for defense. When the Quaker assembly was
once more urged to follow such a policy it again
claimed that the forks of the Ohio were not within the
jurisdiction of their province. This led Croghan to
write: "I Wish with all My hart Some gentelmen
who is an Artist in Philadelphia, and whos Acount
wold be Depended on, whould have the Curiosety to
take a Journay in those parts, whos Return, I Dear
Say, wold give A Ginrel Satisfaction to the whole
Province." [140] The assembly now began to scrutinize
the bills which Croghan sent in and struck out £50
from one and £30 from another. At the end of the year
he complained that during the past years when he was
engaged in official business, sometimes at the risk of his
life, he had never been paid a farthing for his time,
but only for the hire of his packhorses and men; yet for
the mission in January, 1754, Patten was paid £50
while Croghan received no pay though he had served
longer than Patten. This attitude of the assembly
helped to cause Croghan to leave for Virginia. Here
the military operations of Washington were to give
him new fields of opportunity to serve against his old
rivals and enemies.

Among the more important problems which confronted Major George Washington in 1754 were those
of securing supplies and transporting them through
the wilderness, and of maintaining favorable relations
with the Indians. Croghan assisted in solving each
of these problems. Croghan and Trent furnished
Washington with much of the powder and lead which
he used at Fort Necessity. On May 30, 1754, follow-

---

[140] Croghan to Peters, Mar. 23, 1754, in *Pa. Arch.*, II, 133; *Pa. Col. Rec.*,
V, 730, 750, 753, 758-765.

ing a conference with Governor Dinwiddie at Winchester, Croghan contracted to transport to Redstone Creek 10,000 pounds of flour by means of packhorses. He also promised John Carlyle, the commissary for the Virginia forces, to transport an additional 50,000 pounds. Flour reached Washington's soldiers so slowly that at one time they had none for six days. Carlyle explained that neither Gist nor Croghan were fulfilling their agreements. Of Croghan he wrote: "I understand he's not a man of Truth and therefore not to be depended on . . . ", and stated that Dinwiddie was sorry he had put him in a position of trust. Washington, himself, wrote to Fairfax: "The promises of those traders . . . are not to be depended upon; a most flagrant instance of which we experienced in Croghan, who . . . had the assurance, during our sufferings, to tantalize us, and boast of the quantity he could furnish, as he did of the number of horses he could command . . . out of two hundred head he had contracted for, we never had above twenty-five employed in bringing the flour that was engaged for the camp; and even this, small as the quantity was, did not arrive within a month of the time it was to have been delivered." Carlyle and young Washington, placed in positions of responsibility in the midst of serious events, were probably too severe in their condemnation of Croghan.[141]

[141] Fairfax to Washington, July 10, 1754, in Hamilton, Stanislaus M.. *Letters to Washington*, I, 26; Carlyle to Washington, June 17 and 28, 1754, in *idem*, 5, 8, 18; Washington to Dinwiddie, June 10 and 12, 1754, in *Writings*, I, 96ff.; Washington to Fairfax, Aug. 11, 1754, *idem*, 132. – No documents giving Croghan's side of the case were found. He probably encountered the same obstacles that delayed Gist, but he was much more severely condemned. The bitter rivalry between Pennsylvania and Virginia traders probably had much to do with criticisms of Croghan. Gist and Croghan had many incentives to fulfill their agreements if possible.

When Washington started on his retreat to Fort Necessity he impressed the packhorses of Croghan and Trent. As a result, such furs and merchandise as they still had in the woods were left behind for the French to seize.

Croghan was also associated with Washington as an Indian agent. Dinwiddie wrote Washington on June 1, 1754: "Mr. Geo. Croghan, a Gent. well acquainted with Ind'n Affairs, is engag'd by me to serve His M'y as an Interpreter," and added that he was sending some Indian presents in whose distribution Croghan and Montour were to assist and advise him. Washington expected Croghan to enlist the aid of a large number of Indians. The task was a difficult one. Some Indians came to his camp as friends and others as spies. Many of the Indians felt that Washington regarded them as slaves who were to be sent out alone every day scouting and attacking the enemy. In spite of great efforts on the part of Croghan and Montour, but thirty warriors joined Washington and of these not more than half were in service at any one time. Washington was sorely disappointed with the failure of Croghan and Montour. They had stated that their influence with the Indians was so strong that they would be able to enlist a large number to aid him. Their failure is largely explained by Washington, himself, who wrote to Fairfax: ". . . if we depend on Indian assistance, we must have a large quantity of proper Indian goods to reward their services, and make them presents. It is by this means alone, that the French command such an interest among them, and that we had so few. This with the scarcity of provisions, was proverbial; would induce them to ask, when they were to join us, if we meant to starve them

as well as ourselves." The campaign of 1754 gave
Croghan and Washington their first military experience. That the campaign failed was not due to their
conduct.[142]

The news of the defeat at Fort Necessity was
brought to Governor Hamilton by an express sent by
Callender, one of Croghan's partners. After Washington's retreat, not an English flag waved beyond the
Alleghenies and soon nearly all the Ohio tribes drew
their scalping knives to aid the French. Croghan
now left Virginia and because of his debts retired to
Aughwick. About two hundred Indians, still faithful
to the English, without an invitation sought safety by
following their old friend to his new abode. This
farthest outpost in Pennsylvania soon became an important center of activity. Leading Indian traders
and frontiersmen visited Croghan from time to time;
Indian runners brought intelligence from the Ohio
which was sent on to Philadelphia by expresses and
then forwarded to Governors Sharpe of Maryland and
Dinwiddie of Virginia. James Burd, one of Croghan's visitors, wrote on September 25, 1754: "On
Friday night last about 12 o'Clock there arrived at
Auchwick while I was there one of our Indians who
had traveled night and day from the French fort to
give us Intelligence that there was Three hundred
French Indians arrived to make a Divertion upon our
Back Inhabitants. This Mr. Croghan desired me to
acquaint his Honour our Governour which you'l please
do." [143]

---

[142] Washington's Journal, June 21 and 25, 1754, in *Writings*, I, 118;
Weiser's Journal, Sept. 3, 1754, in *Pa. Col. Rec.*, VI, 151-2; *idem*, 195; Dinwiddie to Washington, June 1, 1754, in *Dinwiddie Pap.*, I, 186; *idem*, 255.

[143] *Votes of the Assembly*, IV, 323; Croghan to Hamilton, Aug. 16 and 30,
1754, in *Pa. Col. Rec.*, VI, 140; *idem*, 161; *Pa. Arch.*, II, 173; James Burd to

Croghan soon found thrust upon him the trouble-some problem of providing food for the Indian refugees. They erected some twenty cabins near his house and expected to be provided for by the provin-cial government in accordance with its promise. Game was not plentiful nearby and the Indians feared to penetrate far into the forest. They helped them-selves to such provisions as Croghan's clearing fur-nished, destroying thirty acres of Indian corn. Cro-ghan felt compelled to purchase provisions for them. Unscrupulous traders, supplied by some county offi-cials, sold liquor to the Indians. Some of the Indians traded for liquor even the clothes which they wore and then came to Croghan expecting him to furnish them with new clothing. Croghan endeavored to prevent the sale of liquor. He wrote to Hamilton: ". . . nor do I even keep one Drop in my own House." Later he wrote to Governor Morris: "I am oblig'd to give them a Cag Now and then myself for a frolick, but that is Attended with no Expense to the Govern-ment nor no bad Consequence to the Indians as I Do itt butt onst a Month . . ." In order to determine what should be done, Hamilton in August, 1754, sent Weiser out to investigate and report. He told the Indians in council that they would be taken care of by the government. He brought £300 to Croghan to re-imburse him and enable him to buy provisions until the assembly should determine the policy to be followed. Croghan was also told to present a bill for the damage to his crops and was assured that payment for his services would be duly considered.[144]

As winter came on Croghan's task became more

———, Sept. 25, 1754, in Shippen Corresp., I, 159; Croghan to Burd, Dec. 2, 1754, in idem, 159.

144 Croghan to Hamilton, Aug. 30, 1754, in Pa. Col. Rec., VI, 161; idem,

difficult. Gifts had to be given to visiting Indians
and to messengers and scouts; Virginia accused him of
enticing friendly warriors to leave her soil; the Indians
suspected him of holding back goods when he did not
supply all their wants; the government of Pennsylvania delayed supplying him with funds until it was
necessary for him to secure provisions on his own
credit from inhabitants of the back country; and to
add to his troubles his own government distrusted him.
Weiser had violated the governor's instructions by
leaving with Croghan money for purchasing provisions
instead of purchasing the provisions himself and leaving them with Croghan.   He defended his action by
saying that Croghan "might (if he intended it) pur-
loin a great deal of it, but I have the Opinion of
him that he will do Justice . . . Mr. Croghan
must either be trusted to buy and distribute Provision
or the Government must keep a Man there in whom
they can confide . . ." Croghan felt this keenly
and wrote to Peters, his intimate friend: "I think itt
to hard to be att a Loss by acting for the good of the
Province, besides Laying my Self under a great many
Reflections . . ." After some delay the assembly
paid, one by one, the bills which Croghan presented.
The total cost to Pennsylvania of maintaining the
Indian refugees was about £1,000.[145]

Croghan was glad to be called away from Aughwick
to aid General Braddock.   He offered the free use of

130, 146-149, 219; Weiser's Journal, in *idem*, 150-160; Croghan to Morris,
Dec. 23, 1754, in *Pa. Arch.*, II, 219.

[145] Weiser to Hamilton, Sept. 13, 1754, in *Pa. Col. Rec.*, VI, 149; *idem*,
189, 218, 375; Croghan to Peters, Dec. 2, 1754, in *Pa. Arch.*, II, 212; *idem*,
209, 218; Croghan to Isaac Norris, Mar. 25, 1755, in Misc. MSS., I, 82,
Etting Coll.; Morris to Croghan, Dec. 7, 1754, in Prov. Pap., XIII, 51; Peters
to Croghan, 1755, in *idem*, XVI, 92; *Votes of the Assembly*, IV, 401, 477, 613;
Bd. of Tr. Pap., Proprieties, XIX.

his house to the man who should take care of the Indians in his absence. He informed Governor Morris that all of his packhorses had been engaged for Braddock's expedition and that he therefore could no longer transport provisions for the Indians. He provided Braddock with about fifty packhorses; this was the largest number furnished by one individual. One compensation which Croghan received for his trying services at Aughwick during the year 1754-1755, was a strong recommendation by Peters to the new governor, Robert H. Morris. Also, these services helped in persuading the assembly to pass the act which granted him ten years' relief from his debts.[146]

Croghan was called away from Aughwick to assist in laying out two roads for Braddock's expedition. Braddock planned to advance upon Fort DuQuesne by way of the Potomac and contemplated the establishment of a garrison at the forks of the Ohio. He wished two roads to be built in Pennsylvania that he might be able to secure reinforcements by two different routes and that he might have access by the most direct route possible to the Susquehanna and Delaware valleys – the "bread basket" of the British colonies. One of these roads was to lead through the Cumberland valley to his camp at Will's Creek, the other to run westward from Shippensburg and connect near Fort DuQuesne with the road which he himself intended to build. So important did he consider them that he expressed his intention to postpone his advance until they were finished.[147]

[146] Croghan to Morris, May 20, 1755, in *Pa. Col. Rec.*, VI, 399; James Burd to ———, Mar. 11, 1755, Shippen Corresp., I, 173; Morris to Croghan, Nov. 25, 1754, in *Pa. Arch.*, II, 203; *idem*, 214.

[147] Morris to St. Clair, Feb. 28, 1755, in *Pa. Col. Rec.*, VI, 302; *idem*, 395ff.; Morris to Braddock, July 3, 1755, in *Pa. Arch.*, II, 372.

On February 24, 1755, Governor Morris received a letter from Quartermaster-General Sir John St. Clair asking that these roads be built. He at once went to the speaker of the assembly, who with a committee controlled a fund of £5,000, but they declined to aid. Fortunately, the speaker of the Delaware assembly, who had sole control over a fund of £1,000, agreed to pay the expenses of a survey. This enabled Morris to appoint commissioners to survey routes for the two roads. For this work, which was to be done as secretly as possible, he appointed on March 12, George Croghan, John Armstrong, James Burd, William Buchanan, and Adam Hoops. Croghan furnished pack-horses and Indian scouts and was expected to satisfy the curiosity of the Indians. He was also depended upon to guide the party, as he was the only one of the commissioners who was familiar with the region which was to be penetrated.[148]

The commissioners started from Carlisle on March 29, with two pilots, four packhorsemen, three blazers, two chain-carriers, and some Indians. The shortest route to the Ohio which they found followed an old Indian trail and trader's path; it began south of Shippensburg and then crossed the mountains, following Raystown Creek for part of the way. So dangerous was the work owing to scouting and hunting parties of the French and their Indian allies that the Indians who accompanied the party deserted until but one remained. A good route was found and blazed to within eighteen miles of the forks of the Youghiogheny. Here the approach of a French party caused a hurried return to Fort Cumberland.

---

[148] Morris to Braddock, May 12, 1755, in *Pa. Col. Rec.*, VI, 380; *idem*, 300, 318, 324, 484; Morris to Orme, May 26, 1755, in *Pa. Arch.*, II, 330;

The report of the commissioners to Governor Morris narrates the manner in which they were here received by General St. Clair after they had risked their lives in the service of the army: "We waited for Sir John's coming to camp . . . [he] treated Us in a very disagreeable manner; he is extremely warm and angry at our Province; he would not look at our Draughts nor suffer any Representations to be made to him in regard of the Province, but stormed like a Lyon Rampant. He said our Commission to lay out the Road should have been issued in January last upon his first Letter, that doing it now is doing of nothing, that the Troops must march on the first of May, that the want of this Road and the Provisions promised by Pennsylvania has retarded the Expedition, which may cost them their Lives . . . ; That instead of marching to the Ohio he would in nine days march his Army into Cumberland County to cut the Roads, press Horses, Wagons, etc.; that he would not suffer a Soldier to handle an Axe, but by Fire and Sword oblige the Inhabitants to do it . . . ; that he would kill all kind of Cattle and carry away the Horses, burn the Houses, etc. . . . That he would tomorrow write to England by a Man-of-War, shake Mr. Penn's Proprietaryship, and represent Pennsylvania as a disaffected Province . . . and told Us to go to the General if We pleased, who would give Us ten bad Words for one that he had given." Morris complained to Braddock of St. Clair's words and was assured that the latter was ashamed of what he had said and had been reprimanded. His words, however, had some effect and represented the feelings of the

Accounts of the Commissioners for Burd's Road to the Ohio, in Norris of Fairhill MSS., 3-5.

English officers who were disgusted with the lack of support they received in the Quaker province. Upon the return of the commissioners they were each paid £7, 10s. and all expenses for their twenty-five days of service.[149]

The Quaker assembly finally agreed to pay for the construction of the roads which had been laid out and the commissioners who had surveyed the roads were instructed to supervise the work of construction. Amidst great difficulties and dangers a road was cut westward to a point beyond the present site of Bedford, when the news of Braddock's defeat caused the workmen to hasten back. The entire work had cost the province £3,000. Three years later Forbes made good use of the work that had been done and carried it on to the Ohio. Thereafter, the road which Croghan had helped to lay out remained a great thoroughfare to the West until it was displaced by the canal and the railroad.[150]

Croghan, however, had no part in the actual construction of the road. On April 23, instructions were sent to him to take to Fort Cumberland from Aughwick as many Indian warriors as he could. This was the result of several factors: of the four hundred Cherokees and Catawbas which Dinwiddie and Gist had promised Braddock, not one came; the Iroquois were with Shirley and Johnson; and the Ohio Indians were overawed by the French.[151] When Braddock heard of the refugees at Aughwick he wrote Morris

[149] *Votes of the Assembly*, IV, 30, 190; Report of the Commissioners, Apr. 16, 1755, in *Pa. Col. Rec.*, VI, 368-370; *Md. Archives*, I, 126; Hulbert, Archer B.: *Old Glade Road* (Historic Highways of America Series).

[150] Kitchin's Map of Pennsylvania, 1756; *Pa. Gazette*, June 26 and July 17, 1755; *Pa. Arch.*, II, 294, 317, 363; *Pa. Col. Rec.*, VI, 377-450, *passim*.

[151] Robert Orme's Journal, 314. References to this journal will be to it as printed in Sargent, Winthrop: *Braddock's Expedition*. It is the best

asking him to send the warriors to Fort Cumberland
and to take care at Aughwick of their women and
children.   Croghan received his instructions on the
night of April 30.   The next day he met the Indians
in council and made plans to start the following morning.   Before starting out he sent trusty messengers to
all the Ohio tribes urging them not to oppose Braddock.   The expense of bringing the Indians to Fort
Cumberland was advanced by Croghan, who later had
trouble to collect it from Pennsylvania.[152]

Croghan brought to Braddock about one hundred
Indians.   On May 15, Croghan wrote to Johnson that
he had "forty odd fighting Men and Lads," chiefly
Iroquois.   These warriors refused to leave their
families behind and so the women and children
accompanied them.   Braddock took Croghan and
Montour into his service and to Croghan he gave a
commission.[153]   A separate camp was provided for the
Indians and Braddock issued orders that they were not
to be spoken to nor molested.   On May 12, Braddock
and his officers met the Indians in council and urged
them to join his expedition; a "ceremony of Drams
round" followed.   On the 18th, another council was
held at which the Indians showed their appreciation
of the presents by making "a most horrible noise,
dancing all night."   On the 19th, Braddock again met
the Indians and was informed that they would take
up the hatchet and serve as scouts for him.   Thereupon Braddock ordered "3 Howitzers, 3 12-Pounders,
and 3 Cohorns to be fired, all the drums and fifes play-

source for the services rendered by Croghan and his Indians. Dinwiddie
to Halifax, Oct. 1, 1755, in Va. Pap., I, Bancroft Coll.

[152] Braddock to Morris, Apr. 15, 1755, in Pa. Arch., II, 290; idem, 308;
Pa. Col. Rec., VI, 370-382; idem, 398; Croghan to Morris, May 20, 1755, in
idem, 399.

[153] Johnson MSS., I, 168.

ing, and beating the point of war, which astonished and pleased the Indians greatly. They then retired to their own Camp where they ate a bullock, and danced their war dance . . ." On the 22d they were furnished with arms and clothing.[154]

A mutual interest and curiosity soon developed between the soldiers from Europe and the red men. A visit to the camp of the latter was one of the best diversions available for a soldier when off duty. Richard Peters, after a visit to Braddock, reported that the Indians "were extremely dissatisfied at not being consulted with by the General, and got frequently into high Quarrels, their Squas bringing them money in Plenty which they got from the Officers, who were scandalously fond of them. . ." Peters recommended to Braddock that the women and children be sent home and Colonel Innes acted likewise, adding that all but ten warriors should also be sent home as this number would be sufficient for scouts. When the women and children were ordered home most of the warriors went along as an escort and never returned. Thereafter, Braddock seems to have ceased to give much attention to the Indians. Their number instead of increasing on the march as Croghan had expected, decreased until he had but eight Indians left. At times some Indians from the Ohio would visit Braddock and promise to join him, but they always failed to keep their promise. Gordon wrote: "These people are villains, and always side with the strongest."[155]

[154] The best source for these events is Engineer Harry Gordon's Journal. References to this journal will be to it as printed in Sargent: *Braddock's Expedition*. Here it is printed as "The Morris Journal", with the author unidentified; Parkman in *Montcalm and Wolfe* calls it a "Journal of the Proceeding of the Detachment of Seamen"; Hulbert in *Braddock's Road* identifies the author and also prints the journal. Gordon belonged to the small detachment left by Admiral Keppel to aid Braddock.

[155] *Pa. Col. Rec.*, VI, 397, 460; Croghan to Morris, May 20, 1755, in *idem*,

The service performed on the march by Croghan and his eight faithful Indians, including the two chiefs, Scarroyaddy and Monacatootha, staunch friends to the English, must not be underestimated. Croghan furnished the messengers who kept open the communications between Braddock and Burd's roadcutters in Pennsylvania as they both moved westward into the wilderness. Croghan and the Indians were continually at the front and on the flanks of the army as it marched westward. On June 19, the French captured Scarroyaddy and his son who were saved only by the refusal of the hostile Indians to allow them to be killed. On July 6, during a skirmish with hostile Indians, the British soldiers by mistake fired on their own Indians, killing the son of Scarroyaddy. At times when stragglers were scalped, Croghan and his Indians with volunteers would be sent out to try to retaliate. It was not until they were within a few miles of Fort DuQuesne that Croghan's Indians faltered in securing intelligence. Finally, two of them agreed to go out; they came within a half mile of the fort and brought back the scalp of a French officer. A party which included Croghan and his Indians was then sent out to reconnoitre.[156]

Two days later, on the fatal July 9, 1755, came the French attack. Braddock was not surprised, as is so often stated. Croghan and his Indians, Gist, six mounted Virginians, the engineers led by Gordon, and a detachment of three hundred men headed his march. This vanguard was commanded by Lieutenant-Colonel Thomas Gage, later commander-in-chief of all the

399; Gordon's Journal, 380; Orme's Journal, 314, 340; Franklin's Autobiography, *Writings* (ed. Smyth), I, 400. Innes knew little of Indian affairs; cf. *Pa. Arch.*, II, 321.

[156] Burd to Peters, June 17, 1755, in *Pa. Col. Rec.*, VI, 435; *idem*, 460; Orme's Journal, 336, 342, 348-352.

British forces in America. Gordon first saw the French and Indians advancing in a body led by Beaujeau and dispersing when Beaujeau waved his hat. A few weeks after the battle Croghan told his friend Charles Swaine that he "had a free sight of the Enemy as they approached . . . they were about three hundred, the French in shirts and the Indians naked . . . lead by three French officers with hats in their hands, and with which they gave a Signal for the firing." [157]

No record has been found which tells of Croghan's conduct during the murderous battle which ensued. There is a record, however, which shows that in the disgraceful retreat which followed he manifested a high degree of courage and loyalty to his unfortunate commander-in-chief. Braddock had five horses shot under him and he was finally mortally wounded. His own redcoats fled so precipitately that Captain Orme, his aide-de-camp, could prevail on none to tarry long enough to carry off their dying general – not even when he offered a reward of sixty guineas. Two Americans, Croghan and Washington, helped to place Braddock on horseback and later into a wagon; their fire helped to keep back the enemy as they recrossed the Monongahela. The faithless conduct of the British soldiers added to the terrible defeat and his wounds caused Braddock to insist that he be left upon the field of battle to die like an old Roman. When this was denied him he attempted to seize Croghan's pistols to end his life. Croghan and Washington remained with Braddock till midnight on July 9, when they were

---

[157] Swaine to Peters, Aug. 5, 1755, in Peters MSS., IV, 38; cf. Gordon's Journal, 387. Swaine, Peters, and Croghan were intimate friends.

sent with six light-horse to secure aid from Colonel Dunbar.[158]

With the memories of the bloody defeat fresh in his mind and still subject to imprisonment for debt, Croghan returned during the late summer of 1755 to his home at Aughwick. When the causes for the catastrophe were given, it was charged that the Indian traders and frontiersmen had undermined the morale of the British soldiers by telling them if they fought in their accustomed manner they would certainly be defeated.[159] The failure of the expedition reacted on Croghan by discrediting him with Governor Morris and his council. They ignored him for months to come, even though his services were sorely needed. When Croghan had some advice or news which he felt ought to be given to the governor, he wrote confidentially to his old friend, ex-Governor Hamilton.[160] In spite of these conditions Croghan's temporary service as an imperial official gave him a greater feeling of responsibility for Indian affairs and helped to

[158] Horace Walpole to Sir Horace Mann, Aug. 28, 1755, in *Letters of Horace Walpole* (ed. Toynbee), III, 336. Dinwiddie to Halifax, Oct. 1, 1755, in Va. Pap., I, Bancroft Coll.; Gordon's Journal, 386; James Toby's Journal (MS. in the possession of the Shippen family). Croghan was probably in error when he wrote two years later that "had we had fifty Indians instead of eight, we might in a great measure have prevented the surprise, that day of our unhappy defeat." – Croghan's Transactions with the Indians, etc.; this statement is not included in this document as printed in the *N.Y. Col. Docs.*, VII, 271, nor in Thwaites: *Early Western Travels*, I, 88, but it is included in Sargent: *Braddock's Expedition*, 408, and in the manuscript copies in the Du Simitiere Coll. and in Indian Affairs, I, 51-52, Penn MSS. The common experiences of Croghan and Gordon led to an intimate friendship between these two men. Gordon soon developed an active interest in the West. He engaged with Croghan in land speculation in Pennsylvania, and in 1766, he accompanied Croghan to the Illinois country.

[159] Gage to Albermarle, July 24, 1755, in Keppel, Thomas R.: *Life of Admiral Keppel*, 218.

[160] Croghan to Hamilton, Nov. 12, 1755, in *Pa. Arch.*, II, 483.

prepare him for a permanent imperial appointment.[161]

The defeat of Braddock let loose upon the Pennsylvania, Maryland, and Virginia frontiers a fiendish swarm of savages which gave to the Quaker province its first taste of real Indian warfare. Adam Hoops, a friend of Croghan, wrote from Carlisle on November 3, 1755, to Governor Morris: "We, to be sure, are in as bad Circumstances as ever any poor Christians were ever in, For the Cries of Widowers, Widows, fatherless and Motherless Children, with many others for their Relations, are enough to Pierce the most hardest of hearts; Likewise it's a very Sorrowful specticle to see those that Escaped with their lives not a Mouthful to Eat, or Bed to lie on, or Cloths to Cover their Nakedness, or keep them warm, but all they had consumed into Ashes." [162]

This deplorable condition in Pennsylvania was due to internal as well as external causes. Quaker pacifism, the quarrel of the assembly with the proprietors over the taxation of their estates and with the crown over the issuance of paper money, and the failure to manage Indian affairs properly were the most important internal causes. Croghan wrote that because of the lack of funds little was being done to keep friendly Indians steadfast and that he was glad to have no part in the short-sighted Indian policy which was being pursued.[163] On October 31, 1755, five western leaders sent an appeal to Governor Morris saying in part: "We are all in uproar, all in Disorder, all willing to do, and have little in our power. We have no authority, no commissions, no officers, practiced in

---

[161] Croghan to Johnson, Sept. 10, 1755, in Johnson MSS., II, 212.

[162] Pa. Arch., II, 462.

[163] Croghan to Swaine, Oct. 9, 1755, in Pa. Col. Rec., VI, 642; cf. Peters to Weiser, Oct. 18, 1755, Weiser Corresp., I, 58.

War. . ." Trent wrote to Peters from Carlisle on
February 15, 1756: ". . . all the People have left
their Houses betwixt this and the Mountain, some come
to Town and others gathering into little Forts; they
are moving their Effects from Shippensburgh, every
one thinks of flying; unless the Government fall upon
some effectual Method, and that immediately, of securing the Frontiers, there will not be one inhabitant in
this Valley one Month longer. There is a few of us
endeavour to keep up the Spirits of the People." [164]
    One of these few staunch leaders in the great crisis
was Croghan. While people fled even from Shippensburg and while John Harris, who lived on the
eastern bank of the Susquehanna, was writing, "I have
this day cut holes in my House, and is determined to
hold out to the last extremity. . . ," Croghan was
raising a volunteer company and fortifying himself at
his own expense at Aughwick, forty miles further west
than Harris's Ferry. On October 9, 1755, he asked
Charles Swaine of Shippensburg for the immediate
loan of six guns with some powder and lead, promising
to return them as soon as he received his shipment
from Maryland. He wrote Johnson that he and his
company were ready to serve their King whenever
called upon. After his fort was finished he wrote to
Hamilton: "I have about 40 men with me there, butt
how long I shall be able to keep itt, I realy can't tell."
Doubtless his company was composed of old employees
and associates in the Indian trade. Aughwick became
a rallying place for Indians who still espoused the
English cause. Several times it was reported that
Croghan and his men had been cut off. Friendly
Indians came to warn him to save his scalp, which

---

[164] *Pa. Col. Rec.,* VI, 667; *Pa. Arch.,* II, 575.

would be no small prize to the French. Croghan and his men, however, remained in their little island fortress in the wilderness. Illimitable woods encompassed them and afforded an ideal lurking ground for hostile forces.[165]

At last when conditions reached the nadir, a peaceful political revolution occurred by which the Quakers lost their power. The colony now acted. An appropriation of £60,000 was made for defense and the proprietors offered a land bounty of 1,000 acres to every colonel, 500 acres to every captain, and 200 acres to every private who should enlist. An offer of $350 was made for the scalps of chiefs Shingas and Captain Jacobs and the government offered a bounty of $150 for the scalp of every male Indian above ten years of age and $50 for the scalp of every Indian woman. The Board of Commissioners, appointed by the assembly to supervise the expenditure of funds, planned and had built a chain of forts guarding the passes of the Blue Mountains from the Delaware River to the Maryland border. In spite of all these measures, the stealthy savage, in the dead hours of the night, fell upon the inhabitants at the least suspected points. Safety depended upon the capture of Fort DuQuesne and upon the work of the Indian agent rather than upon the erection of innumerable blockhouses and stockades.[166]

Most of the Indian traders who had been associated with Croghan entered the provincial military service. Callender, Ward, Smallman, and Trent became captains and Crawford, Prentice, and Alexander McKee became lieutenants.[167] On December 2, 1755,

---

[165] *Pa. Col. Rec.*, VI, 642, 655, 779; *Pa. Arch.*, II, 462, 484; Morris to Dinwiddie, Nov. 2, 1755, in Prov. Pap., XVI, 4.

[166] *Pa. Gazette*, Feb. 12 and Aug. 14, 1756; *Pa. Arch.*, II, 619; *Pa. Col. Rec.*, VI, 504.

[167] *Pa. Arch., 5th ser.*, I, *passim*.

the act granting Croghan and Trent ten years' relief
from their debts was passed. On December 18, Croghan was examined before the council on the defense of
the frontier and on the same day Hamilton gave him
a captain's commission. The situation had become so
serious that Hamilton had been called to the council
and while Governor Morris was in the western part of
the province examining the defenses, a *dedimus* had
been given Hamilton, thereby practically giving
Pennsylvania two governors for the time being. Hamilton wrote Morris on December 18: "I have given
Geo. Croghan a Captain's Commission; He is to raise
the men immediately, and Superintend the building
over Susquehanna, as I knew not whom else to employ,
and upon Supposition that He is honest, no body is
fitter for that Service." [168] At last Croghan had
secured the position for which he had yearned. He
at once entered upon his duties with great vigor.

As captain, Croghan received 7s. 6d. per day and
was eligible for a land bounty of 500 acres. He was
ordered to proceed across the Susquehanna and select
sites for, and erect, three stockades. Each was to be
fifty feet square, with blockhouses on each of two cor-
ners and with barracks capable of accommodating fifty
men. On December 17, 200 guns, 300 pounds powder,
500 pounds lead, 2000 flints, 26 brass kettles, and 240
blankets were issued to him; on January 1, 1756, he
also received 1 barrel powder, 1 drum, and 7 casks of
nails. After the forts had been built the men enlisted
for their defense, Croghan was given command of
his own stockade at Aughwick. This was strengthened
and named Fort Shirley. For its garrison of 75 men
Pennsylvania furnished only 30 guns. Additional

---

[168] *Pa. Col. Rec.*, VI, 670; *Pa. Arch.*, II, 537; Morris to Gov. Hardy, July
5, 1756, in *idem*, 689.

guns of a better grade, tools, and other supplies were furnished by Croghan himself. On June 1, 1756, Croghan was paid £200 for the equipment which he had furnished and for the work which he had done on Fort Shirley before the government assumed control over it.[169]

Croghan was stationed at Fort Shirley during the early part of 1756. Here he had charge of routine garrison duty. Patrols were sent out each day to scour the woods; spies as well as friendly Indians visited him. When Washington, who was in charge of the defense of Virginia's frontier, wished three trusty Indian messengers to send to the Ohio and Wabash Indians, Croghan provided them. Morris ordered Croghan to secure all possible intelligence of the movements and designs of the French and Indians. Croghan sent "Delaware Jo" to the Ohio. This Indian reported that all of the Ohio tribes had taken up the hatchet and that a large number of Indians were gathered at Kittanning and had with them more than one hundred prisoners from Pennsylvania and Virginia. This information resulted in Armstrong's daring and successful expedition. It started out from Fort Shirley and attacked Kittanning in 1756. Morris, however, who seems never to have had a high estimate of Croghan, wrote that he "never procured me any [intelligence] that was very material. . ."[170]

Croghan was called away from Fort Shirley for a short time in January, 1756, to assist in the Indian conferences at Harris's Ferry and Carlisle. But one

[169] Trent to Washington, Jan. 21, 1756, in Hamilton: *Letters to Washington*, I, 190; Orders to Croghan, 1755, in *Pa. Arch.*, II, 536; idem, 566, 623, 633; *Pa. Arch., 2nd ser.*, II, 695-696; *Votes of the Assembly*, IV, 620.

[170] *Pa. Gazette*, Feb. 19, March 18, and Apr. 1, 1756; Morris to Hardy, July 5, 1756, in *Pa. Arch.*, II, 690; idem, 571; *Pa. Col. Rec.*, VI, 781.

Seneca and one Mohawk Indian came to Harris's Ferry. When but seven Indians came to Carlisle, where were present Governor Morris, ex-Governor Hamilton, two members of the Board of Commissioners and Weiser, and when Croghan failed to appear until two days before the treaty was to open, he was asked to explain. He replied that he had been busy recruiting men and building forts and that the Indians were out hunting. The attempt to enlist the aid of the upper Susquehanna Indians proved a failure. The contrast between these conferences and the conferences held a few years before show to what extent the tide had turned against the English.[171]

After Croghan returned from Carlisle, news of the preparations at Fort DuQuesne by the French and Indians to attack his fort on about March 1, 1756, was brought to him by his Indian friends. Captain Coulon de Villiers, anxious to avenge the death of his brother Jumonville, set out in the spring of 1756 to attack Croghan's fort, but illness forced him to return. Thinking that Croghan was still at Fort Shirley, he set out again on July 13 with fifty-five men, but lost his way and came upon Fort Granville instead. This he attacked and destroyed. The destruction of Fort Granville, located east of Fort Shirley, together with the weakness of the latter due to its poor water supply, caused Fort Shirley to be abandoned in the fall of 1756.[172]

[171] *Pa. Arch.*, II, 538; *Pa. Col. Rec.*, VI, 753, 779-783; *idem*, VII, 1-7; Bd. of Tr. Pap., Proprieties, XIX. The account sent to England contains some material omitted in the *Pennsylvania Colonial Records*.

[172] Croghan to Burd, Feb. 5, 1756, in Shippen Corresp., II, 25; Villiers du Terrage: *Les derniers Années de la Louisiane Française*, 85-87; Bossu, N.: *Nouveaux Voyages aux Indes Occidentales, etc.*, I, 162; *N.Y. Col. Docs.*, x, 480; Col. Armstrong to Morris, Aug. 20, 1756, in *Pa. Col. Rec.*, VII, 231; *idem*, 242, 278.

Croghan had left Fort Shirley before its abandonment and never returned to Aughwick to reside. He
held his captain's commission but about three months,
resigning it in March, 1756. On March 15, he was
paid in full for his outlays while he was captain. His
successor, Captain Mercer, at once had difficulty in
keeping his company filled. Croghan had raised men
for the defense of the frontier and erected forts in a
very expeditious manner, but not so frugally as the
commissioners thought he might have done. . Disputes
over accounts followed and Croghan, who felt himself
unjustly treated and unappreciated, resigned. In
June, 1756, he informed Morris that he had not received pay upon a warrant from Braddock and asked
him for a recommendation to the new commander-in-
chief, General Shirley. This Morris gave to him and
he left for Albany. Here he soon entered the imperial
service under Sir William Johnson.[173]

From the very beginning of Croghan's official relations to Pennsylvania in 1747 until their end in 1756,
he never possessed the absolute confidence of most of
the colonial officials. Various illustrations of their
lack of confidence have been given in this chapter.
During the years 1754 to 1756 he was charged with
perfidious conduct on three different occasions. He
was suspected of participating in the illicit trade
whereby the French at Fort DuQuesne received not
only guns, powder, and lead, but also intelligence of
the movements of the English. The English traders
at Aughwick and along Raystown Creek were so active
in this trade that Braddock took measures to have it
stopped.[174]

---

[173] Shippen to Burd, Mar. 24, 1756, in Shippen Corresp., II, 35; *Votes of
the Assembly*, IV, 618, 620; *Pa. Arch.*, II, 623, 690.
[174] Braddock to Morris, May 4, 1755, in *Pa. Arch.*, II, 299.

Serious charges were also brought against Croghan because of his relation to the letters written by Captain Stobo, an English hostage at Fort DuQuesne. Stobo, at the risk of his life, wrote two letters to Colonel Innes, a commander of the Virginia forces; in one he enclosed a plan of Fort DuQuesne. These letters he succeeded in sending with two Indians who were going to Aughwick in August, 1754. Croghan, probably not appreciating their significance, opened the letters and sent copies to Hamilton. As a result, the French learned about it and Stobo suffered close confinement. The opening of Stobo's letters prompted Governor Sharpe of Maryland to write to Morris and suggest that Croghan be placed under surveillance. Sharpe accused Croghan of being a Roman Catholic, of harboring at Aughwick other Catholics who were in communication with the French, and of persuading the Indians to keep away from the camp at Will's Creek. Morris replied that he was informed that Croghan was not a Catholic, that Croghan had himself warned the authorities against illicit traders and regretted his indiscretion in opening Stobo's letters. As to the other charges, Morris ordered Weiser to investigate them quietly and wrote Sharpe: ". . . I hope they will not turn out to be anything very Material, or that will effect his faithfulness to the trust reposed in him, which at this time is of Great importance. . ." These secret attacks on Croghan's character were doubtless the cause of some of his troubles at Aughwick and Morris's hesitation to call upon him to help defend the frontier in 1755.[175]

175 Croghan to Hamilton, Aug. 16 and Aug. 30, 1754, in *Pa. Col. Rec.*, VI, 140, 160; Innes to Washington, Sept. 27, 1754, in Hamilton: *Letters to Washington*, I, 49; Corresp. of Gov. Sharpe, in *Md. Archives, 1888*, 153; Morris to Sharpe, Jan. 7, 1755, in *Pa. Arch.*, II, 113; cf. *Pa. Col. Rec.*, VI,

The most serious accusations against Croghan, however, were associated with the famous "Filius Gallicæ" letters to the Duc de Mirepoix, the French ambassador to England from 1749 to 1755. They were written by someone in America in January and March, 1756, and were sent by way of Londonderry, London, and Amsterdam. They were intercepted in Ireland and England. The writer stated that he was French by birth, a Roman Catholic, and a trusted British officer of high rank, but devoted to France; and that there were in Pennsylvania many discontented German and Irish Catholics among whom he could raise from 10,000 to 15,000 troops. To be able to do this, he asked for money, French passports, arms, and military commissions. He gave such accurate intelligence of the English plans that even the British officials in London were enlightened by the letters.[176]

To the statesmen and military leaders who were responsible for the maintenance of the British Empire at the time when report after report came from America telling of reverses and inefficiency, these letters seemed of vast importance. Morris wrote to Governor Hardy of New York: "I am with you in opinion that the French, both in Europe and America, have intelligence of every thing we do, and that we have many Spyes amongst us. . ."[177] The Earl of Halifax, President of the Board of Trade, wrote to

503. As printed, this letter is erroneously headed, "Gov. Hamilton to Gov. Sharpe", and dated 1754. Documents in the *Pennsylvania Archives* and the *Pennsylvania Colonial Records* for the period before 1752 are frequently dated in accordance with the ecclesiastical year which began on March 25.

[176] These letters with the correspondence relating to them are found in C. O., 46. They are printed in the *Annual Report of the Am. Hist. Ass'n, 1896*, I, 660-703. Cf. *Hist* MSS. *Commission of Gt. Br., Fourteenth Report, Appendix* x, MSS. *of the Earl of Dartmouth*, II, 7.

[177] Morris to Hardy, July 5, 1756, in *Pa. Arch.*, II, 689; *idem*, 690, 694; Loudoun to Denny, Jan. 5, 1757, in *Pa. Arch.*, III, 323.

Hardy: "It may be nothing. – It may be an Artifice to draw a little money from France. . . But on the other hand, it may be a matter of the highest consequence. . ." So important were these letters considered that the highest civil and military officials in America were ordered to investigate the matter in person with the utmost secrecy.

The author, however, was never discovered. The Indian traders and Catholics of Pennsylvania and Maryland were especially suspected. Morris had Peters send to Hardy specimens of the handwriting of all the leading Indian traders of Pennsylvania. Lydius, Joncourt, a popish priest, a jesuit of Philadelphia, Washington, and Croghan were mentioned as possible authors. Henry Fox, Secretary of State, wrote to the Duke of Devonshire on April 20, 1756: "One Captain George Croghan, an Intriguing, Disaffected Person, an Indian Trader, in Pennsylvania, was very much suspected. . ." Fox ordered Colonel Webb, commander-in-chief of the British forces in America at the time, to make particular inquiry in regard to Croghan and if he found the suspicion justified, to send Croghan and all his accomplices with the evidence against them to England. John Pownall, Secretary to the Board of Trade, appears to have been responsible for the attention centered on Croghan.

The authorship as well as an estimate of the importance of the "Filius Gallicæ" letters remains one of the unsolved problems of history.[178] It is not probable that Croghan was the author. The letters were not in his handwriting. Hardy and Morris did not consider the suspicions of Croghan justified. Johnson,

---

[178] Professor Archer B. Hulbert of Colorado College, who has been interested in this problem, courteously sent to the writer some transcripts from the Public Record Office which bear upon it.

to whom the records of the case had been opened, revealed his opinion when he appointed Croghan as his Deputy Superintendent of Indian Affairs. All of the relations which Croghan had had with the French for over a decade would lead him to a policy of revenge and not one of coöperation with them. A study of Croghan's character as revealed by his entire life would not lead one to suspect him of playing the part of a traitor.

Because of the very secret nature of the investigation few people ever knew that Croghan was suspected of treachery; he, himself, may never have been aware of it. That he had rivals and enemies whose reports caused English officials to know him as an intriguing, discontented man, unworthy of trust, is evident; this factor was probably one cause of many of his troubles. One direct effect of the shadow cast over his reputation can be traced; the Earl of Loudoun declined Croghan's offer to recruit a company of fearless and skilled white woodsmen similar to the famous rangers of Major Robert Rogers and to enter Loudoun's service at their head. Instead, Loudoun suggested to Johnson that Croghan's services be utilized as an Indian agent.[179]

The mistrust displayed towards Croghan by colonial and imperial officials was due to various factors. He

---

[179] Loudoun to Johnson, Sept. 19, 1756, in Johnson MSS., IV, 120. This suspicion of Croghan was not, as Kingsford states (*History of Canada*, IV, 23), a cause of his resigning as captain. Kingsford is led to make this statement by erroneously placing the date of Croghan's resignation in July instead of in March, 1756. The only persons who were charged to investigate in America the authorship of the letters were the Earl of Loudoun, Governor Hardy, and Colonel Webb. Loudoun did not arrive in America until July 23, 1756. The letters to Hardy were entrusted to Webb, who did not arrive in America until June 7, 1756. The letters first came to the notice of Halifax in England during March, 1756. Before any influence radiating from these officials could affect Croghan beyond the Susquehanna, he had already resigned his commission.

was handicapped as well as aided by certain traits in his character. He was a born diplomat and put into practice Talleyrand's famous dictum that language is made' to conceal thoughts and not to reveal them. This made him a wily and successful Indian agent, but it also engendered distrust. John Connolly, who knew him well, wrote to Washington: "You must well know how specious He is. . . As He is specious where unknown He may impose and carry points. . ."[180] Levi A. Levy wrote confidentially of Croghan: ". . . he is such an Artful person, I make no doubt he will take some person in, in Virginia."[181] Croghan's intimate friend, George Morgan, in a letter to his wife, characterized Croghan as follows: "He can appear highly pleased when most chagrined and show the greatest indifference when most pleased. Notwithstanding my warm temper, I know you would rather have me as I am than to practice such deceit."[182] A second cause of distrust was the fact that Croghan was almost always financially interested in his missions. In these two respects he was in marked contrast to Conrad Weiser and Christian Frederick Post. They had almost no financial interest in their missions and instead of the craft of the diplomat, they possessed the guileless simplicity of the ascetic and the missionary.

Croghan's frequent disregard of official instructions, especially concerning expenditures, made him more efficient, though less trusted as an Indian agent. To eastern officials he seemed profuse in his gifts to the Indians. His lack of respect for legal formalities, so typical of the frontier, is illustrated by the following

[180] Connolly to Washington, June 7, 1774, in Hamilton: *Letters to Washington*, v, 8.

[181] Levi A. Levy to M. Gratz, June 23, 1774, in McAllister Coll.

[182] Morgan to Mary Morgan, July 8, 1766, in *Ill. Hist. Coll.*, XI, 316.

characterization in a business memorandum: "He has Only Acted according to his Usual practice, Which is that of doing what He has no right to do." [183]

The conditions under which he carried on his official duties were also conducive to a lack of trust in him. Eastern officials usually had no other alternative but to employ him or some other Indian trader for their missions to the West and after he entered the wilderness they had no satisfactory means of ascertaining whether he was properly carrying out their instructions. Finally, the machinations of rival traders, the natural prejudice and contempt of many eastern aristocrats and English military officials for a frontiersman, together with the opposition of the dominant faction in Pennsylvania to an aggressive military policy which Croghan and most other Episcopalians supported, helped to arouse and circulate attacks on his conduct and character. Though many of these attacks were unjust, Croghan did not become embittered thereby.

"Were there nothing at Stake between the Crowns of Great Britain and France, but the Lands on that Part of the Ohio included in this Map, we may reckon it as great a Prize as has ever been contended for, between two Nations. . ." wrote Lewis Evans in 1755.[184] It was during the period immediately following 1747 that these two nations first fully appreciated the importance of this great valley. Few Englishmen did more than Croghan to bring the English to realize its great potential value. One of the most important causes of the Seven Years War between England and France was their rivalry for its control.

Few Englishmen had more at stake in this struggle

---

[183] Ohio Co. MSS., II, 15.
[184] Evans: *Analysis of a Map of the Middle British Colonies, etc.*, 31.

than had Croghan.   Loyalty to his King as well as his
own vital material interests caused him to put forth
his best efforts for almost a decade to help stem the
rising French tide.   He was always present at the
places where the struggle was most critical, rendering
daring and efficient service.   In times of crises men
looked to him for counsel and guidance.   In trying to
unite in support of an aggressive western policy the colonists living near the seaboard and those living near the
frontier, with their widely divergent attitude towards
Indian affairs and the West, Croghan suffered many
unpleasant experiences.   The official relations which
Croghan had had with Pennsylvania and Virginia
brought him certain advantages: it increased his prestige among the Indians and for a time this enabled him
to increase his trade; it helped him to keep out of a
debtor's prison; it gave him the opportunity to become
acquainted with the leaders in the east; and finally, the
experience which he had gained as a provincial Indian
agent and as a temporary imperial official under Braddock prepared him for a wider field of service.   He
soon developed a longing to enter permanently the
imperial service.

Deputy Superintendent: Turning the Tide of French Aggression, 1756-1758

Before 1755, the British government had left the management of Indian affairs almost wholly to the individual colonies. This policy was not discarded in order to lessen the powers of local self-government or to increase the authority of imperial officials. The statesmen who were guiding the destiny of the British Empire during this critical period did not even have in mind a well-matured plan when they took the management of Indian affairs out of the hands of provincial officials and placed it in the hands of a new group of imperial officials. It was the very pressing immediate military necessity "to regain the Confidence, and combine the Force of the Savages against a then powerful Enemy" in a great conflict that caused this change to be made.[185] To understand Indian affairs in the English colonies from 1755 to 1775 one must bear in mind that during the French and Indian War the Indian department was made an adjunct to the military department and that after this war was over, in spite of all efforts, the Indian department was never able to free itself from this control.

Indian affairs had been managed by the individual colonies for more than a century. Under their various policies the natives had been continually robbed of their land and cheated in trade until many who had

---

[185] Hillsborough to Gage, Apr. 15, 1768, in C. O., 5:86; Carter, C. E., "The Military Office in America, 1755-1775," in *Am. Hist. Rev.*, XXVIII, 475ff.

been friends of the whites, became their enemies. Many bloody Indian conflicts resulted. Moreover, to the detriment of the general welfare, intercolonial rivalries and jealousies found expression in Indian affairs. In times of peace, Pennsylvania traders were glad to see the Ohio Indians suspicious of the designs of the Virginians, and Virginians trading with the Cherokees and Catawbas were the bitter rivals of the Carolina traders. In times of war, Cherokees and Catawbas went into the service of Pennsylvania, Maryland, or Virginia. They sold their services to the highest bidder, sometimes securing payment from two or more colonies for the same service; to secure scalp bounties in plenty they would show a scalp in one colony, secure a bounty there, and then carry the scalp to another colony and secure a second bounty.[186] Those statesmen who did not discern the irrepressible conflict between the red man and the white man, thought that these evils could be eliminated by an efficient imperial control; wiser men felt that such control would mitigate these evils.[187]

New York had attempted to bring about coöperation in Indian affairs among the various colonies, but had failed. In July, 1754, the Congress of Albany had unanimously agreed that Indian affairs should be controlled and financed by the proposed central government. Imperial management of Indian affairs was achieved, however, not by coöperative agreement, but by royal instructions emanating from the ministry in London. On August 9, 1754, the Board of Trade drew up a "Plan of General Concert" for defense. This

---

[186] Edmund Atkin to Gov. Sharpe of Md., June 12, 1757, in *Pa. Arch.*, III, 183; *idem*, 175, 197, 268.

[187] Gov. Hamilton to Gov. Dinwiddie, Aug. 2, 1753, in *Pa. Col. Rec.*, V, 632.

provided that "the sole direction of Indian Affairs be placed in the hands of some one single person, Commander-in-chief . . . of all Your Majesties' Forts and Garrisons in North America and of all Forces raised therein or sent thither, and likewise Commissary-General for Indian Affairs." [188] On October 29, the Board recommended that William Johnson be appointed Colonel of the Six Nations and that all imperial presents for these tribes be distributed through him. Instructions to Braddock, dated November 25, 1754, directed him to cultivate a policy of friendship and alliance with the Indians; to appoint someone to superintend the affairs of the southern Indians and to watch that presents be fairly and economically distributed.

After Braddock arrived in America, he gave Johnson a commission as "Superintendent of the Affairs of the Six Nations, their Allies and Dependents" and a fund of £2,000 sterling for presents. Later, on February 17, 1756, Johnson received from George II a royal commission as "Colonel of our Faithful Subjects, and Allies, the Six united Nations of Indians and their Confederates, in the Northern Parts of North America" and "Sole Agent and Superintendent of the said Indians and their Affairs . . ." His salary was fixed at £600 sterling per year to be paid out of military funds in the hands of the commander-in-chief. The latter's orders were to be observed and followed by Johnson according to the rules and discipline of war.[189] In a similar manner, Edmund Atkin was appointed

---

[188] Representation of the Board of Trade, Aug. 9, 1754, in *N.Y. Col. Docs.*, VI, 901; *idem*, 919, 961. During the period under consideration, the most important commanders-in-chief were the following: Braddock, Nov., 1754-July, 1755; Loudoun, March, 1756-1757; Abercromby, 1757-Sept., 1758; Amherst, 1758-Nov., 1763; and Gage, 1763-1772.

[189] Royal Commission to Johnson, Feb. 16, 1756, in C. O., 324: 38, f. 445.

Superintendent of the Southern Indians. Atkin was succeeded in 1763 by John Stuart. Stuart held this office until it disappeared during the American Revolution. In the Northern District, Sir William Johnson was superintendent for twenty years. After his death in 1774, he was succeeded by his nephew Guy Johnson. Unlike the Southern District, the Northern District did not disappear as an administrative unit during the Revolution, but thereafter it was confined to Canada.

The Northern District was always considered to be the more important. Johnson recommended that the division of presents for the two districts be in the ratio of two to one. Roughly speaking, the districts were bounded by the Potomac and Ohio rivers. The Board of Trade, in 1764, considered making the Ohio River the line of division, but did not do so because northern tribes exercised jurisdiction and had claims south of the Ohio. Division was therefore indicated by the enumeration of tribes. After the Illinois country was occupied in 1765, both Johnson and Stuart desired to have it included in their district. It was made part of the Northern District.[190]

Much of the prestige of the Northern District and of the entire Indian department was due to the ability and influence of Johnson. He was born in Ireland of a good family and came to New York in 1738. His uncle, Admiral Sir Peter Warren, had extensive lands on the Mohawk and young Johnson was given charge of them. Here he soon acquired a vast estate for himself. On it he erected a fortified mansion, Johnson Hall, where he lived like a semi-feudal lord. Here

---

[190] Johnson to the Board of Trade, Sept. 10, 1756, in *N.Y. Col. Docs.*, VII, 128; Board of Trade to Johnson, July 10, 1764, in *idem*, 635; *Ill. Hist. Coll.*, X, 464.

he entertained his numerous friends, both white and red. His fair dealing, his genial character, and his ability to adapt himself to their ways, soon gave him vast influence over his neighbors, the powerful Iroquois. After the death of his wife he selected a young Mohawk squaw, Molly Brant, to preside over his household.

The year 1755 saw Braddock defeated by the French, but it also saw General Johnson defeat the French army under Baron Dieskau near Crown Point and capture Dieskau, himself. For this victory, King George II created Johnson a baronet and Parliament voted him £5,000. The part he played in the capture of Fort Niagara further increased his military reputation. He was equally at ease in the mansion of a royal governor and in the wigwam of an Indian brave. His remarkable success in Indian affairs was largely due to the fact that, unlike nearly all European military officers, he did not look upon the Indians in the spirit manifested in the following quotation from Dieskau: "They drive us crazy from morning till night. There is no end to their demands. They have already eaten five oxen and as many hogs, without counting the kegs of brandy they have drunk. In short, one needs the patience of an angel to get on with these devils; and yet one must always force himself to seem pleased with them." [191]

Such feelings on the part of the military officials tended to cause them to underestimate the value of the services of those who were given charge of Indian affairs. Atkin, for example, came to New York on October 6, 1756, in order to secure his commission and

[191] Parkman, Francis: *Conspiracy of Pontiac*, I, 90-93; Stone, William L.: *Life and Times of Sir William Johnson*; Parkman: *Montcalm and Wolfe*, I, 297.

instructions from the new commander-in-chief, Lord
Loudoun. After waiting for weeks, he was informed
that Loudoun had set out for Boston on January 10,
1757. Atkin followed him, but Loudoun returned to
New York without issuing the necessary documents.
Atkin followed him back to New York. Here Atkin
reported home on March 1: "So after traveling since
my first Arrival here by Land and Water above 900
Miles, through Severest Frosts and Snow and the worst
of Roads, behold here I am again just where I was the
6th of October; and Still expect not to receive my Dispatches till I reach Philadelphia for which place his
Lordship will set out. . . And I shall accompany
him." [192]

Control over the purse strings of the Indian department by others, was its chief handicap in rendering
efficient service and in achieving an independent position. No sooner was Atkin appointed than he begged
the Board of Trade that he be not sent empty-handed
to the Indian nations. When imperial funds were lacking he fell back upon contributions by the colonies.
Virginia at first supported him loyally, but after a little
more than a year had elapsed, Governor Dinwiddie
wrote to Washington on October 19, 1757: "That
Gent has render'd a monstrous Acco't of Expenses,
which is laid before the Council to Examine." [193]
Johnson's experience was not so trying. In two years
he had secured and spent £19,619 9s. 1½d.[194] But he,
too, wrote home: "I am extremely concerned that the
great expense which this Service hath occasioned,

[192] Atkin to Board of Trade, Mar. 1, 1757, in Bd. of Tr. Pap., Plantations
General, xv.

[193] *Dinwiddie Pap., Va. Hist. Coll.,* IV, 707.

[194] Johnson's Report on Indian Expenditures, March 30, 1755 to October
12, 1756, in C. O., 5: 1067.

should not have produced more favourable Effects.
. . . If your Lordships should be of Opinion that
. . . the Advantages of this Service will not be
adequate to the Expense . . . I shall . . . be
ready and willing to resign my Commission. . ." [195]
At times, the Indian officials had to rely upon charity
or their own private purses to carry on government
business. Such imperial funds as were received had
to pass through the hands of the commander-in-chief
or subordinate military officials.

It was under such conditions, in 1756, the second
year of Johnson's superintendency, that George Croghan was appointed Deputy Superintendent in the
Northern District. Until 1760, Johnson had no other
deputy, but after the surrender of Canada his staff was
increased by the appointment of Daniel Claus in 1760,
Guy Johnson in 1762, and Major Joseph Gorham in
1767. Each drew a salary of £200 sterling. Of these
four deputy superintendents, Croghan rendered by far
the most important services. His appointment was
based solely on his merits, whereas the fact that Daniel
Claus was Johnson's son-in-law and Guy Johnson his
nephew and son-in-law was doubtless responsible for
their appointment. Gorham owed his position entirely
to the political influence of friends in England. This
influence was so strong, that had not Gage and Johnson
objected, he would have received the rank of Superintendent of Indian Affairs and would have had a third
district created for him. [196]

[195] Johnson to Board of Trade, June 25, 1757, in Bd. Tr. Pap., Plantations
General, XVI.

[196] Johnson to the Board of Trade, Nov. 13, 1763, in *N. Y. Col. Docs.*
VII, 579; *Doc. Hist. of N.Y.*, II, 841; *Ill. Hist. Coll.*, XI, 458. The references
to Croghan in the Johnson Manuscripts are almost as numerous as all the
references to the other three deputies combined.

Gorham was assigned to Nova Scotia – a region where the Indian question had long ceased to be very important and where a placeman could draw his salary without much labor. Claus was assigned to Canada and made his headquarters at Montreal; the Indians in this region had lost their spirit of independence and native vigor as a result of living for over a century as neighbors to Europeans. Guy Johnson assisted his uncle in New York in his numerous conferences with the friendly Iroquois and also at times acted as his secretary. To Croghan were assigned the tribes of Pennsylvania and the Ohio valley, including the distant tribes in the Illinois country. Here the friction between the two races over trade and land was greatest. During this period, it was in the Ohio valley that the center of Indian population was located. The formidable power of these tribes was shown in Braddock's defeat, in many bloody raids on the frontiers of Virginia, Maryland, and Pennsylvania, and finally in Pontiac's conspiracy. The Indian agent who entered their country frequently did so at the risk of his life. Probably no man was better equipped to serve his fellow countrymen in this field than George Croghan.

It was while Croghan was with Braddock that he began to develop a longing to enter the imperial service. On May 15, 1755, he wrote to Johnson: "I should be glad to keep up a Correspondence with you and shall by every opportunity let you know what is doing in these parts." [197] After his return to Pennsylvania he wrote again: "If I can be of any Service in the Expedition [against Dieskau at Crown Point] or in Indian Afairs in this Part of the Country I Shall be

_____
[197] Johnson MSS., I, 168.

very Proud to Serve his Majesty and Expects your Interest if you Shall think Me Deserving. . ." [198]

Croghan left Pennsylvania in the spring of 1756 and visited Fort Johnson. Here he at once began to assist Johnson in his task of keeping as many Indians as possible friendly to the English. He accompanied Johnson on his journey to Onondago in June and participated in the conferences held there. Later he assisted in various conferences at Fort Johnson with delegations of Iroquois, Shawnee, and Delawares. After the capture of Oswego by Montcalm, Johnson fell sick and his duties were assumed by Croghan. The latter led an Indian detachment to assist Colonel Webb in protecting the Oneida carrying place. In September, 1756, Lord Loudoun, the new commander-in-chief, planned to attack Ticonderoga. Johnson furnished him with two hundred Indians; of these, one hundred were led by Croghan.[199]

Loudoun recommended to Johnson that they consider employing Croghan in Indian affairs. As a result, before November 19, 1756, Croghan had been made Deputy Superintendent of Indian Affairs. The Board of Trade confirmed the appointment. Johnson suggested that Croghan be granted a commission, but Loudoun considered this unnecessary as Croghan was to act only as Johnson's deputy.[200] This remained Croghan's legal status for the sixteen years that he held office under Johnson. The arrangement worked satisfactorily because of the intimate personal relations that existed between Johnson and Croghan. When Cro-

---

[198] Croghan to Johnson, Sept. 10, 1755, in Johnson MSS., II, 212.

[199] C. O., 5: 1067; Minutes of various Indian Conferences, in *N.Y. Col. Docs.*, VII, 136, 152, 174, 175, 187-190, 196, 211, 230, 232, 236.

[200] Loudoun to Johnson, Sept. 19, 1756, in Sullivan, James: *Papers of Sir William Johnson*, II, 562; *idem*, 762, 764; *N.Y. Col. Docs.*, VII, 167-231; Brant MSS., 1F24.

ghan's difficulties seemed to become unbearable and he felt like resigning, a visit to Johnson Hall would give him new courage. At times, when he happened to be in Philadelphia, the colonial metropolis, he would buy at Johnson's request, such articles as a hat, a pair of breeches, or a saddle for him. If Johnson happened to be ill, Croghan would see a Philadelphia physician and send Johnson some medicines.[201] These two emigrants from Ireland labored together in the greatest spirit of loyalty for their own interests as well as for the interests of their king.

On November 24, 1756, Johnson gave Croghan his first formal instructions. These outlined the Indian policy which was to be followed for the next two years and which proved to be an important factor in enabling General Forbes to capture Fort DuQuesne and thus bring the French and Indian War to a close in the Ohio region. Johnson directed Croghan to proceed to Pennsylvania and (1) to find out the attitude of those Indians who still remained within the English area and to try to keep them friendly and to persuade them to join the English forces; (2) to find out the causes of the alienation of the Delawares and Shawnee and to assure them that if they would return and state their grievances a sincere attempt would be made to grant them justice; (3) to send Indian messengers to the Ohio to secure intelligence and to weaken the alliance of the Ohio tribes with the French. Croghan was also instructed to report to Lord Loudoun or to his representative in Pennsylvania and to keep a journal to send to Johnson.[202]

[201] Croghan to Johnson, Dec. 13, 1768, in Johnson MSS., XVII, 19; *N.Y. Col. Docs.*, VII, 266-7, 321; Croghan to Johnson, Mar. 12, 1763, MS. in Newberry Library.

[202] Instructions to Croghan, Nov. 24, 1756, in *Pa. Col. Rec.*, VII, 355, 435; cf. similar instructions, Feb. 16, 1757, in Indian Affairs, III, 2, Penn MSS.

Croghan encountered numerous handicaps in attempting the difficult tasks assigned to him. Until 1756, Pennsylvania had managed her own Indian affairs, but after 1755 she had no longer seen fit to employ Croghan. Now, by an act of the imperial government, he was given charge over Indian affairs in that province. When Governor Denny informed his council of Croghan's appointment, this body "was not a little surprized at the Appointment, and desired to see his Credentials." The assembly also demanded to know "what Authority Mr. Croghan was vested with," before it would consider granting him aid. Later, when Croghan's instructions were read before the council and it was noted that he was required to report to Johnson and to Lord Loudoun, but not to the governor, the council desired the governor to inform them "what part he proposed to take in it." [203]. At first Denny continued to follow his previous policy and sent out invitations to the Indians to meet with him. Johnson and Loudoun remonstrated, saying that this was contrary to the royal orders and to their plan of war. In spite of this, Denny continued with his plans to hold a treaty at Lancaster early in 1757 and asked that the expenses thereof be met by the imperial officials. Loudoun replied that if Pennsylvania "obstinately insisted on carrying on Negotiations with the Indians," it could also pay the bills entailed; this, he hoped, would cause them to see "that it is their Interest, as well as their Duty, to pay Obedience to the King's Commands, and not to interfere with his Prerogative of making Peace and War." [204] Thereafter, the initiative

---

[203] Minutes of the Provincial Council, Dec. 14, 1756, in *Pa. Col. Rec.*, VII, 355; *idem*, 384.

[204] *Pa. Col. Rec.*, VII, 480, 481, 524; Loudoun to Denny, May 5, 1757, in Indian Affairs, III, 10, Penn MSS.

in the more important Indian affairs was largely left
to Johnson and Croghan, though Pennsylvania continued to hold her own local conferences with the
Indians living on her own soil.

Croghan was also handicapped by the fact that he
was given imperial duties to perform, but no imperial
funds with which to perform them. Upon his arrival
in Philadelphia he wished to send trusty messengers
to the Ohio Indians secretly and quickly. He therefore applied to Governor Denny for funds, but the
latter replied that he had no funds for such purposes;
Croghan next applied to the provincial commissioners
and then to the assembly with the same result; at last,
after five weeks had been lost, a Quaker organization
interested in furthering peace with the Indians, supplied £100.[205] In 1757, on the order of Colonel Stanwix, commander of the forces in Pennsylvania, Croghan purchased clothing for some Cherokee warriors
at a cost of about £200. To secure it he pledged his
own credit for the good of the service. When the account was rendered Pennsylvania refused to pay it.
Several years later, Johnson was still recommending
to the commanders-in-chief that Croghan be reimbursed. During the years 1757 and 1758, Croghan's
major expenses were paid by Pennsylvania. Through
its control over such appropriations, the assembly of
Pennsylvania secured a large influence in Indian
affairs.[206]

The greatest handicap which Croghan met with was
the bitter strife between the proprietary and popular

---

[205] Pemberton to Partridge, Jan. 10, 1757, in Benjamin Franklin, MSS.,
XLVII, 10; *Pa. Col. Rec.*, VII, 382-385, 391.

[206] Johnson to Amherst, July 3, 1762, in Johnson MSS., VI, 56; Johnson to
Gage, Jan. 30, 1766, MS. in Am. Antiq. Soc. Library; *Pa. Col. Rec.*, VII, 498,
660ff., *passim*; *Votes of the Assembly*, IV, 854.

parties in Pennsylvania. The former, led by the governor and council, was intent upon protecting the reputation of the Penns and upon urging a vigorous military policy; it usually had the support of the imperial government. The popular party, dominated by the Quakers, attacked the vested interests of the Penns, opposed the policy of offering bounties for Indian scalps and of declaring war upon the Delaware Indians in Pennsylvania; it tried to make it appear that the chief causes of the alienation of the Indians were the frauds and sharp practices of the Penns in purchasing lands from the Indians. The Quakers organized a strong "Friendly Association for regaining and preserving Peace with the Indians by Pacific Measures" and supported this association with voluntary contributions. Its leaders tried to secure control over Indian affairs. The assembly was usually in sympathy with their actions. It passed a law in 1758 for the regulation of Indian trade. This law aimed to remove the cause of many Indian troubles by establishing in the Indian country provincial trading houses where goods would be sold justly. But the assembly was careful to insist that this system was not to be managed by the governor and council, but by Provincial Commissioners under its own control. Thus the governor and council were being deprived of their formal control over Indian affairs, on the one side by the appointment of Johnson and Croghan, and on the other by the assembly's utilization of its power over the purse.[207]

Croghan and Johnson naturally came into conflict with the Quakers. During the year 1756, largely be-

---

[207] Thomson: *Alienation of the Delawares and Shawanese, etc.*; *Pa. Arch.*, III, 115, 160, 584; *Statutes at Large of Pa.*, V, 320-330, 453; *idem*, VI, 283, 311, 380; *Votes of the Assembly*, V, 97; Address of the "Friendly Association . . ." to Gov. Denny, July 13, 1757, in *Pa. Col. Rec.*, VII, 637-647.

cause of a lack of funds, Governor Morris had acquiesed in letting the Friendly Associaton manage Indian affairs and make the necessary presents. At later treaties with the Indians the Quaker leaders were present. They held their own private conferences with influential chiefs and gave separate presents, and often defeated the plans of Croghan, Johnson, the governor and his council. To them it was repugnant that any particular religious group should attempt to act for the government. The bitter antagonism between these two groups of leaders was illustrated at the Indian treaty at Easton in 1762 where Johnson was reported to have drawn his sword upon the Quaker leader, James Pemberton. "Indian Affairs ought to be considered and conducted upon one public Spirited plan for the good of the whole. . .", wrote Johnson to the Board of Trade.[208]

The Quakers accused Croghan of not having "spirit enough to do his duty". Their antagonism continued until the close of the French and Indian War, though Croghan was on intimate terms with some of their leaders and at times he had the support of the Friendly Association.[209] Governor Denny, on the other hand, wrote: "Mr. Croghan has exerted himself on all occasions for the good of His Majesty's service, and it required his peculiar address to manage the Indians, and counteract the designs of a wretched and restless faction". To Croghan it seemed that all parties in

[208] Croghan to Peters, Aug. 18, 1757, in Offic. Corresp., VIII, 271, Penn MSS.; Johnson to Bd. of Trade, Sept. 28, 1757, in *N.Y. Col. Docs.*, VII, 277; *idem*, 321; Sullivan: *Papers of Sir William Johnson*, III, 822.

[209] Statement drawn up by the Quakers in July, 1757, in Franklin MSS., XLIX, 40; Journal of James Kenny, 1761-1763, in *Pa. Mag. of Hist. and Biog.*, XXXVII, 26, 166, 188, 195, 201. In 1763, the Quakers accused Croghan of being responsible for Pontiac's Conspiracy. – Bouquet to Croghan, June 14, 1763, in Bouquet MSS., A 23-1: 240.

Pennsylvania were working for their own private interests and neglecting the general interest.   When he proceeded to inquire into the grievances of the Indians he found that the proprietary agents tried to stop him.[210]

Finally, Croghan was handicapped by two conditions resulting from the coming of the Cherokee and Catawba warriors into Virginia, Maryland, and Pennsylvania in 1756-1757. Several hundred came and were employed to scout beyond the English line of forts and drive back marauding bands of French and Indians.   Upon one occasion they captured the French leader, Belestre, and brought him to Winchester where he was examined before Washington, Atkin, and Croghan.[211] These southern tribes had for generations been the implacable foes of the Iroquois, Delaware, and Shawnee Indians.   Almost every year saw war parties of young braves from the northern tribes following the trails through western Virginia to western Carolina in order to secure scalps of some southern Indians.   When, therefore, the latter appeared in the north as the allies of the English, it tended to intensify the hostilty of the Delawares and Shawnee, and it caused the Iroquois to declare that they would never fight as allies of the despised Cherokees.

In the second place, the coming of the southern Indians brought on a dispute with Atkin over the question as to whether the jurisdiction of the Indian Superintendents was to be limited by territorial boundaries or by personal relations to certain tribes. Croghan and officials of Maryland and Pennsylvania favored the

[210] Denny to Johnson, Oct. 24, 1758, in Sullivan: *Papers of Sir William Johnson*, III, 10; *idem*, 321.

[211] Croghan's Journal, May 24-July 21, 1757, in Indian Affairs, III, 11ff., Penn MSS.; cf. *N.Y. Col. Docs.*, VII, 280ff.; *Pa. Col. Rec.*, VII, 532, 600.

former, while Atkin and Virginia favored the latter.
The question was brought to an issue in Pennsylvania.
Some sixty Cherokees had pursued some hostile Indians into Pennsylvania and defeated them. To reward and encourage their services, this colony arranged, upon Croghan's advice, to give them a present
at Fort Loudoun. On May 24, 1757, Croghan left
Lancaster for Fort Loudoun with the present, but
while on the way he received an express from Atkin
forbidding him "to send for, speak to, or give any
thing to them, but immediately to come to him at Winchester". At the conferences at Winchester there were
present Atkin and Croghan; Colonel Armstrong, Captain Armstrong, and Captain French, representing
Pennsylvania; and Captain Mercer, Lieutenant
Shelby, and Commissary Ross, representing Maryland.
After a frank discussion Atkin was persuaded that
there was no desire to disregard his authority. He convinced the others that he was not aiming to have the
Cherokees serve Virginia alone, but that it was essential when they desired to employ southern Indians, that
they should do so through him and that the presents in
payment for such services should be given by the provinces to him for distribution. Accordingly, Atkin presented the sixty Cherokees who had followed Croghan
with goods valued at £100. For this Pennsylvania reimbursed him. After the conference was over, Croghan returned to Fort Loudoun with fifty-five Cherokees. These were to serve as scouts. They had been employed by Virginia for four months, but were dissatisfied with the meager presents which Atkin could give
them. Colonel Stanwix of the British army expressed
his attitude towards the entire dispute in the following
words: ". . . I find all those employed as Agents

very jealous of one another, and I can perceive Mr. Croghan so of Colonel Armstrong, and by the enclosed you will find Mt. Atkins so of them all, as well as of the Provinces." [212]

Such were the handicaps with which Croghan had to struggle in carrying out Johnson's instructions to proceed to Pennsylvania and attempt to detach the Indians from the French. To carry out this task, Croghan in December, 1756, went to Philadelphia and conferred with the governor, council and the leaders of the assembly. He then proceeded in midwinter to the frontiers. In January, 1757, he was at Harris's Ferry sending out Indian messengers to the Ohio and upper Susquehanna tribes inviting them to conferences with the English. He returned to Philadelphia in February in order to participate in the conferences which Lord Loudoun was holding with military officials and governors for the purpose of planning the next campaign.[213]

After these conferences, Croghan left to resume his work on the frontiers. When he arrived at Harris's Ferry on March 29, he found about one hundred and sixty Indians belonging to the Six Nations, Delawares, Conestogas, and Naticokes who had come in answer to his invitation. After a conference was held at John Harris's house, some Indians were sent out as scouts and as scalping bands to the Ohio; the remainder came

---

[212] Atkin to Croghan, June 8, 1757, in *Pa. Arch.*, III, 175; *idem*, 146, 187, 197, 268, 272, 288; Stanwix to Gov. Denny, June 12, 1757, in *Pa. Col. Rec.*, VII, 598; *idem*, 534, 600, 630; *Va. Hist. Coll.*, IV, 619, 645. The "Fort Loudoun" mentioned above was in Pennsylvania. Thwaites is in error in stating that it was the fort by the same name, but located in what is today Tennessee. (*Early Western Travels*, I, 100; cf. page 238). Captain Paris, the interpreter for Maryland, was very hostile to both Atkin and Croghan.

[213] Croghan to Johnson, Mar. 14, 1757, in *N.Y. Col. Docs.*, VII, 266; Croghan to Burd, Feb. 14, 1757, in Shippen MSS., II, III; *idem*, 145; *Pa. Col. Rec.*, VII, 382-385, 403.

with Croghan to Lancaster for a more formal conference.   Here they waited in vain for a month expecting the arrival of Teedyuscung, the Delaware chief
who claimed to be leader of ten nations of Delawares
and Iroquois living chiefly along the upper Susquehanna.   In the meantime, Croghan had to take care of
two hundred Indians, men, women, and children, in a
camp two miles out of Lancaster, keeping them sober
and holding them until the conference should open.[214]

Finally, on May 12, 1757, Governor Denny and his
council, ex-Governor Hamilton, Isaac Norris, the
speaker of the assembly, a committee from the assembly, Richard Peters, Conrad Weiser, Colonel Stanwix,
the local magistrates, over a hundred Quakers, and
others met the Indians in conference.   Croghan's
speeches aimed to reëstablish friendly relations and to
soothe the Indians who were angered by the attacks of
frontiersmen and by the fraudulent taking of their
lands.   At the close of the conference the Indians left
for the upper Susquehanna carrying with them another
invitation to Teedyuscung to come to a conference.
Croghan turned his attention to the Cherokees and
went to Winchester to meet Atkin.   During the next
months, Colonel Stanwix relied on him to persuade
the Indians to assist the army in meeting threatened
French attacks.[215]

Efforts were now redoubled to try to arrange a conference with Teedyuscung.   It was hoped that such a
conference would result in ending the Indian ravages
on the northwestern frontier in Pennsylvania and that

[214] Minutes of Croghan's Proceedings, Mar. 29-May 9, 1757, in *Pa. Col.
Rec.*, VII, 506-517; *idem*, 465, 475, 479, 503.

[215] Minutes of the conference at Lancaster, in *Pa. Col. Rec.*, VII, 517-550;
Stanwix to Washington, June 18, 1757, in Hamilton: *Letters to Washington*,
II, 100.

it would bring over the Senecas with their one thousand warriors. The latter constituted the largest tribe of the Six Nations and were pro-French in sympathy. Pressure was therefore brought to bear upon Teedyuscung through Johnson and the Six Nations, at the same time that the Quakers sent him conciliatory invitations. After the most tantalizing delays, Teedyuscung with about two hundred Delawares and one hundred Senecas, men, women, and children, gathered at Easton in July, 1757, to make a treaty of peace.

Governor Denny had written Croghan urging his prompt attendance because the conference would not be opened until his arrival. When it opened there were present Governor Denny and his council, Croghan, Weiser, ex-Governor Hamilton, Secretary Peters, the four provincial commissioners, Joseph Galloway, John Hughes, Joseph Fox and William Masters, and altogether about twenty-five Quakers. Among the latter were the three Pembertons, Jeremiah Warder, Thomas Wharton, Isaac Norris, and Charles Thomson. The commissioners and Quakers belonged to the popular party and had great power because they had absolute control of the presents to be given to the Indians. The proprietary party was at once put upon the defensive when the Indians complained of unjust purchases of lands by the Penns, and asked that the region known as Wyoming be set aside as a permanent Indian reservation and that trade be reopened by the establishment of a trading post at Fort Augusta.

It was unfortunate that the English had to inject their own party differences into an Indian conference in such critical times. These differences came to an issue at Easton over the question as to who should take down the minutes. The proprietary adherents assumed that only Croghan would take down the minutes; they felt that this would be fair to all because each morning the minutes of the preceding day would be read and interpreted to the Indians. This system had been in use for several days when Teedyuscung, probably influenced by the Quakers, asked for his own clerk. When the governor refused his request, he threatened to go home without helping to bring over the western Indians, and the provincial commissioners announced that they would leave with the presents. As a result, on the following day, Teedyuscung "called for Charles Thompson, Master of the Publick Quaker School in the City of Philadelphia; placed him by Mr. Trent at the Table, and said he had chosen him for his Clerk; Whereupon he sat down and began to take Minutes, without asking Permission of the Governor, who took no further notice of it." Thereafter, the crown, the province, and Teedyuscung each had separate interpreters and clerks.[216]

During the hours outside of conferences, each English faction tried to win over the Indians. Since the Indians loved liquor the proprietary party used it and kept Teedyuscung drunk most of the time. On July 23, they celebrated the victory of the King of Prussia with bonfires and liquor; on July 24, they celebrated the arrival of the English fleet; on the follow-

---

[216] Croghan's Journal, May 24-July 21, 1757, in Indian Affairs, III, 12, Penn MSS. The minutes for the treaty of Easton, July 21-Aug. 7, with related documents are found in the N.Y. Col. Docs., VII, 287-322 and in the Pa. Col. Rec., VII, 648-714. Cf. idem, 462, 605, 634. The three versions of the minutes were afterwards compared and an official version agreed upon. Speaker Norris wrote to Franklin: "the Treaty laid before the House is in the Hand of Geo. Croghan . . . but what share he had in these minutes, besides what they were compelled to make and collate at the publick conference you who are acquainted with our Indian Minute Makers need not be informed." – Franklin MSS., I, 50.

ing three days, Weiser, Croghan, and others managed to keep Teedyuscung drunk. On the 28th Thomson wrote to a friend: "He [Teedyuscung] did not go to sleep last night. This morning he lay down under a shed about break of day and slept a few hours. He is to speak this afternoon. He is to be sure in a fine capacity to do business. But thus we go on. I leave you to make reflections. I for my part wish myself at home." The Quakers used more successful methods. They were continually in private conferences with the Indians in small groups; they had control over the presents and the Indians usually came out of such conferences wearing new shirts or silver jewelry, or with other gifts. So successful were the Quakers that when the Englishmen chanced to meet the Indians outside of conference hours, the latter would usually ask in broken English if they were Quakers. ". . . if answer'd No, they wou'd frown and look very stern and illnatur'd upon us, and say we were bad Man – bad Man – Governor's Man; But if we answer'd in the Affirmative . . . they wou'd smile and caress us, and call us Brothers, and say we were good Men, – Quaker good Men – Governors Men bad Men – good for nothing . . ."

The Quakers regarded Croghan as a tool in the hands of the proprietors. Teedyuscung stated that "Croghan was a Rogue, and that he would have nothing to do with him or Johnson. . ." Croghan regarded the Quaker policy as that of madmen. He realized their enmity to him, but felt that he had impartially done his duty and hoped that the imperial government would interpose to check the Quakers.[217]

<hr/>

[217] Thomson to Samuel Rhodes [Rhoads], July 28, 1757, in *Pa. Mag. of Hist. and Biog.*, XX, 422; Depositions of Duche and Peters, in *Pa. Arch.*, III, 274; *idem*, 250, 263, 319; *Pa. Col. Rec.*, VII, 731.

It was agreed at the treaty to refer the land disputes to Johnson; Pennsylvania granted the request for the establishment of a trading post and sent sixty carpenters, masons, and farmers to Wyoming to erect houses for the Indians and to plow their land. Johnson regarded the treaty only as a truce for without the friendship of the Ohio tribes the province was not safe. By mingling informally with the Indians at this treaty, Croghan learned that the French in the west were short of provisions, ammunition, and presents, due to operations of the English navy, and that the Ohio tribes were losing their enthusiasm to fight as allies to the French. This intelligence was acted upon the next year.

During the year 1757, Croghan had held three major and many minor Indian conferences in Pennsylvania. After the conference at Easton, he left for Johnson Hall and for almost a year he made it his headquarters. Here he assisted Johnson in various conferences and in securing intelligence. Early in the spring of 1758, Croghan was on the frontier in the Mohawk valley equipping and sending out white and Indian scouts. In July, Johnson and Croghan led about four hundred Iroquois warriors to assist the new commander-in-chief, Abercromby, in his ill-advised attack on Ticonderoga. They were unable to render much assistance because of his poor tactics. On July 23, Abercromby and Johnson sent Croghan back to Pennsylvania to assist General Forbes in his campaign against Fort DuQuesne.[218]

Unlike Braddock, Forbes appreciated the impor-

---

[218] Croghan to Johnson, Mar. 12, 1758, in Johnson MSS., XXIII, 266; Croghan's Journal, March 18-25, 1758, in *idem*, 269; *Doc. Hist. of N.Y.*, I, 520; Abercromby to Pitt, May 24, 1758, in Kimball, Gertrude S.: *Correspondence of William Pitt, etc.*, I, 258; Croghan to Denny, June 30, 1758, in Emmet Coll.; *Pa. Arch.*, III, 485.

tance of the Indians in relation to the success of his campaign. In the spring of 1758, he, himself, supervised the employment of some seven hundred southern Indians. He spent £6,000 for presents to keep them out scouting, but they gradually went back home before the campaign had really started. This was fortunate, for the presence of the southern Indians would have hindered peace overtures to the Ohio Indians. The exasperating delays encountered by Forbes also proved to be fortunate, for the Ohio Indians were thereby given time to make their decision to be neutral and thus avoid the probability of a severe chastisment for their misdeeds. Few men did more to hasten this decision than Christian Frederick Post. He was sent to the wavering Ohio tribes in July, 1758, by Governor Denny. Heroically and calmly, and with sublime courage he went into the heart of the enemy's country and placed himself in the hands of a treacherous and cruel foe. He met the Indians in conferences west of Fort DuQuesne. Frequently French officers were present, but they could not persuade the Indians to permit them to take Post as a prisoner and they dared not take him without their permission. Post returned by unfrequented forest paths and the good news which he brought came at an opportune time to be of service at the next treaty of Easton.[219]

In the meantime, at the suggestion of Forbes, efforts were made to hold another conference with the Pennsylvania tribes to adjust finally their grievances over land purchases. After many delays, about five hundred Indians, chiefly Iroquois, Delawares, and Shawnee, gathered at Easton for an important conference

---

[219] Forbes to Pitt, May 1, 19, and June 17, 1758, in Kimball: *Correspondence of William Pitt, etc.*, 1, 237, 248 and 278, respectively; Post's *Journal*, in Thwaites: *Early Western Travels*, 1, 177-295, *passim.*

lasting from October 8 to October 26, 1758. Governor
Bernard and the five Indian commissioners of New
Jersey came to meet the Indians. Pennsylvania was
represented by practically the same persons who were
at Easton in 1757. In managing this conference, Croghan had to contend with the same party strife that was
present at the preceding treaty. This time it was the
Quakers who kept the Indians drunk. His task was
lightened, however, by the presence of the Mohawk
chiefs. They overawed Teedyuscung and served as
intermediaries between the other Indians and the
whites. The seriousness with which the Indians regarded this conference is illustrated by the following
brief entry in the minutes for October 17: "The Indians were in Council all Day, and acquainted the
Governors that they could not be ready to meet before
morning."

The Indians finally agreed to return their English
captives, to live as friends with the English, and to
urge the Ohio Indians to follow their example. To
achieve this result, New Jersey paid the Minnisinks
$1,000 to quiet their land claims. Pennsylvania agreed
to open additional trading houses in the Indian country and also made the Indians a large present. This
present included 9 gross of starred gartering, 4 gross of
calimancoe, 28 pieces of red or blue strouds, 50 pairs of
shoes, 3 dozen pairs of women's stockings, 2 dozen
shears, 4 dozen ivory combs, 100 blankets, 160 match-
coats, and 433 plain or ruffled shirts. The Penns also
made great concessions. At the Congress at Albany
in 1754, they had secured from a few Iroquois chiefs
a deed for all of southwestern Pennsylvania. They
had paid, however, for none except the lands east of
the Appalachian divide and south of a line running

east by northeast in central Pennsylvania. In 1757, Croghan had drawn up a memorandum pointing out how the recent land purchases of the Penns had offended the Indians and recommending that the Penns disclaim their rights to most of the purchase of 1754. This memorandum had been sent by Johnson to the Board of Trade and to the Penns in England. As a result, the Penns now deeded back that portion for which they had not yet paid. They also provided Croghan with presents for the Iroquois chiefs and took steps to satisfy Teedyuscung and the Delawares. The treaty of Easton made in 1758 was approved and confirmed by the British ministry. Because of this fact, it was later maintained that the treaty applied not only to Pennsylvania, but that it also forbade Maryland, Virginia, and the other colonies from making settlements beyond the Appalachians till the Indians gave their consent.[220]

Colonel Bouquet, in accounting for the capture of Fort DuQuesne, wrote that this treaty struck the blow "which has knocked the French in the head . . ." Immediately after its terms were known, Post was dispatched to the Ohio with the news. He passed Forbes's army at Loyalhanna and again met the Ohio Indians west of Fort DuQuesne. He succeeded in detaching them from the French in their hour of need and as a result the French burned Fort DuQuesne and retreated down the Ohio. This saved Forbes from an attack such as Braddock had experienced. Meanwhile, Croghan, Montour, and some trusty Indians had joined Forbes. Washington was glad to hear of their coming and in a letter to Forbes expressed the desire that some of them would also serve as scouts with his detachment.[221]

After Forbes had reached the forks of the Ohio in November, 1758, Croghan and Montour crossed this river and visited the Indian villages within a radius of about one hundred miles. Here they met Post who was still working independently among the Indians. The latter were panic-stricken and were planning to flee after the French. They were reassured by the three Englishmen and were invited to a conference with General Forbes at the newly christened Fort Pitt. The self-sacrificing Forbes was forced by a fatal illness to return at once to Philadelphia where he soon died. He left the command to Colonel Bouquet. He with his chief officers and with Croghan and Montour, met the Indians in conferences early in December. The English desired to establish peaceful relations, to re-open trade, to secure the return of prisoners, and to receive formal permission to erect a fort at the forks of the Ohio. The Indians also desired peace and the resumption of trade, but they had suffered so much since a white man's fort had been erected in their country that they yearned to see the English soldiers return over the mountains.

When Post informed Bouquet that the Indians refused to grant permission to erect a fort, Bouquet asked him to persuade them to alter their reply. A private conference between Bouquet, Colonel Armstrong, and Croghan followed. Two days later, Croghan informed Post that the Indians had altered their reply. Post refused to change his record until he, himself, had

221 Bouquet to Chief-Justice Allen, Nov. 25, 1758, in Offic. Corresp., IX, 53, Penn MSS.; Forbes to Bouquet, Sept. 2, 1758, in Bouquet Coll., A 10: 243; Washington: *Writings*, II, 113.

spoken to the Indians. The latter told him that "Mr. Crogan and Henry Montour had not spoke and acted honestly and uprightly. . . We have told them three times to go back; but they will not go, insisting upon staying here." The scarcity of provisions caused the early return of Bouquet and most of the army. Two hundred Virginians under Colonel Mercer remained, however, at Fort Pitt. Croghan also remained to serve the troops which were thus left marooned in the wilderness. The doom of the red man in the Ohio valley was sealed; never again was there to be a day when no representatives of the Anglo-Saxon race were to be found at the forks of the Ohio.

Sir John Sinclair, who had had sixty friendly Cherokee and Catawba warriors in charge on the campaign, had left earlier than Bouquet. Upon leaving he wrote to him: "Adieu, my dear Bouquet. The greatest curse that our Lord can pronounce against the worst of sinners is to give them business to do with provincial commissioners and friendly Indians." For fourteen more years Croghan's official relations continued, not only with provincial commissoners and friendly Indians, but also with hostile Indians, revengeful Frenchmen, unappreciative English military officers, and self-willed frontiersmen.[222]

By the end of 1758, the Indian policy which Johnson had outlined in his instructions to Croghan on November 24, 1756, had thus been successfully carried out. France had lost half of her savage allies and the western frontiers were relieved from the scourge of Indian warfare. Many factors contributed to this end, but

---

[222] Post's Journal, Oct. 25, 1758-Jan. 20, 1759, in Thwaites: *Early Western Travels*, I, 234-295; Croghan's Journal, Nov. 27-Dec. 2, 1758, in *Pa. Arch.*, III, 560-563 (This journal is here erroneously ascribed to Post.); *idem*, 571-574; Parkman: *Montcalm and Wolfe*, II, 139.

probably no single individual contributed more than did Croghan. With the fall of Fort DuQuesne, Indian affairs ceased forever to be of immediate importance to the average Pennsylvania farmer who lived east of the Appalachians and consequently Pennsylvania practically ceased to support Croghan financially. Henceforth, he had to rely on the imperial military commanders for funds and supplies. By the capture of Fort DuQuesne the English had secured their first foothold in the Indian country between the Appalachians and the Mississippi. Wolfe's victory at Quebec and, other English successes gave them permanent possession of this vast wilderness. During the next few years, Croghan was called upon to assist the military department in opening the Great West to English enterprise.

Deputy Superintendent: the Occupation of the West, 1758-1766

The erection of Fort Pitt in 1758 gave to the English control of a strategic point. For over one half a century it was to be one of the most important gateways to the West. Two military roads, Braddock's Road and Forbes's Road, both cut through the wilderness, connected it with the eastern settlements. In their dealings with the Indians, the commanders at Fort Pitt were fortunate in having the assistance of Croghan. He was thoroughly acquainted with the surrounding region and with the natives who inhabited it. His influence was now further increased by the building of "Croghan Hall" on a large farm four miles northeast of Fort Pitt. Here he established his residence until the beginning of the Revolution.

Croghan's field of operations now expanded so greatly that he could no longer carry on the work by himself. His staff came to include two assistant agents at Fort Pitt, one at Detroit, and one at Michillimackinac; a similar number of official interpreters, including one for Fort Miami; one or two gunsmiths for each post; several clerks; and finally a surgeon for each post. Altogether, Croghan's budget for these years called for about £1,000 for salaries. His chief assistant agents were Edward Ward, his half-brother; Thomas McKee, an old Indian trader on the Susquehanna; Alexander McKee, son of the former and later to be Croghan's successor; and Thomas Hutchins. It was probably through his association with Croghan and his group that Hutchins secured much of the material for his books on the topography of the middle colonies. One of Croghan's clerks was a kinsman from Ireland, Daniel Clark, who afterwards became the most prominent American in New Orleans. He became a great landowner and speculator and an associate of Aaron Burr and James Wilkinson.[223]

During the period 1758-1763, Croghan spent more than half of his time at Fort Pitt. Indian problems focussed at this place and from it expeditions were sent out to occupy other French posts. Numerous conferences were held by Croghan or his assistants and the military commanders at Fort Pitt with the Potawatomi, Ottawas, Miami, Wyandots, Shawnee, Delawares, and with those members of the Six Nations who had settled in the Ohio valley. In July, 1759, Colonel Mercer with his chief officers and Croghan with his assistants met about five hundred Indians belongng to these tribes. In October, General Stanwix and Croghan held a similar meeting. The largest conference was held in August, 1760, when General Monckton and Croghan met upwards of a thousand Indians.[224]

In connection with these conferences Croghan encountered the following problems. First, grants of land had to be secured here and there in the wilderness where the English could erect forts and around them have gardens, cornfields, and pastures for the

---

[223] Croghan's Report on his Staff in 1761, in C. O., 5: 61; Report for 1762, in Bouquet Coll., A 25: 230; Sullivan: *Papers of Sir William Johnson,* III, 551, 873.

[224] Papers relating to Indian Affairs, 1750-1775, Chalmers Coll.; Amherst to Pitt, May 19, 1760, in C. O., 5: 58; *Pa. Col. Rec.,* VIII, 382-393, 429-435; *Pa. Arch.,* III, 360ff., 744-752.

needs of the garrisons. Although the Indians were paid in presents for such lands and were assured that the rest of the land was to remain theirs, they only acquiesced in a situation forced upon them.

Again, the release of numerous English prisoners – men, women and children – who had been taken in numerous raids between 1755 and 1758, was to be obtained. This was a difficult and long drawn out process. A few whites desired to remain among the savages; the Indians realized that prisoners served as hostages, that they were a valuable article to barter for rum and other goods not easily obtainable, and that "prices" might rise. A few were usually brought to each conference to be released and for a time individual Indians on visiting Fort Pitt often brought in a prisoner or two. From June, 1759, to October, 1761, Croghan secured the release of 338 prisoners. This entailed a large expense; in January, 1763, alone, Croghan sent in bills totaling £380 for this work. In spite of all efforts, there were still some captives left among the Indians in 1763 when Pontiac's uprising broke out.[225]

Intelligence of what was happening in the wilderness beyond Fort Pitt was to be obtained. This was usually done quietly in informal meetings with individual Indians. Croghan was continually sending out Indian spies. He also secured Indian runners who carried news and dispatches for the English military officials.[226]

[225] Croghan to Johnson, October 12, 1761, in Sullivan: *Papers of Sir William Johnson*, III, 549; Croghan to Bouquet, Jan. 24, 1763; in Bouquet Coll., A 19: 32; *idem*, 45; *Pa. Col. Rec.*, VIII, 776; Johnson's instructions to Croghan, Jan. 8, 1762, in Br. Museum Add. MSS., 21655.

[226] Monckton to Hamilton, July 31, 1760, in Penn MSS., IX, 140; Croghan to Bouquet, July 11, 1759, in Bouquet Coll., A 25: 46; *idem*, A 14: 318; Darlington, Mary C.: *Fort Pitt and Letters from the Frontier*, 112.

The safety of person and of property was also to be secured. It was impossible to prevent the occasional murders of both whites and Indians here and there in the forests and yet each murder usually needed careful attention lest serious consequences should develop. In case an Indian was murdered, condolence presents had to be given with appropriate formalities; in case of the murder of a white man by Indians, demands had to be made for apprehending the murderers, though such demands were usually futile. One of the most tantalizing questions to be solved was the problem of the horse-thief – an individual so ubiquitous on the American frontier. At Fort Pitt during this period packhorses and draft-horses were always numerous and important. After their hard trip over the mountains they were often turned loose to graze and recuperate. They were a great temptation to the Indians who stole them. The military officials expected Croghan to prevent this. The old chiefs usually told him that young warriors, over whom they had no control, were responsible.[227]

Moreover, provisions had to be furnished to needy Indians and to the numerous Indians that came for conferences. An Indian usually expected double the ration furnished to an English soldier. Bouquet and Stanwix had the greatest difficulty to keep the garrisons west of Philadelphia supplied with provisions, ammunition, and clothing. The newly cut roads crossed mountain range after mountain range and passed through a primeval forest. Wagons could be secured only with the greatest difficulty and after they were secured, the roads proved so difficult that packhorses were preferable in many places. Flour, meat,

---

[227] Johnson MSS., VI, 188; *Mass. Hist. Coll., 4th ser.,* IX, 247-412, *passim.*

and ammunition were often spoiled by the weather during transportation. It was difficult to drive cattle through the virgin forests. All supplies were convoyed, but this did not prevent costly attacks by hostile bands of Indians. Consequently, the magazines at Fort Pitt were seldom well stocked. In July, 1759, Croghan wrote Denny that for several days they "had neither Flower, Meat or Salt, except some Milk Cows which some Country People brought here to sell their Milk; we have as many left as will serve us two days, and then we must begin upon our Horses. . ." Fortunately a convoy soon arrived.[228]

The demand for provisions for the Indians was great. Two months after the fall of Fort DuQuesne, Colonel Mercer wrote that the savages "come in Shoals every Day, to live upon us, pretending the utmost Friendship." A few months later he wrote: "We hear of a Number of Distant Tribes being at Hand upon their first Visit, so that there is no appearance of our being able to avoid a vast expense of Provisions. . . [We] can scarcely save an ounce between convoys." In the spring of 1761, Croghan's requests for rations had to be declined almost daily. The demand did not cease; Captain Ecuyer, the new commandant at Fort Pitt, wrote to Bouquet in 1763: ". . . think, that during one month Mr. Croghan has drawn 17,000 pounds, as much flour as beef; that makes one tremble." [229]

The military officials were confronted with a vicious circle. Because garrisons were small, the Indians had

[228] Croghan to Gates, May 25, 1759, in Bouquet Coll., A 14: 249; Crogghan to Denny, July 15, 1759, in Pa. Arch., III, 672; Pa. Col. Rec., VIII, 377.
[229] Mercer to Denny, Jan. 8 and Aug. 6, 1759, in Pa. Col. Rec., VIII, 292 and 391, respectively; idem, 294, 377; Ecuyer to Bouquet, Apr. 23, 1763, in Darlington: Fort Pitt and Letters from the Frontier, 123.

to be kept in good humor; their requests for provisions could not be denied; their consumption of provisions, in turn, hindered the strengthening of the garrisons. Gradually, however, the military leaders curtailed supplies for the Indians and adopted a new attitude. The French had always welcomed the Indians at the posts and overlooked the inconveniences caused by their presence. The English now began to receive them coldly and with contempt. This reflected itself in their attitude toward Croghan. Bouquet wrote to Amherst in 1762: "Our Indian Agents are a kind of Load Stone attracting the Indians, who reciprocally attract Presents, for when they are absent the Savages disappear, and the expence cease; after all in several cases we cannot do without them, but if any address is required it consists rather I think in managing the managers than the Indians." It was natural that the English officers should take this point of view, but it was unfortunate, for it helped to bring on the storm that was to break upon the frontiers in 1763.[230]

Finally, the greatest problem of all concerned the resumption of trade. Peter Wraxall, New York's faithful Indian Secretary, wrote: "The Indians frequently repeat that Trade was the foundation of their Alliance or Connexions with us and that it is the chief Cement which binds us together. And this should undoubtedly be the first Principle of our whole System of Indian Politics." [231] It was absolutely essential that the English supply the needs of the Ohio tribes in a just and fair manner; if they failed in this, then the

---

[230] Bouquet to Amherst, May 24, 1762, in *Mich. Pioneer and Hist. Coll.*, XIX, 144.

[231] McIlwain, Charles H.: *Wraxall's Abridgment of Indian Affairs*, 153.

savages would turn to the French and Spanish traders who operated from New Orleans and the Illinois country and who could easily come up the rivers of the Ohio valley. Johnson, Stuart, and Croghan thought of the Indian trade primarily in terms of its political relations. They sought its extension even where profits were small. The English statesmen and merchants considered primarily the commercial value of this trade. A rough estimate by Johnson of the annual value of the Indian trade in the Northern District places it at about £180,000 sterling.[232]

Imperial officials and colonial traders desired to reopen the Indian trade. The settlers living on the frontiers viewed such action with misgivings, especially when they saw guns and ammunition passing westward. The Indians at almost every conference importunately asked for the immediate reopening of trade. A Delaware chief addressed the conference at Fort Pitt in August, 1760, as follows: "Brother, take pitty on Our Women, Children and Warriors, we are a poor people, and cannot Live without your Assistance; let a Fair and Open Trade be continued to be Carry'd on by your People amongst Us." Before reopening trade the English tried to prevent the return of abuses which had done so much to alienate the Indians. The French system of granting monopolies for small regions was swept aside and the West was now opened to all licensed English traders. These were often the only Englishmen by whom the Indians could judge English rule. Many of the old English traders had been killed or had found other work. With the exception of a few men like Alexander

---

[232] *Ill. Hist. Coll.*, x, 336.

Henry, the new recruits, like their predecessors, were abandoned wretches. Moreover, they had to learn the Indian languages and customs.[233]

Few colonies took a greater interest in the new possibilities for trade than did Pennsylvania. Her agent in London, Richard Jackson, wrote in 1766: "no Colony has sent more Traders among the Indians than Pennsylvania. . ." For this reason, Croghan was ordered by Colonel Stanwix to send Governor Denny copies of the minutes of all conferences held at Fort Pitt. During the period from 1758 to 1765, Pennsylvania granted no licenses to trade beyond the Appalachians, but forbade it under heavy penalty. Instead, it was planned to have the Indians come to a few trading posts managed by the province under the act of 1758. In 1759, such a post was established at Fort Pitt. The way in which this socialistic system worked at Fort Pitt is typical in many ways of government trading posts.[234]

[233] *Pa. Arch.*, III, 747; Gage to Amherst, Mar. 20, 1762, in Bd. of Tr. Pap., Plantations General, XVIII, 63; *N.Y. Col. Docs.*, VII, 961. The following quotation from the contemporary tragedy *Ponteach* by Robert Rogers, page 180, is illustrative:

"A thousand Opportunities present
To take Advantage of their Ignorance;
But the great Engine I employ is Rum,
More pow'rful made by certain strength'ning Drugs,
This I distribute with a lib'ral Hand,
Urge them to drink till they grow mad and valiant;
Which makes them think me generous and just,
And gives full Scope to practise all my Art.
I then begin my Trade with water'd Rum,
The cooling Draught well suits their scorching Throats.
Their Fur and Peltry come in quick Return;
My Scales are honest, but so well contriv'd,
That one small Slip will turn Three Pounds to One;
Which they, poor silly Souls! ignorant of Weights
And Rules of Balancing, do not perceive."

[234] C. O., 5: 67; *Ill. Hist. Coll.*, XI, 429; *Pa. Arch.*, V, 584, 697. Massachusetts had succeeded in eliminating most of the abuses in the Indian trade within her jurisdiction by establishing "truck-houses" at Fort Pownall

The agents in charge of this post, especially the
Quaker, James Kenny, came into continual conflict with
Croghan, with unlicensed traders, and with the private
traders licensed by imperial military or Indian officials.
The largest private trading house was that established
by Croghan's old associates, William Trent, Joseph
Simon, David Franks, and Levi Andrew Levy. They
had formed a partnership in 1760 which lasted for nine
years. Indians who came with peltry to Fort Pitt were
often directed by Croghan to this trading house. Indians would frequently take their peltry to both the
provincial store and to the store kept by Trent in search
of the best bargain. This resulted in a bitter competition. Private traders had the advantage of being
able to grant credit to the Indians and of knowing
their languages better than the provincial agents. The
latter held Croghan responsible for many of their
troubles. They objected to Croghan's power to license
traders. When the Indians complained of high prices
and Croghan secured a modification by mutual agreement, the provincial agents accused him of altering the
prices set by military officers. The sale of liquor also
caused ill-feeling. For a time no private trader could
sell liquor without a permit from Croghan, but the
provincial agent could sell it as he pleased. Croghan
urged Johnson to expose the hypocrisy of the Quakers
for having by law for fifty years forbidden the sale of

on the Penobscot and Fort Halifax on the Kennebec. No profit was made
by the government. Prices were set in Boston and the truckmasters were
allowed a commission of five per cent. One sloop was kept for this trade.–
Report of Gov. Bernard to the Board of Trade, 1764, Bd. of Tr. Pap.,
Plantations General, XXII, 23. Semi-public trading posts had been established
in South Carolina and also in Virginia before Bacon's Rebellion. These
colonial experiences probably suggested to President Washington the policy
of establishing federal government trading houses. The act establishing
such houses was passed in 1796 and repealed in 1822.

liquor to the Indians and now selling it officially in large quantities.[235]

In 1759 and 1760, the Indians brought in great quantities of skins and furs, only to be disappointed because the English were not prepared to take all of them. Soon, however, the Indian trade was again in full swing. Trent and Simon were sending wagon loads of furs and skins to Philadelphia. Thomas Smallman, Croghan's cousin, was busily engaged around Lower Shawnee Town with several men and more than twenty packhorses. The English traders were once more scattered throughout the forests of the upper Ohio region.[236]

The final authority to regulate the Indian trade in the West was vested in the commander-in-chief. Johnson and Croghan, the military commanders, and the provincial governors could issue licenses to trade, but the regulations for trade were given out as military orders and the local commanders helped to enforce them. In 1761, Johnson, with the approbation of Amherst, drew up price lists for each of the western posts. He forbade the purchasing of horses or bells from the Indians and restricted the sale of liquor and ammunition. Croghan was expected to help enforce these regulations. Contrary to the advice of Johnson, Amherst in 1762, forbade any trade in rum and limited the sale of ammunition to such an extent that much suffering resulted among the Indians. They complained of the shortage in many conferences and even

[235] Henry, Alexander: *Travels and Adventures*, 192; Gratz Pap., 1st ser., IV, 8; Bouquet Coll., A 16: 19, A 4: 128, A 25: 75 and A14: 398; Journal of James Kenny, 1761-1763, in *Pa. Mag. of Hist. and Biog.*, XXXVII, 1-47, .152-202 and 395-449, *passim;* Sullivan: *Papers of Sir William Johnson*, III, 301.

[236] Simon to B. Gratz, Aug. 17, and Aug. 29, 1762, and Smallman to John Harris, Mar. 4, 1763, in McAllister Coll.

the Iroquois grew restless. The Ohio tribes began to fear that the English were preparing to make war upon them. Thus, the abuses, restrictions, and insufficiency of the Indian trade contributed to cause an Indian outbreak.[237]

Such were the problems with which Croghan had to deal at Fort Pitt from 1758 to 1763. In the region north and west of this fort his chief duty was to assist in the occupation of the other French forts. Until the fall of Fort Niagara in July, 1759, the small English garrison at Fort Pitt was in a precarious situation. No strong fortifications were erected here for more than a year and the English convoys of supplies were frequently attacked by parties of French and Indians sent out from Fort Venango. Vaudreuil planned to bring to the upper Ohio all the French militia from Illinois and Detroit with numerous western Indians to retake Fort Pitt. As reports of these preparations kept coming to Croghan from his Indian spies he redoubled his efforts to maintain the friendship of the Ohio Indians. The situation was not relieved until the capture of Niagara forced the French to abandon Forts Venango, Le Beouf, and Presque Isle.[238]

In July, 1760, Bouquet and Mercer, accompanied by Croghan and his assistants, moved northward from Fort Pitt to occupy the abandoned forts. Croghan visited the Indian villages along the route and acquainted the natives with the purposes of the expedition, asked them to assist the English, and invited them

[237] Johnson's Regulations, 1761, in Br. Museum Add. MSS., 21655; Amherst to Bouquet, Jan. 16, 1762, in Bouquet Coll., A 4: 83-1; Sullivan: *Papers of Sir William Johnson,* III, 597.

[238] Papers relating to Indian Affairs, 1750-1775, Chalmers Coll.; Croghan to Bouquet, July 11, 1759, in Bouquet Coll., A 25: 46; *idem,* A 14: 249; Bouquet to Mercer, May 8, 1759, in *idem,* A 22: 118; *N.Y. Col. Docs.,* X, 952; *Pa. Col. Rec.,* VIII, 393-396.

to Fort Pitt to renew peaceful relations and to receive presents. The expedition was watched by Indian spies sent from Detroit, but it accomplished its purposes without any losses. "The Indians are in good humor, and Croghan takes Pains to keep them so," wrote Bouquet to Monckton.

The occupation of the important French fort and town of Detroit was more difficult. Croghan prepared the natives for it by sending Indian emissaries from Fort Pitt to the tribes around Detroit months before the English army started. On October 21, 1760, Croghan again left Fort Pitt with a band of friendly Indians for Presque Isle. Here he joined the expedition under Major Robert Rogers which was to occupy Detroit. The French and Indians at Detroit had been good neighbors as long as the Indians living in 1760 could remember. It was, therefore, with great alarm and confusion that the savages heard of the coming of Rogers. Whenever the expedition stopped, Croghan assembled the neighboring Indians in order to establish friendly relations. At one conference he met the Ottawa chief, Pontiac, then of no special prominence. The fact that Croghan had traded here in years past helped to prevent attacks. Upon one occasion, Croghan wrote in his journal that they met some Ottawa Indians "who received us very kindly they being old Acquaintances of mine." Near Sandusky Bay, the deputies whom Croghan had dispatched to Detroit brought delegations from the Wyandots, Ottawas and Potawatomi to meet the English. A formal conference followed, in which the Indians promised to be friendly, to return their English prisoners, and to furnish deputies to accompany Rogers to Michillimackinac. The English agreed to reopen trade and

presented gifts. Detroit was soon reached and occupied. Another Indian conference was held similar to
the previous one. From Detroit a detachment was
sent to occupy Fort Miami on the Maumee. It was
accompanied by an interpreter whom Croghan had
provided with instructions, speeches, wampum, and
presents. When Rogers set out to occupy Michillimackinac, Croghan assisted him in the same way.
Winter, however, forced his return and this post was
not occupied till 1761. Croghan with a few Indians
and whites returned by canoe to Sandusky Bay. From
here they proceeded on horseback along the "Great
Trail" and arrived at Fort Pitt on January 7, 1761.
"The Western Indians would never have suffered us
to take possession of Detroit but from the precaution
I took in sending Mr. Croghan to prepare them for it,"
wrote Johnson.[239]

Mutterings of discontent among the western Indians,
the discovery of a plot to attack Detroit, Niagara, and
Pittsburg simultaneously, and the desire to gain first
hand detailed information caused Johnson in 1761, to
decide to visit Detroit in person with a large Iroquois
delegation. In order to prepare an impressive entry
for Johnson, Croghan left Fort Pitt accompanied by a
delegation of Delaware and Shawnee Indians who
helped to bring up the cattle and presents. On the
way he studied the causes of discontent, selected the
site for Fort Sandusky, and prepared the Indians for
its erection. Johnson arrived at Detroit on Septem-

---

[239] Croghan's Journals, July 7-Aug. 31, 1760 and Oct. 21, 1760-Jan. 7,
1761, with related documents, in *Mass. Hist. Coll., 4th ser.,* IX; Hough,
Franklin B.: *Journals of Major Robert Rogers,* 184, 186; Johnson to Gage,
June 9, 1764, in *Ill. Hist. Coll.,* x, 263. Parkman's highly colored picture
of the meeting with Pontiac in *The Conspiracy of Pontiac,* I, 165, is based
upon Roger's *Concise Account of North America,* written in 1765. The
entry in Croghan's contemporary journal is doubtless truer to the actual facts.

ber 3, 1761. During the ensuing days a conference was held with the Potawatomi, Wyandots, Chippewas, Ottawas, representatives from the tribes around Lake Superior, Delawares, Shawnee, and Iroquois. So many were present that Johnson, Croghan, and Captain Campbell held the meetings in the open air. The ceremonies were long and accompanied by lengthy speeches, wampum belts, and glasses of rum, but in the end friendly relations were again declared, better trading facilities were promised, and arrangements were made for the occupation of the far distant posts. Large presents including 150 silver ear bobs, 200 silver broches, and 90 crosses were then distributed. Johnson left on September 17; Croghan accompanied him as far as Sandusky Bay and then again returned to Fort Pitt.[240]

By 1762, English garrisons had been established at Pittsburg, Venango, Le Boeuf, Presque Isle, Niagara, Sandusky, Detroit, Miami, Michillimackinac, Sault Ste. Marie, St. Joseph, and Green Bay. At this time England was following the expensive policy of maintaining in the conquered region numerous forts scattered from Florida to Illinois and Canada, in order to hold in subjection the new French and Spanish subjects, to overawe the natives and secure their trade, and to encourage colonization in the West. This policy was pregnant with unseen results. It led first, to attempts to tax the colonies, then to revised plans for colonization and Indian trade, and finally, to the abandonment of nearly all of the inland posts. Each of these posts was surrounded by vast primeval forests.

[240] James Kenny's Journal, in *Pa. Mag. of Hist. and Biog.*, XXXVII, 15; Stone: *Life and Times of Sir William Johnson*, II, 145; Johnson's diary, 1761, in *idem*, 441-468; *Mich. Pioneer and Hist. Coll.*, XIX, 85; Sir William Johnson's Indian Conferences, 1761-1763, MSS. in N.Y. Hist. Soc. Library.

The smaller posts were garrisoned by from fourteen to twenty-five men under the command of a minor officer. Life for them in their isolated forts was most monotonous and they were practically at the mercy of the savages. To reach the nearest English settlements they had to travel hundreds of miles through the wilderness and cross the Appalachians. Croghan now planned to keep one of his assistants traveling from fort to fort to transact such business as was necessary and appointed Thomas Hutchins for this task. The French were still in control of Vincennes on the Wabash River and of the entire Illinois country. Bouquet planned to go down the Ohio early in 1763 to complete the occupation of the West. He asked Croghan to accompany him, but Croghan declined because of his proposed trip to England and because Amherst would not supply the necessary quantity of Indian presents. The English were not aware that at this very time Pontiac was secretly marshalling his forces for an attack which was to force a long postponement of Bouquet's plans.[241]

With the exception of short trips to Philadelphia early in 1759 and to New York in 1761, Croghan remained away from civilization for about three years. He longed to return east and wrote Johnson to "plese to Lett [me] know whether your honour Intends to keep Me heer Till I grow Gray." Early in 1762, he was called to Bedford to see his dying mother; he remained in the east during the entire summer of 1762. In June he assisted Johnson in an Indian conference at Easton. This was the fourth conference held at

241 Croghan to Johnson, Mar. 31, 1762, in Sullivan: *Papers of Sir William Johnson*, III, 662; Croghan's Instructions to Hutchins, Apr. 3, 1762, in Bouquet Coll., A 25: 216; Croghan to Bouquet, Mar. 19, 1763, (two letters) in *idem*, A 19: 98, 101.

this place since 1756 and it did not differ materially from the earlier ones. Shortly after this conference, Teedyuscung withdrew his charges of land frauds and in return was paid £400 by the Penns.[242]

In August, 1762, Croghan managed the Indian conference at Lancaster. Pennsylvania's repeated invitations to the Ohio Indians had been finally accepted; representatives of the Delawares, Shawnee, Miami, Kickapoo, Wea, and Six Nations came and brought thirty white prisoners to be released. Five hundred and fifty-seven Indians from the upper Susquehanna region were also present. Governor Hamilton, a committee of the assembly, and the usual group of Quakers came to meet them. Croghan went to Fort Lyttleton to assist Post in conducting the Indians and to secure agreements before the Quakers could influence the Indians. Johnson, fresh from his own experience at Easton, felt elated to hear that Croghan had successfully combatted the Quaker attempt "to exercise corrupt and illegal influence over Indian affairs." The usual topics were discussed, peace was formally renewed, and presents valued at £2,000 were distributed. Upon leaving, some of the Indians threw away their presents. This was a significant manifestation of their discontent which was soon to find expression in revolt. After this conference Croghan returned to Fort Pitt.[243]

After 1761, serious friction arose between Croghan and his military superiors over the question of expenditures. Practically all of his expenses were now paid

---

[242] Croghan to Johnson, Jan. 13, 1761, in Sullivan: *Papers of Sir William Johnson*, III, 301; *Mich. Pioneer and Hist. Coll.*, XIX, 144; *Acts of the Privy Council, Colonial Ser., Unbound Papers*, 343.

[243] Minutes of the Conference at Lancaster, 1762, in *Pa. Col. Rec.*, VIII, 721-774; *idem*, 676, 690; Sullivan: *Papers of Sir William Johnson*, III, 873; Johnson to Croghan, Dec. 30, 1762, in Johnson MSS., VI, 188; Croghan to ———, July 31, 1763, MS. in N.Y. Pub. Lib.

out of Amherst's military funds; salaries were paid
through Johnson and other bills through the military
commanders at the posts. This consumed time and
often forced Croghan to advance his own money or
credit for the department. Within certain limits Croghan could incur such expenses as he thought necessary
and this accounted in part for his successes. "An Indian Agent," wrote Johnson, "cannot support his Consequence or be of so much use if it is not in his power
to bestow favors upon them, because the Indians never
can believe a man to be of Consequence, or that he has
proper Authority unless it is in his power to shew
them kindness as they call it." [244]

In 1760, Canada was completely conquered and
George II was succeeded by George III; soon the
great war minister, William Pitt, was displaced by
Lord Bute. Amherst was now asked to curtail expenditures. He soon ceased to follow Johnson's advice and
began to view all Indian expenditures with disfavor.
During 1761, Croghan's expenditures were especially
heavy. He presented his accounts amounting to £4,400
in person to Amherst at New York in December, 1761.

[244] Johnson to Gage, Mar. 15, 1766, in *Ill. Hist. Coll.*, XI, 189. What
Johnson meant by "kindness" is illustrated by the following entries in his
"Expense Account to October, 1756", given in C. O., 5: 1067:

	£	s	d
To an old blind Indian to buy some bread	0	2	0
To a Tuscarora Warrior, Cost to buy something for his Sick Wife	0	8	0
To an Indian 3 Dollars for a Gun	1	4	0
To an Oneida Indian going to War for his family 3 Dollars	1	4	0
To a poor Squaw lost her husband viz. Thomas at the Lake	0	8	0
To 2 Mohawk Inds who lost 2 Horses by the 44 Regmt. They were shott. To make them easy	0	8	0
To a Doctor for curing a young Ind's hand which was shott by Accident	9	15	6
To an Entertainment given to 4 Mohawk Familys come from Ohio to settle at the Mohawk	3	17	6

To Amherst they seemed to "amount to a prodigious expense," and he refused to pay them until Croghan took them to Johnson for approval. For the next half year, Croghan submitted an account of £317, exclusive of salaries. Even this Amherst thought too much, though it was certified by Bouquet.[245] Among other economies, Amherst now forbade giving guns, ammunition, knives, vermillion, and food to northern warriors passing Fort Pitt on their way to attack southern Indians. This perennial warfare was encouraged by Johnson and Croghan for, without harm to the English, it gave turbulent young braves in both districts the diversion from hunting which they demanded. During the Cherokee war against Carolina in 1760, Croghan had advanced his own money to equip one hundred warriors to send southward. After Amherst's new orders, northern warriors passing Fort Pitt, when refused supplies, showed such ill temper that Croghan, rather than see the service suffer, used his salary to buy them small presents. "I Can say Now I Serve the King for nothing . . .", he wrote to Johnson in 1763.[246]

Amhersts's zeal for economy grew apace. Croghan was instructed to "retrench all Indian expences, and make use of all the Oconemy which the good of the Sirvice will in any wise admit of. . ." His budget for salaries was cut forty per cent in 1762. Instead of securing the release of captives by paying for them, Amherst ordered the suppression of all presents until after they had been released. "As to appropriating

[245] Amherst to Bouquet, Jan. 16, 1762, in Bouquet Coll., A4:83-1; Amherst to Johnson, Dec. 30, 1761, in Sullivan: *Papers of Sir William Johnson*, III, 597.
[246] Johnson to Stuart, Sept. 17, 1765, in Bd. of Tr. Pap., Plantations General, xxv, 623; *Pa. Arch.*, III, 733; Croghan to Johnson, Mar. 31, 1762 and May 10, 1762, in Sullivan: *Papers of Sir William Johnson*, III, 662, 732; Croghan to Johnson, Mar. 12, 1763, MS. in Newberry Library, Chicago.

a particular sum to be laid out yearly to the warriors in presents, etc., that I can by no means agree to," wrote Amherst; "nor can I think it necessary to give them any presents by way of *Bribes,* for if they do not behave properly they are to be punished." As an additional check on Croghan, Amherst forbade Indian agents to incur any expenses except upon the written orders of the commandants at the posts. Croghan was now thoroughly disgusted. He wrote to Johnson that he had done all he could to serve his King as frugally as possible, but that for the future he would never incur even the smallest expense without a written order, no matter what happened. The most intelligent Indians now began to ask Croghan why the English had repeatedly called them into council and given them presents during the war, but since were ignoring them. Croghan wrote to Bouquet: ". . . I do nott aprove of General Amhersts plan in Distressing them too much although as in my opinion they will not consider consequences if too much distrest tho' Sir Jeffrey thinks they will. How itt may end the Lord knows Butt I ashure you I am of opinion itt will nott be long before we shall have some [quarrels] with them." [247]

From Amherst's point of view it was not consistent with the financial condition or the dignity of England to adopt the policy of the defeated Bourbon enemy, especially when it could not insure the friendship of the Indians for any length of time. He saw no need of calling the Indians into conference in 1763 and giving

---

[247] Johnson's Instructions to Croghan, Jan. 8, 1762, in Bouquet Coll., A25: 211; *idem,* A4:140, A4:83-1; Parkman: *Conspiracy of Pontiac,* I, 174 note; Sullivan: *Papers of Sir William Johnson,* III, 732; Croghan to Bouquet, Dec. 10, 1762 and Mar. 19, 1763, in Bouquet Coll., A18-2: 534 and A19: 98, respectively. Parkman in quoting Croghan usually corrects his spelling and English. Parkman's *Conspiracy of Pontiac* is the classic account for this period.

them presents in order to properly announce to them
the terms of the peace of 1763 and thus prevent the
French traders from spreading false impressions.[248]
Croghan wrote at this time: "Since the Reduction of
Canada the several Indian Nations . . . has been
very jelous of his Majesty's growing power in this
country Butt this last Account of so much of North
America being ceded to Great Britain has allmost drove
them to despair." ". . . they . . . say the
French had no right to give away their country." To
this Amherst replied: "whatever idle notions they may
entertain in regard to the cessions made by the French
Crown, can be of very little consequence, as it is their
interest to behave peaceably, and while they continue
to do so they may be assured of His Majesty's Protection." This blustering and arrogant reply was
written only a few weeks before news came out of the
West which was to show Amherst that to follow a
policy based on military force was not a simple matter
in dealing with a foe possessed of no forts, or towns, or
valuable property, and who in the tangled woods was as
alert and active as a lynx. It was possible, as Bouquet
proved in 1764, to follow temporarily such a policy
and at times it was perhaps desirable to demonstrate
to the savages that a peaceful policy was not based on
a fear of their power.[249]

Johnson and Croghan, on the other hand, advocated
an Indian policy based, not upon force, but upon winning the friendship and confidence of the Indians by

[248] Stuart was able to hold such a conference for the Southern District;
cf. Carter, Clarence E.: "British Policy towards the American Indians in
the South," in *Eng. Hist. Rev.*, XXXIII, 38.

[249] Croghan to Amherst, Apr. 30, 1763, in Bouquet Coll., A4: 227; Amherst
to Croghan, May 10, 1763, in *idem*, A4: 233.

treating them as human beings and, in a kindly way, adapting policies to their primitive manners and customs. A keg of rum, a few thousand rations, or presents valued at £100, were to Johnson and Croghan a small matter when it meant the saving of the profits of the Indian trade or the prevention of all the costs and woes entailed by an Indian war. "The British and French Colonies since the first settling of America has adopted the Indian Customs and manners by indulging them in Treaties and renewing friendships making them large Presents which I fear won't be so easy to break them of as the Giniral may imagine . . .", wrote Croghan. In following this policy Johnson and Croghan probably tended to spend imperial funds rather freely. Johnson summarized the matter well when he wrote: "The more Indians get, the more they will Expect nevertheless there is a necessity for Expenses, and nothing Can be done with them without it but, in that point Judgment is required, when it shall be incured, and how favors shall be dispensed." [250]

When Amherst refused to modify his orders, Croghan began to consider resigning his office. On December 10, 1762, he wrote to his friend Bouquet: ". . . I don't chuse to be beging eternally for such nesesarys as is wanted to carry on the service nor will I suport itt att my own expense." Three months later he wrote again saying that he could no longer see any occasion to keep an agent at Fort Pitt since no regard was paid to any intelligence sent in or to any opinions expressed. Rather than condescend to act under Amherst, Croghan wrote that he would "content myself

[250] Croghan to Bouquet, Mar. 27, 1762, in Bouquet Coll., 25: 213; Johnson to Gage, Aug. 24, 1768, in Johnson MSS., XVI, 144; N. Y. Col. Docs., VII, 559, 581, 603, 648.

att the Tayl of a plow somewhere on the fronteers."
Amherst, however, refused to let Croghan resign.[251]

Other causes, besides those described thus far, contributed to the revolt of the natives. Those on the
upper Ohio feared the on-coming tide of English settlers; the genius of Pontiac united and enthused the
natives; the French traders spread rumors to incite
the savages against the English. Pontiac later spoke
of his uprising as being really a "Bever War". So
well planned and wide-spread was Pontiac's conspiracy
that by midsummer in 1763 the English remained in
possession of but three of the French posts which they
had just occupied. Nine forts were surprised and captured, two thousand English soldiers, traders, and
settlers captured or killed, often with the foulest bar-
barity, some thousands of English settlers driven to
beggary, and traders and troops plundered of goods
valued at nearly £100,000.[252]

Croghan had left Fort Pitt for Carlisle late in April,
1763. He had been gone but a few days when Captain
Ecuyer began to suspect trouble. In the hour of need
Croghan's services were appreciated; Ecuyer wrote:
"It is well that he should not delay, for those rascally
Delawares are coming. . . I am surrounded with
scamps." [253] Ecuyer was to be beseiged for weeks by
the savages. Croghan was surprised when the first
news of the rising came to him. He knew that the
Indians were uneasy, but he did not expect such a wide-
spread revolt at the time. On June 8, he wrote Bou-

---

[251] Croghan to Bouquet, Dec. 10, 1762, Mar. 19, Mar. 30, and Oct. 11,
1763, in Bouquet Coll., A18-2: 537, A19: 98, 109, and 474, respectively.

[252] *Ill. Hist. Coll.*, XI, 53; *idem*, X, 256-7.

[253] Ecuyer to Bouquet, May 4, 1763, in Darlington: *Fort Pitt and Letters
from the Frontier*, 106; *idem*, 124.

quet: "I Need Say Nothing Now on the Subjectt as itt will Nott Bear Laffing att as usual by his ——." [254] Amherst was greatly surprised and gathered relief expeditions as fast as he could. To Bouquet he wrote: ". . . I wish there was not an Indian Settlement within a Thousand Miles of our Country, for they are only fit to live with the Inhabitants of the Woods being more nearly allied to the Brute than the Human Creation." "I wish to hear of no prisoners, should any of the villains be met with in arms. . . Could it not be contrived to send the Small Pox among those disaffected tribes of Indians?" [255]

In the feverish activity which followed Croghan rendered all the service he could. He coöperated with Bouquet in preparing the region from Carlisle to Bedford for eventualities. He instilled courage into the hearts of fleeing frontiersmen. Without waiting for authorization he engaged and supplied twenty-five men at his own expense to garrison Fort Lyttleton. For this Pennsylvania later reimbursed him. When the justices of the peace of Cumberland County could persuade no one to help convoy powder and lead to Fort Bedford, Croghan took charge and led the convoy himself. When he arrived, Lieutenant Ourry, who was holding Fort Bedford, wrote Bouquet: "His company as you may well imagine is a great relief to me as his generosity has been to many a starving family." Here Croghan remained for two months assisting Bouquet in arranging for the relief of Fort Pitt. In September, 1763, when the worst of the storm had blown over, and when it was evident that at this time, force and not

---

[254] Darlington: *History of Col. Henry Bouquet, etc.*, 131, 134, 150, 190; Croghan to Peters and Clark, June 15, 1763, in Prov. Pap., xxxiii, 89.
[255] Parkman: *Conspiracy of Pontiac*, ii, 38-40.

diplomacy must be used, Croghan left for Johnson Hall. His chief assistant, Alexander McKee, who had been in charge of Indian affairs at Fort Pitt during the siege, took charge of Croghan's work during the next year and a half. This he did with credit to himself.[256]

Johnson and Croghan discussed with great earnestness the future of their department. It had failed to detect and prevent Pontiac's uprising and therefore had not served the British Empire as it should. The opening of the French and Indian War had begotten it and now the close of that war threatened to see its early decline, if not its demise. Should this occur, Johnson and Croghan would lose not only the opportunity to serve their king, but also the prestige, the great influence, and the salary connected with their imperial offices. They dreamed of an Indian department with its own financial resources. They hoped to occupy a position similar to that of the surveyors-general of the king's customs, the vice-admiralty judges, the surveyors-general of the king's woods, or the proposed surveyors-general of the king's lands. This would make them coördinate and not subordinate to the military department.

The time for attempting to realize these hopes was now most opportune. British statesmen were engaged in shaping a new imperial system; the lessons of Pontiac's uprising were fresh in men's minds; and the Board of Trade was makng a detailed study of Indian

---

[256] *Pa. Col. Rec.*, IX, 34; Ourry to Bouquet, June 23, 1763, in Bouquet Coll., A12-2: 499; Croghan to McKee, Dec. 4, 1764, in *idem*, A23-2: 470. Croghan and Bouquet corresponded very frequently during this exciting period, sometimes exchanging two letters a day. – Cf. *idem*, A19: 173, 184, 207, 210, 262; A23: 240; A4: 265, 292. Trent was made captain of the militia at Fort Pitt and some letters passed between him and Croghan. – Trent's Journal at Fort Pitt, 1763, in *Miss. Valley Hist. Rev.*, XI, 390ff.

affairs. The Board had written to Johnson and to various other officials in America for detailed information and advice. In reply, Johnson prepared a long memorial on Indian affairs. Croghan had been planning for some time to go to London to assist in securing restitution for the losses of the Indian traders before 1755 and to secure a grant of 200,000 acres of land in New York. It was therefore decided to have Croghan present Johnson's reply to the Board of Trade and support it in person with detailed explanations. Croghan was to sound the ministry on the question of establishing a definite Indian boundary line and to help the Penns to get it moved far westward in Pennsylvania.[257] He was also to aid Johnson to secure several land grants in New York and reimbursement for his extraordinary services and for his personal expenditures for official purposes. To assist them in these various projects, Johnson and Croghan enlisted the influence of influential friends in both England and America.

From Johnson Hall Croghan went to New York to secure from Amherst leave of absence to go to England. Nearly all of those who had held positions of trust under Amherst in the West felt as Croghan did and wanted to resign. Captain Gladwyn at Detroit, Lieutenant Blane at Fort Ligonier, and Bouquet asked Amherst to approve their resignations. "For God's sake let me go and raise cabbages", wrote Captain Ecuyer from Fort Pitt. Amherst was in no mood to grant Croghan's request, especially since Croghan would probably testify against him. He wrote to Bouquet: "I have absolutely refused to comply with his request, as I think if his presence ever was of any consequence . . . it certainly is so at this present time." Am-

---

[257] Thomas Penn to Croghan, Jan. 9, 1768, in Penn Letter Bk., IX, 213.

herst asked Croghan to join Bouquet and assist in the
relief of Fort Pitt, but this, to the great disappointment
of Bouquet, he absolutely refused to do. Instead, he
sent in his written resignation to Amherst. "I know
many people will think I am wrong", wrote Croghan to
Bouquet "butt had I continued I could be of no more
service than I have been this eighteen months past
which was none ataul." [258] It was not until Amherst
was superceded by Gage that Croghan withdrew his
resignation.

From New York Croghan proceeded to Carlisle and
Bedford. He sold several thousand acres of land in
this region to raise funds for his journey and he gave
to Edward Ward and Joseph Dobson power of attorney
to conduct his business affairs in his absence. He then
returned to Philadelphia where he engaged a man to
make a map showing the colonial frontiers. Here he
also participated in a series of conferences of far-reaching importance with twelve of the leading traders and
merchants of Pennsylvania, who along with Croghan
were seeking restitution for their losses in the Indian
trade before 1754 and in 1763. He sailed from Philadelphia on December 30, 1763. When his ship, the
Britannia, reached the coast of Normandy it was completely wrecked. Croghan lost everything but his
papers. "I Traveld about 140 Miles in france Butt
Never See So Much pride and poverty before," he
wrote to Johnson.[259] The *ancien regime* presented
great contrasts to the frontiersman.

---

[258] Amherst to Bouquet, Sept. 25, 1763, in Bouquet Coll., 4: 413; Johnson
to Amherst, Sept. 14, 1763, in Haldimand Coll., 220: 555; *idem*, 588; Croghan to Bouquet, Oct. 11, 1763, in Bouquet Coll., A19-2:474.

[259] Day: *Calendar of Sir William Johnson* MSS., 182; *Mass. Hist. Coll.,
4th ser., X*, 508; Winsor is probably in error in stating (*Westward Movement*, 8) that Croghan was also to further the interests of the Ohio Company of Virginia and of the claimants to Dinwiddie's military grants.

The "vanities of London", to use Croghan's phrase, made a similar impression. His letters to Johnson contain the following striking observations on the political conditions in England on the eve of the American Revolution.[260] He wrote that "the Cheefe Study of the pople in power hear att present is To Lay Heavy Taxes on the Colenys and tis Talkt of Laying an Internal Tax on them Next Cesion of parlament." "Tho I have been hear Now a Month Nothing has been Don Respecting North aMerrica – the pople hear Spend thire Time in Nothing butt abuseing one aNother & Striveing who Shall be in power with a view to Serve themselves and thire frends, and Neglect the publick. Itt was butt yesterday that your State of Indian affairs was Read att the Board of Trade tho I Delivered itt the 13th of Last Month." "Was I to Spake My Mind I wold say they are all R-g-e-s [Rogues] aLike." It ought to be added that Johnson, Croghan, and many of the Revolutionary leaders were not entirely free from similar personal material interests in politics.

Croghan arrived in London on February 11, 1764. Johnson had given him letters of introduction to such leaders as Lord Halifax, Secretary of State for the Southern Department, Lord Hillsborough, President of the Board of Trade, John Pownall, Secretary to the Board of Trade, ex-Governor Thomas Pownall, and Thomas Penn; with these and with other influential leaders Croghan held various conferences. English noblemen who desired to speculate in western lands in America sought interviews with him. During the ensuing months, the Board of Trade very seriously

---

The relation of Croghan's visit to England to the traders' losses and to western lands will be discussed in succeeding chapters.

[260] Johnson MSS. (Ill.), VIII, 169; IX 19, 43, 53, 112, 132; VII, 218, 251; XXIV, 216.

considered Indian affairs; its journal shows that often entire meetings were given over to this subject. On June 7 and 8, Croghan was called before the Board to discuss the problems presented in Johnson's letters. He drew up a long formal letter on Indian affairs which was read before the Board on June 8.[261] Croghan continued working for his various projects during the following summer and then returned to New York in the autumn of 1764.

It is difficult to estimate the results of Croghan's visit. He did not succeed in his efforts to secure land grants or restitution for Indian traders, but his visit doubtless increased the interest of many Englishmen in the West and it probably helped him later on to secure grants of land. · In Indian affairs, he was more successful for the Board of Trade adopted many of the ideas advocated by Johnson and Croghan. The new ministry, headed by Grenville, Halifax, and the new president of the Board of Trade, Lord Hillsborough, were much more favorably disposed toward the Indian department than were their predecessors. The lessons taught by Pontiac's uprising were easily seen. "Gineral Amhirsts Conduct is Condem⁴ by Everybody and has been pelted away in the papers. the army Curse him in publick as well as the Merchants," wrote Croghan.

Pontiac's uprising hastened the partial announcement of a western colonial policy by the imperial government in one of the important documents of American colonial history, the royal proclamation of October 7, 1763. The Board of Trade under the leadership of the industrious Shelburne had been engaged all

---

[261] Bd. of Tr., Journal, LXXII: 257-260 and *passim*; Croghan's letter, in Bd. of Tr. Pap., Plantations General, XIX, R54; *N.Y. Hist. Soc. Coll.*, 1871, I: 35.

spring and summer in studying the great problem of
formulating a comprehensive colonial policy for all
the territories acquired in 1763. Two points had been
agreed upon before the news of Pontiac's uprising
came: first, the establishment of civil governments for
Florida and Nova Scotia and the encouragement of
emigration to these colonies in order to settle these out-
lying colonies and to relieve the pressure upon the
Indian's land, and second, the drawing of an Indian
boundary line from Canada to Florida beyond which
no settlements were to be permitted. This line was
gradually to be moved westward as the pressure of
population made this necessary; but this was to be accomplished, not by private purchases of land from the
Indians which had so often been accompanied by
fraud, but by purchases made by the imperial government. Beyond this line colonial governors were forbidden to grant warrants of survey or patents; squatting
upon the Indian's land was also forbidden. Criminals
who fled into the Indian country for a place of refuge
were to be returned by the military and Indian officials.
It was hoped that this system would remove permanently one of the chief causes for Indian wars and that
it would help immediately to allay the fears of Pontiac's adherents. When Hillsborough, the new president of the Board of Trade, drew up the proclamation
rather hastily and crudely, these two major points were
included. Other points were added, some good and
some bad. Two of these related to Indian affairs.
Because of the necessity for haste, the Indian boundary
line was not rationally marked out for surveying, but
was located at the Appalachian divide where the Indians could easily identify it. The Indian trade was
opened to all who secured a license from a governor or

from the commander-in-chief and who obeyed the regulations.

The more mature policy of the ministry was expressed in the "Plan for the future Management of Indian Affairs" which was finally drawn up on July 10, 1764, by the Board of Trade.[262] This provided for a permanent Indian department with two districts with a superintendent over each. There were to be three deputy superintendents for the Northern and two for the Southern District. Each district was to have four missionaries. To protect the Indians from abuses in trade all colonial laws governing it were to be repealed and it was to be regulated solely by imperial officials. It was to be open to all English subjects who secured a license from a governor or the commander-in-chief specifying the particular place where trade was to be carried on and who gave bond to obey the imperial regulations. As soon as a trader entered the Indian country he would pass under the direct supervision of the Indian department. In the Southern District trade was to be confined to the Indian villages; in the Northern District, to about twelve posts. In each village and post there was to reside an interpreter, a smith, and a commissary. The latter was to have strict supervision of trade for which tariffs were to be established. No rum, swan shot, or rifled barreled guns were to be sold to the Indians, nor credit extended to them in excess of fifty shillings. The superintendents or their deputies were to visit each village and post annually to inspect conditions, to meet the Indians, and to make them presents. Only the officials of the Indian department were to hold conferences with the Indians. To

---

[262] Printed in *N.Y. Col. Docs.*, VII, 637ff. Criticisms are found in Bd. of Tr. Pap., Plantations General, XXII.

protect the Indians against settlers and land speculators, it was provided that all purchases of their land
must be made through the Indian department. The
governors, military commanders, and Indian officials
were to be independent of each other, but they were
to coöperate and act in concert. To further such
action the two superintendents were to be ex-officio
members of the council of each colony in their respective districts. The superintendents, deputies, and commissaries were to be made justices of the peace in order
to be able to apprehend criminals in the Indian country
and to decide all civil cases between traders or between
traders and Indians involving less than £10. In all
such cases the testimony of Indians was to be received.
Civil cases involving more than £10 and criminal cases
were to be tried in the regular colonial courts. All
Indian officials were forbidden to engage in trade with
the Indians or to receive grants of land from them. It
was estimated that this plan would cost £20,000 annually; this was to be raised by levying an export duty
on furs and skins of five percent or by taxing the trade
at the posts.

This plan was at once subjected to severe criticism.
Many traders, merchants, and colonial and imperial
officials maintained that it did not meet the needs of the
situation and that it was too costly. It was declared
unwise to prohibit the sale of rum, while to confine
trade to the posts would materially decrease profits for
distant Indians could not visit a post frequently nor
bring many goods; the presence of a trader among the
Indians with a supply of such articles as the Indians
wanted encouraged them to greater activity; moreover,
many Indian families would often be seriously incon-
venienced and distressed when they lost or broke their

hatchets, knives, gun-locks, or had their gunpowder spoiled. A policy of *laissez faire* was declared preferable to government regulation. It was also argued that it was unwise to repeal the colonial laws which were drawn up to meet local needs and that there would be great danger of corruption if so much power was vested in a few autocratic officials responsible only to the ministry. Governor Bernard of Massachusetts wrote to the Board of Trade that with all due respect to Johnson, he was opposed to making him " a Governor within my Government". Governor Murray of Quebec wrote that giving the Superintendent sole control over Indian affairs "is establishing a Power within another power, the Policy of which I do not comprehend."

The plan could be put into full effect only through an act of Parliament. The ministry, however, were afraid to lay it before Parliament for it would subject their entire American policy to attack and they would be accused of false professions of economy; the Board of Trade had even waited until Parliament had adjourned before announcing its plan. Croghan was told that until Parliament acted, the commander-in-chief would furnish the Indian department with the funds which it needed. This was the crux of the whole matter and it presaged the ultimate defeat of the plans of Johnson and Croghan. Meantime, the Board instructed Johnson and Stuart to put the plan into operation so far as possible. Stuart proceeded to do so at once, but Johnson delayed for two years, probably because of the expense involved. By 1764, the Indian department had thus reached its height and it had become an important phase of the new imperial system. Croghan felt elated and wrote to McKee: "I have been able to settle the Department of Indian Affairs, on a new system. . . The sole management of Indian Affairs and the Regulation of Indian Trade is invested in the Superintendent and his Agents independent of the Officers Commanding at any of the posts which I make no doubt will be no small mortification to some people." [263]

While Croghan was in England, Pontiac's plans had been frustrated. Colonel Bradstreet had relieved Detroit and Bouquet, after winning the battle of Bushy Run, had relieved Fort Pitt and then marched beyond into the heart of the Indian country and forced the Delawares and Shawnee to sue for peace. English garrisons were again established at various posts in the West. After 1763, Indian affairs presented many of the same problems as after 1758. One old problem remained unsolved – the occupation of the Illinois country. Here, on the banks of the Mississippi, two years after the peace of Paris had been signed, the *fleur de lis* was still flying over Fort de Chartres, one of the strongest fortresses in America. In the villages of Kaskaskia and Cahokia and in neighboring settlements lived several hundred French peasants and traders. The savages within a large radius regarded the French as their friends and fathers. Closely associated with these French settlements were Vincennes and Ouiatenon on the Wabash. After Croghan's return to America, his first and perhaps his greatest service was to assist in occupying the Illinois country. Pontiac had retired into this region and refused all overtures of peace. Instead, he attempted to retrieve his cause and determined to defend his last place of retreat against the hated English. He was led by the

---

[263] Croghan to McKee, Dec. 4, 1764, in Bouquet Coll., A23-2: 470.

French traders to believe that their king would send a large army to help him. They were especially influential in 1765 because the formal transfer of Louisiana to Spain caused several hundred French traders to come up the Mississippi with a large convoy of goods.

To the Englishmen of 1765, the Illinois country seemed as far distant and as difficult to occupy as the wilds of central Africa or the Antarctic region would seem to us today. Hutchins considered the Western Confederacy "more difficult to conquer with an armed Force than the taking of a dozen such places as the Havana with its Moro Castles." Numerous desertions from the 34th regiment occurred as soon as it was announced that this regiment was to be sent to occupy the Illinois country. Gage used Detroit, Fort Pitt, and Mobile as bases from which to occupy Illinois. Both Johnson and Stuart sent deputies to the Illinois tribes and there was much rivalry as to which of the two should first succeed. Before success was finally attained, six missions were sent to Illinois. Some of these were forced to turn back before reaching it; those who did reach it often had their men stripped, beaten, and threatened by drunken Indians. Only the intercession of Pontiac or the French commander, St. Ange, enabled them to drop secretly down the Mississippi at night for New Orleans. One military force composed of over 300 men under Major Loftus while going up the Mississippi in 1764 to occupy Illinois, was fired upon by the Indians and helplessly forced to retreat after it had gone only 240 miles. All of these attempts, however, helped to prepare the way for Croghan.[264]

[264] Hutchins to Johnson, Aug. 31, 1765, in *Ill. Hist. Coll.*, XI, 80; *idem*, 58; *Pa. Gazette*, Aug. 15 and 22, 1765; Carter, Clarence E.: *Great Britain and the Illinois Country, 1763-1774*, Chapt. III; Journal of Capt. Morris, in

"It admits of no doubt but the Way of Negotiation is the only one admissable at present. . . Mr. Croghan is the fittest Person in America to Transact that Business . . .", wrote the seasoned Indian fighter, Bouquet, to Gage; and the latter reported to the ministry that "it must be confessed, that the operations are delicate, and that they require caution, skill and Artful management." Croghan wrote to Benjamin Franklin in London: "I returned from England last winter, when I found the General not a little distressed – In that, all his endeavours had hitherto failed, with respect to gaining the Ilinois. I therefore thought it the Duty of my Department, to propose to him that I should use my best endeavours with the Natives (with whom I had been long acquainted and flattered myself, had some influence) to obtain their consent to His Majestys Troops, peaceably, possessing that Country. – Which proposition he cheerfully accepted off." [265]

Croghan with great exuberance of spirit now sent McKee a message for the Indians around Fort Pitt. In it he told of his coming and asked them to have their peltry collected and to be ready to transact busi-

Thwaites: *Early Western Travels*, I, 301-328. The success of Major Farmar the next year on a similar expedition was due to Croghan's successful mission and to the preparation made by Stuart. Stuart supplied three Choctaw chiefs who accompanied Farmar to Natchez and made the smaller tribes forget their hostility; at Natchez, 80 Choctaws joined Farmar; further up the river 125 Chickasaws met him, 14 of whom accompanied him all the way to the Illinois country, hunting buffaloes for the expedition and overawing the natives; and finally, a band of Cherokees came to meet him at the mouth of the Ohio. Stuart also furnished Farmar with presents and agents to distribute them all along his route. – Farmar to Stuart, Dec. 16, 1765, in Bd. of Tr. Pap., Plantations General, xxv-2, 656.

[265] Bouquet to Gage, Jan. 5, 1765, in Bouquet Coll., A7: 111; Gage to Lord Halifax, July 13, 1764, in *Ill. Hist. Coll.*, x, 283; *idem*, xi, 80. All students of Croghan's missions to Illinois are greatly indebted to Professors Alvord and Carter for their work in collecting and editing the original documents contained in the *British Series* of the *Illinois Historical Collections*.

ness. He wrote McKee: "You are under no necessity of acquainting any officer what instructions you receive from me. . . You will present my compliments to any gentlemen you please, or none at all as you shall think proper. . ." Bouquet wrote Captain Murray at Fort Pitt to open the letter, send him a copy of it, and should the message be contrary to his Indian policy, not to permit it to be delivered. Bouquet complained to Gage that Croghan gave him no notice of his plans and that by prematurely opening the Indian trade he would counteract the good accomplished by his expedition. He added that he was glad that under the new system the military officers would have no further duties in Indian affairs, "tho' at the same time we cannot but regret that Powers of so great importance to this country, should in this instance have been trusted to a man so ill[it]erate, impudent and ill-bred, who subverts to particular purposes the wise views of the Government, and begins his functions by a ridiculous display of his own importance, and an attempt to destroy the harmony which ought to subsist between the different branches of the service." [266]

Meanwhile, Croghan had been in conference with Gage at New York and probably with Johnson at Johnson Hall, and had proceeded to Philadelphia. Lieutenant Fraser had volunteered to accompany Croghan as Gage's representative to St. Ange. He spoke French and supplied other qualifications lacking by his colleague. Gage generously supplied Croghan with £2,000 sterling and with presents valued at £1,200. Gage issued orders to all military officers stationed along the road to Fort Pitt to permit Croghan's pres-

---

[266] Croghan to McKee, Dec. 4, 1764, in Bouquet Coll., A23-2: 470; Bouquet to Murray, Dec. 14, 1764, in *idem*, 473; Bouquet to Gage, Dec. 22, 1765, in *idem*, 474; *idem*, A7: 122, A8: 508, A24: 250, and A26: 60.

ents of ammunition, dry goods, and liquor to pass un-
molested, and to furnish him with provisions and at
Fort Pitt with batteaux. Croghan left Philadelphia
for Carlisle on January 24, 1765, in advance of his convoy of presents. He then followed the military road
which seven years before had been cut across the mountains. It passed along crags and chasms and still
abounded in stumps, roots, and stones. On either side
stood the grim, leafless forest. During this season of
the year the traveler could secure a good view of the
interminable ranges of waste and lonely mountains.
The traveler over this road could stop here and there
at a friendly English fort. To Croghan this stern life
had a fascination that made all other existence seem
tame.

Shortly after his arrival at Fort Pitt, news came
that the "Black Boys" had attacked his convoy, burned
most of his presents and threatened his life if he ever
returned to Cumberland County. The frontiersmen
of Pennsylvania had overlooked the Indian attacks
of 1755-1758, but after 1763 they could not again over-
look the burning of their homes and the scalping of
loved ones. They objected to the immediate reopening of trade with the savages, to making them such
large presents, and especially to letting them have guns
and ammunition. Their past sufferings and their
narrow horizon prevented them from seeing the larger
aspects of the problem. The Indian trade had not yet
been legally opened. When the frontiersmen saw the
size of Croghan's convoy and heard rumors that the
firm of Baynton, Wharton, and Morgan were illegally
sending their goods along with the king's presents,
they acted quickly in a manner characteristic of the
frontier. Thirty of them with blackened faces and

dressed like Indians, led by Captain James Smith and two other justices of the peace of Cumberland County, stationed themselves in ambush on Sideling Hill, seventeen miles west of Fort Loudoun. When the convoy of eighty-one packhorses came along, they fired, killing many of the horses. The frightened drivers, thankful to escape alive, soon had their goods and saddles piled up as directed and saw them burned or taken. Some of the drivers with seventeen horseloads escaped to Fort Loudoun.[267]

This led to open hostility between the imperial troops and the frontiersmen. Prisoners and arms were taken on both sides and exchanged under flags of truce. At one time 300 riflemen surrounded the fort. At another time, they seized the commandant and left him tied to a tree. Goods passing westward were inspected and passes such as the following were more effectual than passes issued by Governor Penn or General Gage: "As the Sidling Hill Volunteers have already Inspected these goods, and as they are all private property, it is Expected that none of these brave fellows will molest them upon the Road, as there is no Indian Supplies amongst them. – Given under my Hand, May 15, 1765 – James Smith."[268] Expresses carrying news and dispatches were censored. Governor Penn issued proclamations and removed the three justices of the peace from office. Gage wrote Penn placing all the troops in Pennsylvania at his disposal to suppress the lawless banditti who seemed to be in an actual state of rebellion. His words were prophetic. Gradually, the activity of the Pennsylvania frontiersmen decreased, but it never ceased entirely before the Revolution.

[267] Withers, Alexander S.: *Chronicles of Border Warfare*, 110ff.
[268] *Pa. Arch.*, IV, 220; *Pa. Col. Rec.*, IX, 265-270, 293.

With his presents destroyed and charged with corruption, Croghan, now at Fort Pitt, faced his work
with serious handicaps. For the moment he felt that
he ought to resign. In the emergency, he went to the
firm of Trent, Simon, Levy, and Franks and asked for
goods out of their warehouse. He inspired them with
enthusiasm for his vision of the future of the West and
partially repaired his loss with goods to the amount of
£2,037, 11s, 10½d. He gave his own personal note as
security in spite of his previous experience under similar circumstances.[269]

After Croghan and Fraser arrived at Fort Pitt they
encountered various delays. The hostages, whom the
Delawares and Shawnee had left at that place, had
fled. These tribes had promised Bouquet after he had
chastised them that they would send a delegation to
Johnson to make peace, but only one chief came. Time
after time Indians came to Pittsburg with loads of
peltry; when they were told that trade was not to be
opened till they fulfilled their promises, they grew
sulky and sullen. McKee had sent belts to the upper
Ohio tribes and to Pontiac inviting them to conferences
with Croghan, but they reluctantly came dropping in,
band after band, with such slowness that weeks passed
before enough were present to open a council. Fraser's
orders did not permit long delay and therefore he left
in a canoe in March, outfitted by Croghan. Fraser
.arrived safely at Fort de Chartres, but when Croghan's
arrival was delayed, he was forced to drop down the
Mississippi to save his life.

Croghan labored for two months sending out messages to individual Indians and holding private interviews with such Indians as he could reach. Finally,

---

[269] Original bill, note and receipts, in McAllister Coll.; Byars: *B. and
M. Gratz*, 73.

he was able to open a formal and difficult conference
on May 8.   Over 500 Delaware, Shawnee, Seneca, and
Sandusky warriors, most of whom had participated in
the rising in 1763, together with many of their women
and children were present.   Croghan's speeches informed them that if they would return their English
captives, leave hostages at Fort Pitt, send delegates to
Johnson to make peace, and provide a deputation to
accompany him to Illinois, then trade would be reopened.   The Indians asked that they be treated with
more consideration than had been the case before 1763
and that trade in rum, guns, and ammunition be allowed.   They agreed to fulfill the conditions laid
down by Croghan.   "We will go with you and do
everything in our power to promote the good work of
Peace," said one speaker.   Presents were then distributed.   Croghan enclosed a copy of the minutes of
the conference in a letter to Governor Penn and the
latter then issued a proclamation throwing wide open
the Indian trade.   Croghan had patiently laid the
foundation for the success of his mission.[270]

On May 15, he left Fort Pitt on a journey that was
to occupy a memorable place in western annals.   His
company included Thomas Smallman and a deputation of Delaware, Shawnee, and Seneca chiefs.   In his
two batteaux were a goodly supply of presents and
gold and silver money.   He dropped down the Ohio
at the rate of twenty to ninety miles a day.   The interest and anxiety with which his friends, military and
civil officials, and eastern business leaders awaited the
outcome of his perilous undertaking is shown by con-

---

[270] Croghan's Journal of Transactions with the Indians at Fort Pitt
in 1765, in *Pa. Col. Rec.*, IX, 249, 264 (another version is found in the
Gratz-Croghan MSS., I, 12); Wharton to Franklin, 1765, in Franklin MSS.,
LVIII, 88; *idem*, I, 19.

temporary notices in the *Pennsylvania Gazette* and in Johnson's wide correspondence. To many persons his mission rivaled the Stamp Act in interest. Many business interests hoped to profit more by it than they ever expected to lose through new taxes. Rumors soon began to come out of the West to these persons. One rumor said that Croghan and all his party were burned at the stake; another, that Pontiac "had prepared a large Kettle, in which he was determined to boil them, and all other Englishmen that came that Way."[271]

Meanwhile, Croghan was proceeding down the Ohio.[272] He tarried at the mouth of the Scioto to hold

[271] *Pa. Gazette,* July 18, Aug. 15, et al, 1765; *Doc. Hist. of N.Y.,* II, 820, 833. Capucin, a leading French merchant at Vincennes, wrote on June 7, 1765: "Les Anglois que Maisonville a conduit Aux Ilinois, sont tous echapez de la fureur des Sauvages, comme ceux qui etoint venûs en premier lieu, ils n'ont pas mieux reûssoi l'un que l'autre. *Mr. George Croghan* est bien attendû, mais je pense que s'il arrive il ne sera pas mieux reçu que les Autres, je croi qu'il a eût plus de prudence que les premiers envoyés, on bien il a eté defait dans la Belle Rivierè." – Bd. of Tr. Pap., Plantations General, XXV-1, 157.

[272] Croghan's two journals of this expedition are important documents for the history of the west. One journal, emphasizing the Indian negotiations, was evidently prepared for English officials; the other, emphasizing topography, soil, trees, game, etc., was evidently prepared for land speculators and projectors of inland colonies. Croghan referred to the latter as his "private" journal. No paragraph in one is the same as any paragraph in the other, yet there is nothing contradictory in the two journals. Croghan to Franklin, Feb. 25, 1766, in C. O., 5: 66. Croghan sent a copy of both journals to Franklin. – Croghan to Franklin, Dec. 12, 1765, in C. O., 5: 66.

There are several versions of each journal, varying in phraseology and in length. Versions of the "official" journal are found in (1) the Penn MSS., Indian Affairs, IV, 49ff., (2) C. O., 323.23 (copy sent by Croghan to the Board of Trade), (3) C. O., 5: 66 (copy sent by Croghan to Franklin), C. O., 5:83, (4) Durrett Coll., University of Chicago, and (5) MSS., Division, Carnegie Library of Pittsburgh. The "official" journal has been printed in (1) Perkins, J. H.: *Annals of the West,* 1846, (2) Albach, J. R.: *Annals of the West,* 1856, (3) Hildreth, S. P.: *Pioneer History of Ohio,* 68ff., 1848, (4) the *N.Y. Col. Docs.,* VII, 779ff., 1856, and (5) in the *Ill. Hist. Coll.,* XI, 38ff., 1916.

Versions of the "land" journal are found in (1) Hutchins MSS., III, 94ff.,

a conference with the Indians and to secure seven French "Incendiaries". From here he wrote Gage and Johnson. He was about to enter the region which had been closed to him as a trader and into which but few Englishmen had ever ventured. As his party floated and rowed down the Ohio they encountered only the stillness and solitude of the leafy banks which might at any point harbor a lurking foe. On June 7, Croghan's servant who had left the camp to look for wood did not return. Croghan waited in vain and concluded that he had become lost, but he had been captured by Indians who learned from him the nature of the expedition. At the mouth of the Wabash Croghan found a breastwork which had been thrown up by the Indians. He now thought it wise to dispatch two Indians overland to Fort de Chartres with letters to Fraser and St. Ange. The next day he encamped. The story of the attack which followed is best told in his own words: "June 8th at Day Break we were attacked by a Party of Indians consisting of Eighty Warriors of the Kicapers and Musquatimes [273] who Killed

and (2) among the papers of George Morgan, though the latter copy may no longer be in existence. The "land" journal has been printed in (1) the *Monthly Journal of American Geology*, I, 257ff., 1831, (2) Butler, Mann: *History of Kentucky, Appendix*, 1834, (3) Craig, N. B., *Olden Time*, I, 403ff., 1846, (4) a pamphlet, published by Thomas at Burlington, N.J., in 1876 and (5) in the *Ill. Hist. Coll.*, XI, 23ff., 1916. In Thwaites: *Early Western Travels*, I, 126ff. (1904) the "official" and "land" journals have been combined and printed as one journal.

Croghan furnished Dr. William Smith, Provost of the College of Philadelphia, with a copy of one of these journals for use in a projected history of "all the Indians and their countries" annexed to England in 1763. (Smith to Johnson, Jan. 13, 1766, in Johnson MSS., Library of Congress). James Adair probably used them for his *History of the American Indians*. From that day to this, these journals have been utilized by historians. Parkman used them extensively for his *Conspiracy of Pontiac*. The best printed versions are found in the *Ill. Hist. Coll.*

[273] Probably the Kickapoo and Mascoutens, staunch allies to the French; cf. *Ill. Hist. Coll.*, XI, 3n.3 and 57n.2.

two of my men & three Indians wounded myselfe and
all the rest of my party Except two White Men and one
Indian then made myselfe and all the White men Prisoners plundering us of everything we had. A Deputy of the Shawnesse who was Shot thro the Thigh having concealed him selfe in the Woods for a few Minuets
after he was Wounded not then Knowing but they
were Southern Indians who are always at war with the
Northward Indians: after discovering what Nation
they were he came up to them and made a very bold
speech telling them that the Whole Northward Indians
would join in taking Revenge for the Insult and murder of their People this alarmed thoss Indians very
much they began excusing themselves saying their
Fathers the French had spirited them up telling them
the Inglish were coming with a body of Southern Indians to take their Country from them and inslave them
that it was this that induced them to commit this Out-
rage after having divided the plunder they left great
Part of the heaviest Effects Behind not being able to
carry them they sett of with us to their Village at
Cautonan [Ouiatenon] in a great Hurry being in dread
of a Pursuit from a large Party of Indians they suspected they were coming after me: Our Course was
thro a thick Woody Country crossing a great many
Swamps Morasses and Beaver Ponds we traveled this
Day about 42 Miles."

"I got the stroke of a Hatchet on the Head," wrote
Croghan to Captain Murray, "but my skull being
pretty thick, the hatchet would not enter, so you may see
a thick skull is of service on some occasions." [274] Immediately after the attack his Indian deputies were at

[274] Croghan to Murray, July 12, 1765, in Eng. and Am. 1764-5, 414, Bancroft Coll.

once released and they faithfully proceeded overland to Fort de Chartres. The white prisoners, many of whom were wounded, were compelled to proceed northward to Vincennes by forced marches. They suffered exceedingly with the heat and the lack of water. For a time they feared that they might be burned at the stake. After they reached Vincennes, Croghan procured with difficulty scraps of paper upon which he wrote his journal in disguised characters, unintelligible to the French.

At Vincennes, Croghan found eighty French families whom he describes as "an idle lazy people a parcel of Renegadoes from Canada and are much worse than Indians." They took secret pleasure at his misfortune and enriched themselves by securing his gold and silver specie from the Indians for mere trifles. They told him of Fraser's escape from Illinois and allowed him to send a letter to St. Ange and to buy some clothing and horses for the journey to Ouiatenon. This journey took him through the region inhabited by the Piankashaws, with whose chiefs he had traded at Pickawillani fifteen years before. His old acquaintances frankly informed him of the situation, refused to accept any of the plunder and upbraided the Kickapoo and Mascoutens for beginning "a War for which our Women and Children will have reason to Cry. . ." The fear of the dreaded Iroquois brought the Indians to terms. They were soon abjectly begging Croghan to intercede for them with the Shawnee, Delawares and Six Nations and offered to conduct any troops to Fort de Chartres and to be forever, faithful allies to the English.

In the meantime, the chiefs of the Wabash tribes, who had gone to Illinois to await Croghan, returned. Croghan met them and reconciled them to English rule. On July 1, the Englishmen were set free and on July 12, Croghan was permitted to write Johnson, Gage, Murray, Farmar, and Campbell. The following day, Croghan held a formal conference with the Ottawa, Piankashaw, Miami, Ouiatenon, Mascoutens, and Kickapoo Indians. They confessed that "they never had much sense" and expressed sincere repentance. Finally, their chiefs made a pathetic appeal to both the English and the French, to help reëstablish peace.[275]

Shortly after this conference, Maisonville arrived with a message from St. Ange inviting Croghan and the Indian chiefs to come to Illinois to meet Pontiac. They set out on July 18. On the trail they met Pontiac, himself, with a train of dark, malignant followers and the Indian deputies who had left Croghan after the attack. Pontiac had read the handwriting on the wall and had finally decided to smoke the calumet with his triumphant enemies. All now returned to Ouiatenon where a grand council was held; Croghan was informed that he might rest satisfied that whenever the English came to take possession of the Illinois country they would be received with open arms. "Pondiac and I are on extreme good terms," wrote Croghan to McKee, "and I am mistaken if I don't ruin his influence with his own people before I part with him. . . Had I arrived safe to the Ilinois it would not have been in my Power to have carried this Point. . . nothing but their Killing the People with Me, would have brought them to Reason." Later he wrote Johnson that "Pondiac is a shrewd Sensible Indian of few words, and commands more respect amongst those

[275] Speeches of the Indians of the Oubache to Mr. Croghan, in C. O., 5: 83.

Nations, than any Indian I ever saw could do amongst his own Tribe." [276]

Indian runners were dispatched to notify Captain Stirling at Fort Pitt that he could now leave for Fort de Chartres. This he did. Under trying circumstances, without sufficient presents or an Indian agent to help him, he occupied and held it until Major Farmar came up the Mississippi to establish securely English rule in Illinois.

Since there was now no need to proceed to Fort de Chartres, Croghan left for Detroit, accompanied by Pontiac and many chiefs. Croghan met many old Indian friends as he journeyed along the Maumee River. English prisoners were brought to him. He arrived at Detroit on August 17, and was at once engaged in the midst of important Indian negotiations. In response to inviations sent them by Colonel Bradstreet, thirty chiefs and upwards of five hundred warriors, representing the Ottawa, Potawatomi, Ojibway, Wyandot, Wea, Piankashaw, Kickapoo, Mascoutens, and Miami tribes, had assembled. Le Grand Sauteur, or Minavavana, the chief coadjutor of Pontiac who had so successfully led the attack on Fort Michillimackinac in 1763, was among those who came to make peace. Pontiac played an important part in the proceedings. Colonel Campbell and deputies from the Six Nations sent by Johnson assisted Croghan. The Indians agreed to return their prisoners, to permit the occupation of posts in their country, and to recognize the English as their fathers. In return, they asked that trade be reopened on favorable terms and that they be paid a yearly rental in presents for the land around the posts.

[276] Croghan to McKee, Aug. 3, 1765, in C. O., 5: 83; *Ill. Hist. Coll.*, XI, 53. Through the efforts of Professor George W. Brown, now of Peru,

After this second signal success, Croghan left Detroit in a canoe for Niagara. Here he héld a council with the Senecas, informed them of his recent treaties, and asked them to spread the news thereof. He then proceeded down Lake Ontario and at Ontario held a similar council with the Onondago sachems. He arrived at Johnson Hall early in November after an absence of almost a year. The final epilogue to the Seven Years War in America had closed; England's hereditary foe was crushed and the cause of the savages irretrievably ruined. The Illinois country was permanently opened to Anglo-Saxon civilization.

Croghan's contemporaries regarded his mission as a brilliant diplomatic achievement which surpassed the most sanguine expectations. Letters to Johnson in 1765 and 1766 abound in congratulations; Gage felt relieved and satisfied; the assembly of Pennsylvania sent a message to Gage expressing their approbation of Croghan's success and their gratitude that the Illinois country had been occupied without an immense expenditure of blood and treasure and that the fur trade could now be extended into vast regions hitherto never visited by English traders.[277]

To the Philadelphia merchants, whose ocean-going trade was suffering from the results of non-importation agreements, the prospect of opening a rich inland trade was welcomed. Vast fortunes were supposed to await them in the rich peltry trade of the Illinois country and its rich lands. Speculative colonial leaders were lured on to risk life and fortune in the West. They considered that Forbes's Road and the Ohio River

---

Nebraska, a monument has been erected in Edgar County, Illinois, marking the approximate place where Croghan and Pontiac first met.

[277] *Ill. Hist. Coll.,* XI, 87, 116, 207, 336, 340, 383; *Pa. Gazette,* Nov. 28, 1765, and May 15, 1766.

offered as good a route to the interior as did the Mississippi from New Orleans. Two rival Philadelphia firms were especially interested in the West – Baynton, Wharton, and Morgan, predominantly Quaker, and David Franks and Company, predominantly Jewish. The latter included Barnard and Michael Gratz, William Plumsted, William Murray, James Rumsey, and Alexander Ross and was closely associated with the partnership of Simon, Trent, Levy, and Franks. Simon and Levy were the leading Jewish merchants in Lancaster. Franks and Company, through Moses Franks in London, kept in close touch with British politics. Croghan was closely associated with both firms; in the beginning his major business dealings were with the Quaker group, but about 1767 they shifted to the Jewish group. In some matters the two groups worked together and then Croghan served as a connecting link. For over a decade they were competitors at Philadelphia, Lancaster, Pittsburg, Kaskaskia, and London.[278]

Baynton, Wharton, and Morgan were the first to send cargoes westward. In 1765, they had sent goods valued at £3,000 with Croghan's convoy. These were lost in the attack by the frontiersmen. In 1766, they engaged shipbuilders to go to Pittsburg and build 65 batteaux; rivets, burrs, oakum, pitch, and other shipbuilding supplies were carried over the mountains. One shipment of supplies for employees at Pittsburg included 30 cattle and 20,000 pounds of flour. Numerous wagons and 600 packhorses were employed on the road between Philadelphia and Pittsburg, while on the Ohio some 300 boatmen were soon busily engaged

---

[278] Gratz Pap., 1st ser., VII, 106ff., IX, 39, X, 28, and XI, 74; Byars: *B. and M. Gratz*, 71, 86, 87, 93, 120; Kohler, Max: "The Franks Family as British Army Contractors", in *Am. Jewish Hist. Soc., Pub.*, XI, 181ff.

in the trade of this firm. Each batteau usually carried five or six men. Gage estimated the value of the goods sent westward by this firm in 1766 at £50,000. Through Benjamin Franklin, the batteaux and their cargoes were insured at a cost of two per cent of their value by Richard Neave and Son, merchants in London specializing in goods for the Indian trade. Bands of hunters were employed to bring in furs and skins; they also secured buffalo meat and tallow in what is today Illinois and western Kentucky for sale to the garrison and settlers in the Illinois country. Several years before Daniel Boone made his famous journey to Kentucky, Baynton, Wharton, and Morgan were thus engaged in the far West in one of the significant commercial undertakings of their generation. Johnson and Croghan were deeply interested in the success of this venture and in the ventures of traders, for unless the wants of the Indians were supplied by the English they would continue their attachment to the French and Spaniards. "He not only ought to have the prayers of our Congregation, but of every well wisher to North America, as the peace of it is intimately concerned in his undertaking," wrote Baynton when Morgan started with the first large cargo for Kaskaskia in 1766.

Meanwhile, Croghan had been preparing for a second journey to the Illinois country. He had left Johnson Hall for New York, where he had consulted with Gage. He then proceeded to Philadelphia and in the spring of 1766, he left for Pittsburg. His presence was needed in Illinois for although most of the western tribes had acknowledged the King of England as their father in 1765, many Indians still cherished their old French alliance. In this they were encouraged by French traders who traveled freely among them. English traders did not yet risk their lives far from the posts. Major Farmar had written Gage late in 1765 that "in order to keep the different Nations Contiguous to this place in Peace and quietness it would be absolutely necessary for some Indian Agent to Come here early in the Spring with a Proper Assortment of Presents for them." [279] In addition to the meeting at Fort de Chartres, Johnson planned for a meeting at Oswego with Pontiac and other representatives of the western tribes. Croghan was instructed to make the arrangements for such a meeting. This he did; Hugh Crawford, who had been one of Croghan's associates in the Indian trade before 1755, conducted Pontiac safely to Oswego where the treaty of friendship was renewed and presents given. [280]

While Johnson and Gage were laying plans for holding the conferences in Illinois and Oswego, they also agreed, as part of their Indian policy for the year 1766, to put into operation the plan for Indian management as recommended by the Board of Trade in 1764. After he had received the news of the successful occupation of Illinois, Johnson had written Stuart on September 17, 1765: "This is agreeable Intelligence but we must Advantage ourselves of it, and by the Appointment of the Commissaries and other Officers at the different Posts keep up the Pacifick disposition of the Indians now manifest. Otherwise all will Come to Nothing." Upon Croghan's recommendation, Alexander McKee was now appointed by Johnson as commissary at Pittsburg. Croghan recommended Thomas Smallman, his nephew, as commissary at Detroit, but this post went

---

[279] Bd. of Tr. Pap., Plantations General, xxv-2, 657; *idem*, 621, 622.

[280] Johnson to Croghan, Feb. 21, 1766, in the library of the Hist. Soc. of Oneida Co., N.Y.; Johnson to Croghan, Mar. 15, 1766, in the library of the Am. Antiq. Soc.

to an army officer. Edward Cole was appointed commissary for Illinois. Gunsmiths, interpreters, and
surgeons were also appointed for these and other posts.
The salaries of commissaries were usually £200, gunsmiths £100, interpreters £80, and surgeons £80.[281]
Thus the Indian policy of Gage and Johnson in 1766
entailed a great outlay for salaries and presents.

Croghan's proposed visit to the Illinois country was
to be the first formal visit of importance by an Indian
agent since that country was occupied. Hence the Indians would expect generous presents. Gage ordered
twenty large silver medals made for presentation to the
most influential chiefs. Croghan asked Gage for over
£3,000 to be spent for presents and requested that before he again entered the wilderness sufficient cash be
advanced to cover his expenses. On his previous
journey he had incurred a debt of £2,037 for which his
estate would have been liable had he been killed.
This debt, together with a sum of £1,450 for similar
advances made before 1763, he asked Gage to pay
before the latter again sent him to the Illinois country.

The delays in paying Croghan's previous drafts had
so injured his credit that merchants hesitated to honor
any of his new drafts. This, together with the fact
that Indian goods were very hard to obtain because of
the non-importation agreements, caused Croghan to
feel well satisfied when he succeeded in purchasing
from Baynton, Wharton, and Morgan at a reasonable
price sufficient goods to be delivered to him out of their
storehouse at Pittsburg. He paid for them with a
draft on Gage. Croghan now waited impatiently for
six weeks. His draft was not honored for some time
and his instructions were not sent. Neither was he

[281] List of officers in the Northern District, Dec., 1766, in C. O., 5: 84.

supplied with other necessary funds. He wrote to
Gage on May 1, 1766: "[I] have often embarked
my own Money and Credit in the Service and think
now it would be best to appoint some other person in
my stead in whom greater confidence can be pleaced".
He hoped that before his return Gage and Johnson
would appoint his successor.

His final instructions from Gage, dated April 16,
1766, are significant for they mark the beginning of
a return to the same system and attitude of mind which
had been in existence before 1763 under Amherst.
They read in part as follows: "Before your departure
from Fort Pitt you will transmit me an exact list of the
quantity of merchandise, silver-ware, wampum, etc.,
that you take with you for to conciliate the affections
of the Indians on the Miss[issippi] and you will follow
the mode before prescribed to you in the distribution
thereof, by delivering them in the presence of the commanding officers of the several posts where your presence may be required and obtaining from them certifi-
cates of the delivery of the several articles which you
will transmit to me as accounting for the same." Arrangements were finally completed and Croghan left
for Pittsburg. Upon his arrival in May, 1766, he
found the Indians in an ugly mood because of murders
committed by frontiersmen in Virginia and Pennsylvania and because of the encroachment of squatters
upon their lands. The old chiefs found it difficult to
restrain the young warriors. Croghan with Major
Murray, the commandant at Fort Pitt, held a treaty
with the Delawares, Shawnee, Six Nations, and Hurons
whereby they "happily renewed and confirmed the
Chain of Friendship with them." Croghan then persuaded a delegation of about fifty Indians to accom-

pany him to Illinois. They were to be an important factor in the success of his mission.[282]

On June 18, a flotilla of seventeen batteaux left Fort Pitt for the voyage of over a thousand miles. One batteau carried Croghan, his staff, and some presents. Another was occupied by his intimate friends and past associates, Captain Harry Gordon and Ensign Thomas Hutchins. They had been ordered by Gage to accompany Croghan and to report on the condition of the English forts, to map the courses of rivers, and to take the latitude and longitude of various places. Two batteaux carried provisions for Fort de Chartres. The remaining thirteen belonged to Baynton, Wharton, and Morgan and carried large cargoes of Indian goods. This shipment was in charge of George Morgan. These four leaders were on the best of terms; they messed together morning, noon, and evening during their long journey. It was to be the only time that Croghan traversed *La Belle Rivière* from its source to its mouth, around whose waters all the dreams and ambitions of his life centered.[283]

The first stop was made at the mouth of the Scioto where Croghan held a conference with two hundred Shawnee, twenty of whom had just returned from Illinois. His Indian deputies distributed presents valued at £1,800, all of which Croghan purchased from Mor-

---

[282] *Pa. Gazette,* July 10, 1766; Baynton, Wharton, and Morgan to Franklin, Aug. 28, 1766, in Franklin MSS., Misc., I: 50 (Library of Congress); Croghan's Journal, in *Pa. Col. Rec.,* IX, 322-4.

[283] Hutchins: *Topographical Description of Va., Md., and N.C.;* *Ill. Hist. Coll.,* XI, *passim*; Croghan to Gage, Jan. 16, 1767, in *idem,* 487ff. In this letter Croghan gives a long, formal report of his mission. His letter to Johnson, dated January 18, is identical with it, save for the opening and closing. The latter is in the possession of the Albany Institute and Historical and Art Society. It is in the handwriting of a clerk, but signed by Croghan. His letters to Gage and Johnson probably took the place of a journal for this mission.

gan.   So heavily laden were his batteaux that the sale of these goods was scarcely noticeable.   The next stop was made at "Big Bone Lick" in what is now Boone County, Kentucky.   Here the party leisurely examined the beaten buffalo trace ten feet wide leading to the "Great Licking Place" and the vast boneyard which surrounded it.   Here were the remains of numerous animals which from time immemorial had been attracted by the salt deposits.   There were some remarkable bones which resembled the bones of elephants, teeth which weighed four pounds and still had their enamel well preserved, and ivory tusks six feet long. Croghan took with him some of the best specimens which he later sent to London to Lord Shelburne and Benjamin Franklin.[284]

From Big Bone Lick Croghan proceeded with sleepless caution.   At two different times, Indian deputies were sent on ahead to prevent a recurrence of the dis-

---

[284] Croghan to Shelburne, Jan. 16, 1767, in Shelburne MSS., XLVIII, 78, 95; Franklin to Croghan, Aug. 5, 1767, in *Writings*, V, 39; *idem*, 92. Croghan's shipment aroused much scientific curiosity and speculation in England. Franklin sent a tooth to a French savant to determine whether it came from a herbiverous or carnivorous animal. He also made comparisons with similar specimens from Peru and Siberia and speculated that the climate on the Ohio must once have been very warm. Franklin presented his collection to the Royal Society. Shelburne presented his to the British Museum and promised to aid further investigation on the Ohio. Two papers were later read before the Royal Society on the subject. In one, Collinson, advanced the theory that the specimens sent by Croghan were the remains of a vast animal, different in size and shape from any animal yet known, which probably browsed on trees and shrubs. The existence of similar specimens in Siberia was explained by the washing northward of carcasses of drowned elephants from Africa and Asia at the time of the deluge. "But what system, or hypothesis can, with any degree of probability, account for these remains of elephants being found in America . . . is submitted to this learned Society", concluded Collinson. – Royal Society of London, *Philosophical Transactions*, LVII, 464ff., and LVIII, 34ff.; Hutchins Papers, I, 60. – Croghan was also interested in the origin of oyster shells which he found in the Allegheny Mountains. Halsey, Francis W.: *A Tour of Four Great Rivers*, 47.

aster of 1765 and to ask the Illinois tribes to assemble
to meet him. Finally, after a long and fatiguing
journey during the heat of midsummer, he arrived
safely at Fort de Chartres on August 20. After meeting Colonel Reed, Croghan with his Indian deputies
went to Kaskaskia. Here, in a preliminary conference, with Croghan acting as mediator, the Northern
and Western Confederacies made peace. The latter
acknowledged that they had transgressed in making the
attack in 1765 and they accepted the status of "younger
brothers" to the Northern Confederacy. The main
conference was held at Fort de Chartres, beginning
August 25. About one thousand Indians were present,
representing the Kaskaskia, Cahokia, Peoria, Michi-
gamea, Piankashaw, Wea, Kickapoo, Mascoutens,
Miami, Sacs, and Foxes. These were grouped into
twenty-two tribes which made it difficult to carry on
negotiations. Three tribes, influenced by the French,
did not come to make peace till chiefs returning from
the main conference urged them to do so.

In these conferences, Croghan's aims were to secure
information, to keep open communications between
Pittsburg, Detroit, Michillimackinac and Illinois, and
above all to encourage an extensive trade. He sent
deputies across the Mississippi inviting the Missouri
and Arkansas Indians to come to Kaskaskia to trade.
The Indians ratified and confirmed the peace made in
1765. They agreed to acknowledge the King of England as their father, to return prisoners and stolen
horses, and to permit the establishment of posts. Presents were then distributed. This peace lasted as long
as the British flag remained in Illinois. There were
minor outbreaks at times and the British commandant
often feared a general Indian war, but not even the

murder of Pontiac caused an attack on the English. Much of the credit for this condition belongs to Croghan for his skillful and courageous management in 1765 and 1766.

Croghan had found upon his arrival that most of the officers and soldiers at Fort de Chartres were suffering from ague and malaria fever – the curse of Illinois. He, himself, soon contracted the fever and became too weak to write. Instead of attempting the tiresome journey overland to Pittsburg, he borrowed a batteau from Morgan and accompanied Gordon down the Mississippi. After touching at New Orleans, Pensacola, Mobile, Havanna, and Charleston, he arrived at New York in January, 1767. He made a journey to Philadelphia and Pittsburg during the following spring and then proceeded to Johnson Hall. Here he assisted Johnson in conferences with the Six Nations during the summer of 1767.[285]

After his arrival in New York in January, 1767, Croghan tendered Gage his resignation as Deputy Superintendent. Various factors were responsible for his action. In the first place, he was accused of corrupt relations with the firm of Baynton, Wharton, and Morgan.[286] These charges were made in 1765 when

[285] Baynton, Wharton, and Morgan's Account Bk. D; *Pa. Gazette,* Feb. 12, 1767; Day, Richard E.: *Calendar of Sir William Johnson* MSS., 335, 340; Croghan to Franklin, Oct. 2, 1767, in Franklin MSS., II, 97; Croghan to Franklin, Jan. 27, 1767, in *Ill. Hist. Coll.,* XI, 501.

[286] Johnson to Croghan, Apr. 4, 1765, in Johnson MSS., XXIV, 256; *Pa. Arch.,* IV, 215, 216, 226; *Ill. Hist. Coll.,* XI, 61. The convoy was said to have taken a road through the woods to avoid showing a pass at Fort Loudoun. However, there may have been other reasons for selecting the route followed for it would be impossible to avoid showing a pass at other forts, particularly at Fort Pitt. It was also charged that affidavits were made in Philadelphia by representatives of the firm that the goods were for the use of the crown, but that later Wharton went to see Johnson and stated that the goods were the private property of his firm. These statements are not necessarily contradictory.

Croghan permitted this firm to send westward a large cargo of goods for the Indian trade under cover of his pass for presents. This would enable it to be the first to take advantage of the legal opening of the trade. Croghan knew that it was highly important that the wants of the western Indians be promptly supplied by English traders as soon as Illinois should be occupied. Therefore, when this firm inquired whether trade would be permitted after the occupation of Illinois and whether they might send a cargo to be lodged in the King's store at Pittsburg until trade was opened, Croghan referred the matter to Bouquet. The latter gave his approval to such an arrangement. Later, Croghan admitted that he made a mistake to have these goods and his presents pass westward in the same convoy.[287]

The unscrupulous business methods employed by Baynton, Wharton, and Morgan, their relations with the Indian department, and their personal relations with Croghan made it easy to bring charges of corruption against Croghan. This firm tried to secure the contract to supply the garrison at Fort de Chartres by offering a bribe to an under-secretary in London. With a view to increasing their profits from the Illinois trade, Morgan wrote to his senior partners: "It would be well worth your while to make Mr Sinnot or Mr. Stewart [Stuart] a present of a Thousand Pounds to put a stop to the French coming up the Mississippi."[288] For a few years after Croghan's return from England, his personal wants while in the

[287] Croghan to Johnson, Nov., 1765, in C. O., 5: 66; Ill. Hist. Coll., x, 509, 522; Johnson to Gage, Apr. 3, 1767, in Doc. Hist. of N. Y., II, 846; Bouquet to Gage, Mar. 29, 1765, in Bouquet Coll., A7: 129.

[288] Ill. Hist. Coll., XI, 473; Morgan to Baynton, Wharton, and Morgan, July 11, 1768, in Gratz Pap., 1st ser., VIII, 62.

West were supplied by Baynton, Wharton, and Morgan. They served as his bankers and from them he secured such articles as the following: a gold watch, a barrel of loaf sugar, green Bohea tea, a barrel of pork, a box of candles, some linen, calico, and flour. He was also closely associated with this firm through land operations. "Our Company you know Sir, are much indebted to him, in respect of Landed Matters, therefore their Gratitude would naturally oblige them to cordially wish him well in every respect," wrote Baynton. In 1763, Croghan conveyed to this firm various lands on the frontier for which he was paid in Indian goods; these Johnson purchased for the Indian department. Baynton, Wharton, and Morgan secured most of the goods they used in the Indian trade from Richard Neave and Son in London. When Croghan drew up a list of goods, suitable for presents to the Indians, he recommended that they be purchased from Neave and Son since they were best acquainted with choosing and sorting Indian goods.[289]

Most of the presents which were distributed in large amounts at Pittsburg and Fort de Chartres in 1765, 1766, and 1767 were furnished by Baynton, Wharton, and Morgan. They furnished McKee and Murray with presents valued at over £1,200. These were given to the Indian deputies who went to Johnson Hall, to those who went with the various expeditions to Illinois, and to the Shawnee as gifts to condole them for the loss of their chiefs who were killed while with Croghan in 1765. At Pittsburg they also furnished Croghan with

---

[289] Baynton, Wharton, and Morgan's Account Books, particularly No. D; John Baynton to Abel James, Dec. 13, 1769, in Baynton's Private Letter Bk.; Johnson MSS. (Ill.), IX, 2 and 35; List of Goods for the Indian trade, in Ohio Co. MSS., I, 37; Croghan to R. Neave and Son, June 24, 1767, in Dreer Coll.

presents valued at £459, 10s. 3d. For this sum Croghan gave them his personal note guaranteeing payment. Croghan's total expenses on his second journey to Illinois amounted to £8,408, 9s. 7½d. of which £6,480 went to Baynton, Wharton, and Morgan. Cole, the commissary at Illinois, was under special obligations to this firm and not only purchased from them large amounts of goods for presents, but also supported all their undertakings in Illinois. He with Colonel Reed purchased from them large amounts of goods for the Indians. This firm honored drafts for the salaries of Indian officials in the West.[290]

Evidently, there was a close connection between "big business" and the government in the West. The evidence discovered does not show that Croghan received pecuniary rewards for his actions, nor does it enable us to fathom the motives impelling his conduct. He cleared himself of all charges to the entire satisfaction of Gage. Johnson wrote: "I believe he has been used very ill, and traduced at a time when he was doing his utmost for the service". Croghan, himself, felt keenly the "false and scandalous Reports" which he asserted were circulated by enemies and rival traders.[291]

The second reason why Croghan tendered his resignation in 1767, was because of the new attitude of the home government and Gage towards the Indian department. This attitude was rapidly crystalizing in 1766 and 1767 and rendered futile the efforts of Johnson to have his department established on a firm, independent basis through an act of Parliament. As it existed, it had no definite funds nor adequate salaries;

[290] *Ill. Hist. Coll.*, XI, 258, 283, 330, 364, 367, 388, 473, 511. Croghan's note, June 1, 1767, in the library of the Hist. Soc. of Pa.

[291] Croghan to Johnson, Nov. 1765, in C. O., 5: 66; *Doc. Hist. of N.Y.*, II, 846.

it was at the mercy of executive caprice; and it lacked authority based on law. His own powers and those of his deputies and commissaries were "very trifling, uncertain and in general disregarded and disputed." Should they attempt to detain an Indian trader, a frontiersman, or land speculator who was defrauding the Indians, they themselves would be liable to be prosecuted and thrown into jail. The beginning of the decline of the Indian department was evident when Shelburne wrote to him: "The System of Indian Affairs as managed by Superintendants must ultimately be under his Direction. . . It is therefore necessary that the Superintendants should take the orders of the Commander in Chief on all material Occasions. . ." [292]

The plans for a strong Indian department were in part frustrated by factional party strife in London. Shelburne, who had become Secretary of State for the Southern Department in 1766, believed that the plan of 1764 did not meet the needs of those interested in the Indian trade and he favored less interference by the government in Indian affairs. Barrington, who had become Secretary of War in 1765, formulated a plan for dealing with the West in which he stated that "The Country on the Westward of our Frontier quite to the Mississippi was intended to be a Desert for the Indians to hunt in and inhabit." He favored the restriction of settlement to the proclamation line of 1763, the abandonment by the army of the numerous small posts in the interior and the concentration of troops nearer the seacoast, and decreasing the powers

---

[292] *Doc. Hist. of N.Y.*, ii, 835, 845, 851, 883; *Ill. Hist. Coll.*, xi, 450; *N.Y. Col. Docs.*, vii, 872, 891, 964. When Roberts at Michillimackinac attempted to enforce the proclamation of 1763 he was sued and imprisoned. – Bd. of Tr. Pap., Plantations General, xxix, 89-95.

of the Indian department. The increasing, sinister influence of the Bedford faction was also beginning to work against the success of Johnson and Croghan's plans. Gage's attitude was naturally influenced by the changing attitude of the ministry in London.[293]

He was also influenced by the failure of the anticipated boom in the Indian trade to materialize after Illinois was occupied. In return for the large expenditures which this occupation entailed, England was expected to reap the benefits of a large trade from this region. The Indians, however, prefered to trade with their old friends and the Mississippi afforded the natural outlet to the sea. Hence, New Orleans and Paris, and not Philadelphia and London, profited from the peltry trade of Illinois. The disillusionment of Baynton, Wharton, and Morgan was bitter. Wharton was responsible for their entry into this field; he, and not Morgan was originally scheduled to take charge of this trade. The buoyant optimism of Morgan and Baynton in 1766 was soon displaced by deep pessimism. Morgan looked upon himself as "a son of affliction" when he had to return "to the accursed Illinois". Baynton wrote of "our business in this hateful Country" and he spoke of Morgan's journey in 1769 as "another Ordeal Tryal". In 1770 he writes: "Mr. Morgan setts off to Day or to Morrow for that shocking Country the Illinois – My Familys Distress on this grevious Occasion beggars Description." As a result of their failure in Illinois and their losses in 1763 and 1765, this firm had to conduct its business under the supervision of its creditors and a bitter personal feud arose between Wharton and Morgan. Gage had sensed the situation as early as 1766.[294] Upon Cro-

293 Alvord, Clarence W.: *Mississippi Valley in British Politics.*
294 Morgan to Wharton, Jan. 13, 1772, in Baynton, Wharton, and Mor-

ghan's return from his second journey to Illinois he
found that Gage anticipated but little benefit to English trade from the occupation of Illinois.   Croghan
thought that Gage's opinion was influenced by New
York merchants who were illicitly supplying the
French traders at New Orleans.

The lack of necessary funds was the main reason for
the refusal to favor the establishment of a strong Indian
department.   As long as the Seven Years War was
undecided, money was not difficult to obtain.   But
after the fighting was over and England found herself
"reeling under a national debt of nearly 140 millions,"
a policy of economy and retrenchment was adopted.
In 1765, the Lords of the Treasury ordered Gage "to
issue no more warrants nor to incurr any farther Expense, but in Cases of urgency wherein there is not
time for knowing his Majesties pleasure, even then the
reasonableness of accounts are to be Judged of at home
and approved or rejected as they shall see fitting.   And
also Voucher's must be produced for every article of
Expense, even for the Delivery of them to the Indians."
This order made the royal officials personally responsible for all expenditures not fixed by Parliament or
previously approved by the crown.   It greatly per-
plexed and embarrassed Gage, Bouquet, and Johnson
in the performance of their duties.[295]

Croghan first felt the effect of the new system after
his journey to Illinois in 1765. The debt of £2,037 which
he had incurred at Fort Pitt was very tardily paid
in four installments; the last one being made almost

gan's Letter Bk. A; John Baynton to Abel Smith Nov. 28 and Dec. 13,
1769, and Feb. 20, 1770, in Baynton's Private Letter Bk.; Joseph Galloway
to Franklin, Sept. 6, 1767, in Franklin MSS., XLVIII, 134.

[295] Johnson to Croghan, Apr. 4, 1765, in Johnson MSS., XXIV, 256; *Ill.
Hist. Coll.*, X, 453, 502, 527; *idem*, XI, 122, 501.

two years after his personal note guaranteeing payment
was due. His losses and expenses resulting from the
attack in 1765 amounted to £1,732, 11s. 10d. Gage
refused to pay this and other bills until they had been
referred to England. Croghan felt very bitter at such
treatment. He wrote to Johnson that Gage "Did Nott
Trate Lift Freser in that Maner fer on his Return he
paid him all his expenses and Made him a present of
Six Hundred Pounds, Butt its to be Considered that
he is a Gentleman of the army and Not an Indian
agent." Croghan was forced to send his account to
Gage with a memorial to the Lords of the Treasury;
these papers Gage then forwarded to London with his
endorsement. Croghan wrote to Franklin asking him
to support this memorial.[296]

The year 1765 brought new hopes to imperial officials both in England and in America. The passage
of the Stamp Act was expected to result in supplying
sorely needed funds. Johnson and Croghan now had
hopes that the Indian department might be established
as planned in 1764. But the opposition to the Stamp
Act soon caused such hopes to vanish. The Lords of
the Treasury were now more than ever alarmed at the
growing expenses in America; heavy accounts and
drafts were continually coming in. Gage scrutinized
and curtailed expenses as much as possible at every
post and in every department under his command.

It was unfortunate that just at this time the expenditures of the Indian department should be heavy. After
a conference with Croghan in New York in January,
1767, Gage wrote to Johnson: "Mr. Croghan has incurred a very great Expense in this Tour to the Ilinois,

of which he is now giving his Account." Cole, whom
Croghan had left in charge in Illinois, sent in accounts
totaling from £6,000 to over £10,000 annually. On
one occasion Gage wrote to Johnson concerning Cole's
account: "This is really so monstrous an account that
I hardly know what can be done with it." Meanwhile, Major Rogers, the commandant at Michillimackinac, was buying immense quantities of goods
from English traders and presenting them to the Indians who flocked to his post in response to his invitations. Over 7,000 came – the largest number that ever
assembled at this post. Even the chiefs of the far distant Sioux came. When the local commissary objected
to his lavish gifts, Rogers promptly degraded and confined him. Rogers sent in his account of over £5,000
to Gage, but Gage and Johnson, who were not pleased
with the manner of his appointment, refused to pay
them. In September, 1767, Gage ordered Rogers to
meet Croghan at Detroit; the latter bore a letter from
Gage telling Rogers of his dismissal.[297]

Johnson feared that in the zeal for economy the
gains which had been achieved at such great costs
might be lost. He assured Gage that with the work of
occupation completed, expenditures should greatly
decrease. He instructed all commissaries to reduce
their expenses; he instructed Gorham to meet the Indians in council only once a year; and he wrote Gage
that he had "given Mr. Croghan positive orders for
retrenching Expenses and I am certain he will Strictly
follow them. . ." Johnson feared, however, that
such a policy might again lead to disaster as in 1763.
In spite of Johnson's assurances Gage wrote to Shel-

[297] Doc. Hist. of N.Y., II, 835, 850, 863, 865; Clements, William L.:
"Journal of Major Robert Rogers," in Proc. of the Am. Antiq. Soc., 1918;
Hough: Journals of Major Robert Rogers, 223.

burne that "tho' I hope many Expenses before incurred, May now be retrenched, yet I fear those Depart-
ments will be always a heavy Charge." He suggested
that the Board of Trade set a definite limit to the number of officials in the Indian department, to the number of councils to be held, and to the size of the presents to be delivered. Since the colonies had been relieved of the costs of managing the Indian trade he
suggested that they ought to contribute a proportionate
sum and "lighten a heavy Burthen bore by the Mother
Country". A few months later, Benjamin Franklin,
after having dined with Shelburne and Conway, wrote
confidentially to his son: "They have it in contem-
plation to return the management of Indian affairs into
the hands of the several provinces . . . the treasury being tired with the immense drafts of the superintendents, etc." [298]

Such were the forces at work which created the conditions that caused Croghan to tender to Gage his resignation in January, 1767. As soon as his resignation
became known, applications for his position began to
come to Johnson. After tendering his resignation,
Croghan proceeded to Johnson Hall. It was probably
through an appeal to personal friendship, loyalty to
their King, and to personal gain that Johnson persuaded Croghan to withdraw, for the second time, his
resignation. On April 1, 1767, Johnson was able to
write Gage: "Mr. Croghan is now here and is to continue in his office. . ." Henceforth, Croghan delegated most of the work in his district to McKee and
other subordinates; a tacit understanding with Gage
and Johnson existed whereby Croghan's services were
to be held in reserve for important negotiations. This

[298] Benjamin Franklin to William Franklin, Aug. 28, 1767, in *Writings*,
v, 45; *N.Y. Col. Docs.*, VII, 981; *Ill. Hist. Coll.*, XI, 553.

enabled him to draw his salary and give most of his time to his numerous land operations which were becoming highly important.[299]

By her victories during the Seven Years War, England secured legal possession of the region extending from the Appalachians to the Mississippi and lying on both sides of the Great Lakes. To secure a *de facto* control over this region, it was necessary that the French forts controlling strategic points in the heart of the Indian country be occupied by English garrisons, that the Indian tribes should transfer their alliance from the French to the English, and that the latter reopen the Indian trade and conduct it in a manner satisfactory to the natives. It was to this work that Croghan gave his attention from 1758 to 1766. His operations centered at Pittsburg, though he held numerous Indian conferences at various places in the region limited by Johnson Hall, Detroit, Kaskaskia, and Pittsburg. Though the Indian department had rendered valuable services during this period, by 1766 its prestige and powers had begun to decline, largely as a result of the failure of the plans of the imperial government to tax the colonies. Thereafter, Croghan's major interests ceased to be associated with his official position. The completion of the work of occupation in 1766, opened the first business connections between the Illinois country and the Atlantic seaboard and it greatly stimulated the desire of traders, land speculators, and settlers to exploit the Great West.

---

[299] Day: *Celendar of Sir William Johnson* MSS., 343, 348, 350; Johnson MSS., XVIII, 133 and XXI, 68; Johnson to Gage, Apr. 1, 1767, in *Doc. Hist. of N.Y.*, II, 845.

Deputy Superintendent: the Irresistible Pressure upon the Indian's Land,
1759-1772

Towards the end of the period during which the West was occupied, Indian politics and trade were displaced by land relations as the most important phase of Indian affairs. As a result of victory in a great war the British subject felt that he possessed the right to exploit the West. The prize available was described by Franklin as follows: "The great country back of the Appalachian Mountains, on both sides of the Ohio, and between that river and the Lakes is now well known . . . to be one of the finest in North America, for the extreme richness and fertility of the land; the healthy temperature of the air, and the mildness of the climate; the plenty of hunting, fishing, and fowling, the facility of trade with the Indians; and the vast convenience of inland navigation. . . From these natural advantages it must undoubtedly, (perhaps in less than another century) become a populous and powerful dominion. . ." [300]

The frontiersmen were just getting ready to enter this realm of wild and waste fertility when war with France broke out again. Good lands east of the mountains had been engrossed by settlers or speculators and fertile lands were rare among the mountains. Vir-

---

[300] "Plan for settling two Western Colonies in North America with Reasons for the Plan," in *Writings* (ed. Smyth), III, 358.

ginians had organized the Ohio Company in 1749 and the Penns had arranged for a large Indian purchase in 1754. A few log cabins began to appear along the upper Juniata and its Raystown branch, and far out in the Monongahela valley.

During the period from 1754 to 1765 various military and political conditions served to drive back these normal forces of expansion. First, there was the war itself which caused a bloody retreat all along the frontier. Then came the treaty at Easton in 1758, with its promise to the Indian that his lands beyond the mountains would not be settled. In 1761, came Bouquet's proclamation enforcing this treaty.[301] In the same year the imperial government assumed control in royal colonies of all purchases of land from the Indians. In 1763, came Pontiac's war and the proclamation of October 7. To this were added governors' proclamations and colonial laws forbidding settlement in the Indian country. One example of the result of all of these conditions is the fact that no new counties were organized in Pennsylvania during the period from 1750 to 1771.

The immediate motive back of these prohibitions was the desire to avoid further Indian wars. No sooner were the English established at Fort Pitt than the normal westward movement began again. On February 8, 1762, Bouquet wrote to Governor Fauquier of Virginia: "For two years past these Lands have been over run by a Number of Vagabonds, who under pretense of hunting, were Making Settlements in several parts of them, of which the Indians made grievous and repeated Complaints, as being Contrary to the Treaty made with them at Easton. . . Notwithstanding

[301] The proclamation with relating correspondence is printed in the *Canadian Archives Report, 1889,* 72-80.

what I have done, they still in a less degree, Continue the same Practices, and two days ago an Indian . . . complained to me that he had discovered ten New Hutts in the Woods and many Fields cleared for Corn." Bouquet's proclamation forbade hunting or settling on lands west of the mountains unless by permission of the commander-in-chief or of a governor; violators were to be court-martialed at Fort Pitt and have their cabins burned. Bouquet, like a true soldier, tried to enforce his order, but it was a physical impossibility to be prepared at all times to send troops to any place in the wilderness when needed. Virginia land speculators, greedy to engross the best lands, tried to bribe Bouquet by inviting him to become a member of the Ohio Company and thus secure a claim to 25,000 acres; when the gallant Bouquet declined to be concerned they made it so unpleasant for him that he asked to be removed from this region.

Bouquet here encountered one of those great social movements which roll on in their might, unimpeded by laws, by proclamations, by treaties, or by battles lost. These were mere incidents – temporary obstructions to be overcome by the irresistible westward movement of the Anglo-Saxon. Its vital dynamic forces were typified in the impulses of unknown and obscure men seeking new homes in the wilderness – men whom Bouquet called "Vagabonds" and Gage "Lawless Banditti", living under "loose and disorderly governments". In vain did Lord Hillsborough announce the mercantilist policy that it was for the best interests of Great Britain to confine the colonists along the seacoast where millions of acres were still uncultivated. ". . . I have learned from experience", wrote Governor Dunmore of Virginia, "that the established

Authority of any government in America, and the policy of Government at home, are both insufficient to restrain the Americans; and that they do and will remove as their avidity and restlessness incite them. They acquire no attachment to Place: But wandering about Seems engrafted in their Nature; and it is a weakness incident to it that they Should forever imagine the Lands further off, are Still better than those upon which they are already Settled." [302]

Official exceptions to the general prohibition of settlement in the Indian country were made only for military bounty claimants and for settlers around inland forts and along the lines of communications leading to such forts. Along no other line of communication were these as important as along Forbes's Road and Braddock's Road. The traveler who started from Fort Pitt for Philadelphia would travel fifty-six miles through the Indian country before he came to the next fort, Ligonier; forty-five miles farther east was Fort Bedford, nestled among the mountains; beyond this, as he approached Fort Loudoun, log cabins began to appear with greater frequency and after he reached Carlisle the country assumed a settled appearance. The garrisons of these forts usually consisted of from twenty to two hundred and fifty men. Clarkson passed over this road in 1766 and left a diary describing his journey.[303] In it he tells of meeting galloping expresses, small groups of soldiers going from one post to another, droves of cattle, wagon loads of pork in barrels, packhorses loaded with flour – all for the western garrisons, and horse loads of furs and skins bound for Philadelphia. At night he stopped at flea-infested log

---

[302] Thwaites and Kellogg: *Documentary History of Lord Dunmore's War*, 371.

[303] Printed in *Ill. Hist. Coll.*, XI, 355ff.

taverns or camped in the open. This was the road which Croghan traversed so many times.

In order to supply the needs of the garrisons and to provide conveniences along the line of communications the commander-in-chief or the general in charge of the western district granted, free of charge, licenses to settle along the roads and around the forts. The consent of the Indians to such settlements was secured without difficulty. Usually the land within cannon shot of a fort was considered as belonging to it, but at Fort Pitt a larger area was secured. Here Gage proposed to grant lands in 100 to 150 acre tracts on the semi-feudal condition that the settler supply annually a specified number of hogs or cattle, or a quantity of provisions to the garrison. Such military licenses gave to the holder the first opportunity to secure a title in fee simple when the lands should formally be opened to settlement by the Penns or by the crown.[304]

On November 25, 1758, two days after Fort Du-Quesne had been burned, Bouquet wrote to Chief Justice Allen at Philadelphia, that he needed "A Number of Cows and Bulls, Mares and Stallions, Garden seeds, etc. every moment is precious and the Land so rich, and the pastures so abundant that everything would thrive and the Garrison would soon be able to support itself." [305] Fort Pitt soon became a bustling frontier community. Sawmills, tan-yards, lime-kilns, brick-kilns, coal-mines, and trading-houses were in operation. Land was cleared and orchards, meadows, and fields were fenced in. Turnips and other vegetables, hay, corn, and the cereal spelt were grown. Great profits were realized by raising corn

---

[304] Bouquet to Amherst, April 1, 1762, in *Canadian Arch. Rep., 1889,* 77; Bouquet Coll., A8, *passim.*

[305] Official Corresp., IX, 53, Penn MSS.

and hay and by feeding cattle for the use of the garrison and Indian traders. Among those most interested were William Plumsted and David Franks, British army contractors for Pennsylvania and the West.[306]

A census taken in 1760 showed that the population of Pittsburg consisted of 88 men, chiefly Indian traders, 29 women, and 32 children, and that it had 146 houses and 36 huts. The next year the population had almost doubled. The taverns were frequented by traders, trappers, mule drivers, and pioneer farmers. Nearly all were hard drinking men and many were fugitives from eastern justice or escaped debtors. The natives frequented Pittsburg and drunken Indians staggering and yelling through the village were a common sight. Most of the Indian traders had a squaw and some of them a white woman as a temporary wife. This community was without any minister till after the Revolution and the garrison was frequently without a chaplain. Some of the inhabitants, however, were of a high character.[307]

The leading citizen in this community from 1758 to 1775 was Croghan, usually referred to as "the Colonel". Like others, he acquired lots and houses in Pittsburg and also lands nearby; but he based his land claims upon a private Indian purchase made in 1749. The military authorities were embarrassed, but acquiesced. One large tract was located twenty-five miles from Pittsburg in the Youghiogheny valley. To develop it he entered into a partnership with Colonel Clapham; settlers were brought in and improvements made.

306 Croghan to David Franks, Dec. 25, 1770, MS. in Newberry Library, Chicago; Max Kohler, "The Franks Family as British Army Contractors", in *Am. Jewish Hist. Soc. Pub.*, XI, 181ff.

307 *Pa. Mag. of Hist. and Biog.*, II, 303 and VI, 344; Jones: *Diary*, II, 20, 21; McClure: *Diary*, 45, 46, 53, 101.

Croghan sold a half interest in his improvements and
live stock to Plumsted and Franks for £2,500. During
Pontiac's uprising Clapham was murdered and Croghan lost horses, cattle, hogs, and buildings valued at
£2,500.[308]

Croghan's other tract was located just northeast of
Fort Pitt. In earlier years he had his trading post on
Pine Creek just across the Allegheny River from his
new location. It was an excellent tract of rich bottom
land extending northward along the river for several
miles and eastward to a ridge of hills that lay from a
quarter to three-quarters of a mile from the river. Here
he erected a house and other buildings, all of which
were burned by the Indians in 1763, causing a loss of
£2,000 to Croghan. These were soon rebuilt; the new
residence was named "Croghan Hall". An index to the
manner of living at this place is found in the fact that
servants were kept, that a number of families were
brought in to live on the plantation, and that its plate
was of sufficient value to be used as security for a
goodly sized loan. Distinguished visitors, both white
and red, frequented this landmark. Missionaries from
the east brought letters of introduction and were received kindly and assisted. Washington, on his tour
to the Ohio in 1770, dined at but two places while at
Pittsburg, viz., Fort Pitt and Croghan Hall. Captain
Edmonstone, while commander at Fort Pitt in 1771,
stated that Croghan had more property around Fort
Pitt to lose by an Indian war than any other private
subject of the King in that country.[309]

[308] Croghan to Peters and Clark, June 15, 1763, in Prov. Pap., XXXIII, 89.
[309] Edmonstone to Gage, Mar. 9, 1771, in Johnson MSS., XX, 129; Darlington: *Fort Pitt and Letters from the Frontier*, 108, 130; Day: *Calendar
of Sir William Johnson Manuscripts*, 146; Gratz-Croghan MSS., II, 35; Croghan to Thomas Wharton, Dec. 9, 1773, in *Pa. Mag. of Hist. and Biog.*, XV,

Not all who desired to migrate westward had influence sufficient to secure a military permit, nor could all have been accommodated along the roads or around the forts; moreover, not all frontiersmen were disposed to ask permission to settle in the Indian country. As a result, after peace had been insured in 1765, fresh clearings and crude cabins began to appear here and there in fertile spots in the Indian country and desirable lands were surveyed and their boundaries blazed on trees. The desire to preëmpt the best lands in anticipation of their early opening to settlement was a strong motive for making such improvements. The settlements which were to give the most trouble were those in the Monongahela valley along Cheat River and Redstone Creek. Here the boundary dispute between Pennsylvania and Virginia made it easier for the squatters to settle. Probably 2,000 whites settled here between 1765 and 1768.[310]

Such were the conditions with which Croghan had to deal during his last years as Deputy Superintendent. The Indians had just been quieted when the irrepressible conflict threatened to break out again. There were various causes for the fresh discontent of the Indians. The chief cause was the encroachment upon their lands with daily threats of more invasions of their property for which they could obtain no justice. Rumors of proposed colonies in the heart of their country added to their discontent. Johnson wrote Shelburne on April 1, 1767, that "The affairs of Lands are more immediately interesting and alarming to the Indians than anything else, yet the avidity manifested by most people here in pursuit of them increases every day in

---

436; Bouquet Coll., A17: 237; Thwaites and Kellogg: *Frontier Defense on the Upper Ohio*, 200, 250.

[310] *Acts of the Privy Council*, V, 205; *Pa. Col. Rec.*, IX, 509.

so much that the American Govern^{ts} I believe find it
impracticable to prevent them." [311]

Other causes increased the discontent. Distant
tribes found the English trade inadequate and others
were dissatisfied with the way in which it was carried
on. The English traders and soldiers did not manifest
the same tolerant and sympathetic attitude and interest
that the French had manifested. Bands of young
braves on the war path to attack the Cherokees stole
horses on their way through the back country and were
attacked by the whites. Instances of murders on both
sides ocurred. One incident made a deep impression
upon the Indians and led to much correspondence
among English officials. Stump, a Pennsylvania frontiersman, and his servant were visited by ten Indians –
men, women, and children. These Indians were made
drunk, killed with an ax, scalped, and their bodies
burned. Governor Penn offered a reward of £200 for
the arrest of the murderers, but when they were placed
in jail a mob of eighty frontiersmen rescued them.
Stump was retaken and tried, but the jury refused to
convict him. The most prominent Indian aggression
was the attack on two batteaux on the Ohio River
belonging to Baynton, Wharton, and Morgan causing
a loss of fourteen men and goods valued at £3,000.
Hunting parties were also attacked.[312]

Croghan first called attention to the situation in a
letter to Gage written on May 26, 1766, at Pittsburg
while on his way to the Illinois country. In it he stated
that unless the causes be removed "the Consequences
may be dreadful, and We involved in all the Calamitys

[311] *N.Y. Col. Docs.*, VII, 914.

[312] *Pa. Col. Rec.*, IX, 420ff.; Baynton and Wharton to Macleane, Oct.
9, 1767, in Bd. of Tr. Pap., Plantations General, XXVI, T46; Croghan to Gage,
June 17, 1766, MS. in Newberry Library.

of another general War".[313]   Gage at once asked Governor Penn to remove all Pennsylvanians who had illegally settled west of the mountains. When he requested funds for this purpose from the assembly, Penn was asked first to secure the coöperation of Governor Fauquier of Virginia. Both governors then issued proclamations warning the settlers to leave, but little regard was paid to them. A letter now came to Penn from Lord Shelburne urging him to energetic action and to coöperate with Gage.   "It is a matter truly alarming and requires the utmost attention and consideration of the Legislatures of these Middle Colonies", wrote Penn to Gage. It was difficult to get the colonial assemblies to enforce the imperial proclamation of 1763 and Penn wrote Shelburne that it would be wisest for the military power to take charge of the matter since the civil power could not compel obedience.   Soldiers were sent upon two different occasions from Fort Pitt to oust the squatters, but no sooner had they returned to their fort than the squatters returned in greater numbers than before. Finally, on February 3, 1768, the assembly of Pennsylvania passed a law to be in force for one year, whereby all illegal settlers on Indian lands were required to remove within thirty days after being notified under penalty of death without benefit of clergy; persons making surveys or marking trees with a view to settlement were to be fined £50 and imprisoned for six months.[314] Official commissioners were now sent to the settlers on Cheat River, Redstone Creek, and at three places on the Youghio-

---

[313] *Pa. Col. Rec.*, IX, 323. The pages following give most of the documents for the succeeding narrative.

[314] *Stat. at Large of Pa.*, VII, 152. A similar act was passed when this act expired to help make the new Indian boundary of 1768 effective.– *Idem*, 260.

gheny to read this law and the governor's proclamation to them and to explain the situation. When they could not assure the settlers a first option on their improvements as soon as the Indian title should be extinguished the settlers refused to leave.

Meanwhile, in the Indian country, mysterious movements were going on which baffled Indian officials. Belts were being passed secretly from village to village and a great council of twelve nations was to be held at the mouth of the Scioto River. In the autumn of 1767, Johnson quickly went to meet the Six Nations and he sent Croghan to investigate and to meet with the Indians at Fort Pitt, on the Scioto, and at Detroit. The Scioto meeting was postponed till March, but Croghan learned at Detroit that its purposes were to make peace among the tribes, to consider grievances against the English, and to organize a confederacy of northern and western tribes.[315] Gage prepared to put Fort Pitt and Niagara on a war footing by strengthening the forts and storing up provisions. Shortly after Croghan had departed again for the east, anxious chiefs kept coming to Pittsburg from all parts of the West to ask McKee whether he had heard from Johnson or the General and if Croghan was coming back. McKee tried to quiet them for the time being. Croghan reported to Johnson that in his opinion nothing would now prevent a war but an Indian land purchase. He also presented the situation in person to the frugal assembly of Pennsylvania. It acted promptly and in February, 1768, appropriated the large sum of £3,000 for pacifying the Indians; £500 was to be used to apprehend Stump and his servant; £1,300 was sent to Johnson as

---

[315] Croghan to Franklin, Oct. 2, 1767, in Franklin MSS., II, 63; *idem*, LVIII, 82; *Votes of the Assembly*, VI, 9-11.

a condolence present for the Six Nations who had lost
some members through murders in Pennsylvania;
£1,200 were to be used for presents to moderate the
resentment of the Ohio Indians.[316]

On February 29, 1768, Johnson wrote Croghan who
was then in Philadelphia, asking him to take immediate charge of a mission to the Ohio Indians and to
send at once invitations to the Ohio tribes to meet him
at Fort Pitt. The situation was felt to be so serious
that Croghan left for Fort Pitt on the same day that he
received his instructions. When he reached Lancaster
his friends in Cumberland County informed him that
the frontiersmen were again in the greatest commotion
and that the "Black Boys" had resolved that no council
should be held. They threatened to seize all presents
sent out and to take Croghan's life if he attempted to
hold a conference. He now awaited the coming of an
escort of thirty-five soldiers from Philadelphia to convoy his goods. When an express met the convoy and
brought the news that the Indians were leaving Fort
Pitt and holding conferences in the woods, Croghan
left his escort and hurried to Fort Pitt.[317]

On April 26, he was able to open the conference.[318]
There were present Colonel Reed with twelve officers,
McKee, the local Indian commissary, John Allen and
Joseph Shippen, the two Pennsylvania commissioners,
and over 1,100 Indians, chiefly Delawares, Shawnee,

[316] *Ill. Hist. Coll.*, XII, 88, 170, 209, 270; Franklin: *Writings*, (ed.
Smyth), V, 499.

[317] Johnson to Croghan, Feb. 29, 1768, MS. in Newberry Library; Croghan to Johnson, Mar. 18, 1768, in Johnson MSS., XVI, 53; *idem*, 56.

[318] The minutes of this conference are found in manuscript form in the
Library of Congress and in almost the same form in the *Pa. Col. Rec.*, IX,
514ff.; they were printed in Philadelphia in 1769 by William Goddard.
See also *Ill. Hist. Coll.*, XII, 323, and Croghan to Thomas Wharton, April
17 and May 7, 1768, in *Pa. Mag. of Hist. and Biog.*, XV, 430.

Six Nations, Wyandots, Munsies, and Mohicans. The Indians were much discontented and in a sullen temper and asked that the English forts be demolished and that navigation on the Ohio cease. By private meetings with the chiefs, however, Croghan was able to accomplish his ends. The Indians discussed all their grievances with their friend and by the judicious use of presents valued at £1,150 Croghan was able to settle all questions except that of the removal of settlers; its settlement was postponed until the proposed Indian purchase should be made. Negotiations concerning it could now proceed. Gage was gratified and felt that an Indian war had been avoided.

The only real relief to the entire situation was to be had through the shifting of the Indian boundary line westward from the line established in 1758 and 1763. Expansion had become a vital necessity for Pennsylvania with her large German and Scotch-Irish immigration and it also vitally interested the Virginia planters. It was difficult to persuade the British government to act because of the opposition of merchants interested in the Indian trade, of politicians still adhering to mercantilist theories, and of treasury officials zealous for economy. Croghan and Johnson, after a conference in the fall of 1767, used all their influence to secure action. Both wrote letters to the Board of Trade and Croghan persuaded Governor Penn, Governor Franklin, Peters, Galloway, and Wharton to write to their friends in England. The Pennsylvania assembly instructed Benjamin Franklin and Jackson, its agents in London, to urge action. Finally, early in 1768, instructions were sent to Johnson to make the desired purchase.[319]

319 *Ill. Hist. Coll.*, XII, 180; Franklin: *Writings* (ed. Smyth), v, 65.

Croghan and Johnson had for several years been preparing the Indians for the purchase, but to assemble at Fort Stanwix representatives of all the Iroquois tribes took all summer.   The conference which followed was one of the most important Indian conferences ever held in North America.   Between three and four thousand Indians came.   Governors Penn and Franklin with commissioners representing their colonies, and commissioners representing Virginia were present. Johnson was assisted by interpreters and by his three deputies, Croghan, Claus, and Guy Johnson.   William Trent and Samuel Wharton came to try to secure a private grant for the traders who had lost heavily in 1763.   Croghan also intended to secure a grant around Fort Pitt for himself.   Twenty boats heavily laden with presents came up the Mohawk.   These were judiciously displayed; some were privately presented to leading chiefs at critical times during conferences. Days and nights for weeks were spent in difficult negotiations.   Most of the real work was done in private conferences with the leading chiefs.   Croghan was busy looking after the interests of the empire, the Penns, the traders, and himself.   While in England he had had conferences with the Penns in regard to the boundary line and he had an understanding that in return for his influence to secure a desirable line, Thomas Penn would use his good offices in London to further Croghan's petitions for land grants.

In return for presents valued at £10,000, the Six Nations ceded their claims to the vast tract of land lying between the Appalachian divide and the Ohio

Most of the persons named had hopes of benefiting through securing private grants of lands at the sale. This phase will be discussed in the next chapter. The best collection of documents bearing on the treaty of Fort Stanwix is found in the *N.Y. Col. Docs.*, VIII.

River; it included a small strip in central New York, southwestern Pennsylvania, modern West Virginia, and northern Kentucky as far as the Tennessee River. The boundary line was ratified by the home government the next year. An examination of the map will show that rivers formed most of the boundary line. The part that was not thus indicated had to be surveyed and marked by blazing the trees on both sides in a zone fifty feet wide. Croghan, in the spring of 1769, supervized a party of surveyors and blazers engaged in this work.[320]

The barriers were now removed and the trickling stream of lonely pioneers which had already been crossing the mountains became an irresistible tide of westward moving settlers. One of the phenomenal westward movements of American history followed. Most of the settlers were real homeseekers, but the agents and surveyors of speculators like Washington were also present and a few pioneers took up claims only to sell them at a profit. The Penns opened their portion to settlement on April 3, 1769, and on the first day they received 2,790 applications, each for 300 acres; in four months 1,000,000 acres, including all the good lands were sold.[321] Croghan wrote in 1770: "What number of families has settled, since the congress, to the westward of the high ridge, I cannot pretend to say positively; but last year, I am sure, there were between four and five thousand, and all this spring and summer the roads have been lined with wagons moving to the

[320] Croghan to Johnson, Oct., 1768, in Johnson MSS., XVI, 191; Samuel Wharton to Franklin, Dec. 2, 1768, in Franklin MSS., XLIX, 77; Thomas Penn to Croghan, Dec. 4, 1768, in Penn Letter Bk., IX, 309; Croghan to Gage, Jan. 1, 1770, in C. O., 5: 88; Pa. Mag. of Hist. and Biog., XV, 430.

[321] New Purchase (1768) Applications, Department of Internal Affairs, Harrisburg.

Ohio." [322] In Virginia over 6,000,000 acres, lying chiefly in what is now West Virginia, were granted or petitioned for. Wade wrote Johnson on April 20, 1774, that families with from ten to fifty negro slaves crossed the mountains and that it was not uncommon to meet twenty to thirty wagons a day in the fall of 1773 all going to the Ohio country. A traveler reported in 1773 that for one hundred and fifty miles below Pittsburg the country was thickly settled, that a large acreage was in grain, and that gristmills were being erected. New counties were being organized: in Pennsylvania, Bedford County was organized in 1771, Northumberland in 1772, and Westmoreland in 1773; in Virginia, Botetourt County was organized in 1770, Fincastle in 1772, and the District of West Augusta in 1774. The political status of the territory which was being settled was to become one of the great problems of the next twenty years. [323]

Soon, however, the old causes of conflict between the Indians and the English again came to the surface, and in 1769, 1770, and 1771, English officials were apprehensive of a new Indian war. The Delawares and Shawnee were incensed because their claims had been entirely disregarded at Fort Stanwix. We read of 150 horses stolen at Fort Pitt, of 200 cattle shot, of murders committed on both sides, of the renewal of the plan for a great Indian conference on the Scioto, of the "Black Boys" seizing 25 horses loaded with Indian goods on the way to Fort Pitt, and of the garrison at Fort Pitt keeping their drawbridge always up and placing

---

[322] Alvord: *Mississippi Valley in British Politics*, II, 113. This masterly work is indispensable to the student for the period 1763 to 1775. *Acts of the Privy Council*, V, 205.

[323] George Washington to Charles Washington, Jan. 31, 1770, in Washington MSS., XI, 1453a; Johnson MSS., XXI, 213; *Pa. Mag. of Hist. and Biog.*, XXX, 320.

a double sentry at the gate. Croghan, however, remained in the east much of the time and had McKee manage affairs at Fort Pitt. He, himself, took part in only a few small conferences at Fort Pitt. By 1773, Gage and Governor Penn were again both issuing proclamations warning trespassers off of lands across the new boundary line. Until after the Revolution, however, the area east and south of Ohio proved adequate to meet the needs of actual settlers, though not of scheming land speculators who wanted to organize new colonies in the interior.[324]

The drawing of a new boundary line was the first of four important measures affecting the West which were decided in the year 1768 and which were carried out by the new Pittite-Bedford ministry. The second measure provided for the abandonment of most of the western forts and the concentration of the troops along the seacoast; the third guaranteed the permanency of the Indian department, but took away from it the oversight of Indian trade; the fourth rejected all plans for the establishment of new colonies in the far West, along the Great Lakes, or the Mississippi. These four measures were all interrelated and constituted the most important imperial decisions with regard to the West that were made between 1764 and 1774. The policy announced in 1768 was neither reactionary nor radical, nor did it incorporate all of the measures advocated by any one cabinet member; it was a compromise influenced largely by the failure of imperial plans to tax the colonies, by the desire of the merchants interested in the Indian trade to be freed from restrictive regulations, and by the ominous desire to have the army

---

[324] *Pa. Gazette,* Aug. 17, 1769; *Pa. Arch.,* IV, 411, 433; Johnson MSS., VIII, 187; *N.Y. Col. Docs.,* VIII, *passim*; Croghan to Gage, Jan. 1, 1770, in C. O., 5: 88; *Pa. Col. Rec.,* X, 95; *American State Pap., Public Lands,* II, 209.

nearer the seacoast ready for action. That it marked a decline in the Indian department is self-evident.[325]

This department had always relied upon the assistance of the commanders of the forts and when these were abandoned, the local Indian officials often found their positions untenable. In 1768, the cabinet authorized Gage to abandon all interior forts except Niagara, Detroit, Michillimackinac, Pitt, Chartres, and either Crown Point or Ticonderoga. In 1771, he was ordered to abandon Fort Pitt and Fort de Chartres, demolish their works and carry their cannon to Philadelphia. Fort Pitt, which had been erected at a cost of £60,000, was now destroyed and all the materials in the buildings and walls were sold for £50. The settlers viewed this with surprise and grief. When one of the officers was asked the reason for destroying a fort so necessary for the safety of the frontiers, he replied: "The Americans will not submit to the british Parliament, and they may now defend themselves". The Indians were glad. Croghan wrote to Johnson that he had talked to many and that they had always had the suspicion that the troops were being kept to be used some day against them. The removal of the troops quieted them. Gage had offered Croghan the house of the commanding officer with other property, but the house was pulled down. Croghan did take over an old barrack, an

---

[325] Shelburne's famous letter to the Board of Trade dated October 5, 1767, and the Representation to the King dated March 7, 1768, replying to it, are found in the *N.Y. Col. Docs.*, VII, 981ff. and VIII, 19ff., respectively. A detailed discussion is given in Alvord: *Mississippi Valley in British Politics*. During the Stamp Act troubles in 1765, Gage had written Governor Sharpe of Maryland that Fort Pitt was the nearest place from which troops could be sent to his assistance and that its communications were extremely weak. The troops were so scattered over a vast continent that it would be difficult to meet a sudden emergency. – Gage to Conway, Sept. 23, 1765, in America to 1765, 535, Bancroft Coll.

orchard, garden, and fields and tried to hold them until it was proven that they lay within Pennsylvania.[326]

The desire to abandon most of the forts was an additional reason for abandoning the attempt to regulate the Indian trade through imperial officials. The cabinet decided in 1768 to maintain the Indian department for the purpose of controllng political relations with the Indians and making purchases of their lands; but the department was to be subordinate to the military department and its control over the regulation of Indian trade as planned in 1764 was to be taken away and left to the colonies. The merchants of England were almost unanimously against the plan of 1764. Local needs, they argued, could be best judged by each individual colony. Moreover, Gage reported that it was impossible to enforce imperial regulations because most of the Indian traders were nearly "as wild as the Country they go in, or the People they deal with and by far more vicious and wicked". Should Indian wars arise, under the new system the colonies would bear the major expenses.

Johnson was ordered to discharge all commissaries and to reduce drastically the number of other officials. Gage wrote him on March 19, 1769: "Mr. Croghan will order the Commisarys away from the Posts in his District immediately, The Smiths and more particularly the Interpreters must remain. . ."[327] It was felt unwise to act until the colonies had had time to appoint the successors to these officials, hence their discharge was delayed for several months. Gage asked the province of Quebec to appoint and provide

---

[326] *Calendar of Va. State Papers*, I, 278; McClure: *Diary*, 101; Croghan to Johnson, Dec. 24, 1772, in Johnson MSS., xxv, 118; Croghan to Haldimand, Oct. 4, 1773, in Haldimand Coll., series B, 70: 269; *idem*, 104.

[327] Gage to Johnson, Mar. 13, 1769, in Dreer Coll.

salaries for the local officials at Michillimackinac, New
York to be responsible for those at Niagara and
Detroit, and Pennsylvania for those at Pittsburg and
Kaskaskia. The governors of the colonies were instructed to have their assemblies pass proper laws for
regulating the trade and for preventing encroachments
on the Indian's land.

Johnson summarized the situation well when he
wrote that "none of those conversant in these matters
expect they will do anything material. . . ." New
York, Pennsylvania, and Virginia were the colonies
most interested. Colonial assemblies in 1769 and 1770
were giving little heed to requests from London or to
recommendations made by royal governors. Delays
ensued. The New York assembly provided for a
small appropriation and for commissioners to consult
with representatives from the other colonies. Virginia
also provided for such commissioners. In Pennsylvania the assembly informed Governor Penn that they
already had laws governing the two questions involved
and that they could do no more alone; that it was vain
to think of extending the jurisdiction of Pennsylvania
to cover posts outside its limits or over traders from
other colonies in such regions. After repeated urgings,
Pennsylvania, in 1770, provided for commissioners to
meet with commissioners from Quebec, New York,
New Jersey, Maryland, Delaware, and Virginia for
the purpose of formulating a general plan for the regulation of the Indian trade and stated that until this
was done it could do nothing further. In view of the
revolutionary movements on foot, the imperial government thought it wise to prevent such a colonial conference.[328]

---

[328] *Pa. Col. Rec.,* IX, 555, 582, 592, 646, 656, 708, 709; *N.Y. Col. Docs.,*
VIII, 151, 185, 222, 225, 254; *Stat. at Large of Pa.,* VII, 339.

Matters now drifted along and the Indian trade was thrown into chaos and confusion. There was no longer any check on rapacious traders. Non-importation agreements were making goods for the Indian trade so scarce that when Johnson and Croghan wanted goods valued at £3,000 there were not £10 worth to be had in Philadelphia. Conferences without presents could scarcely be held. When the Indians saw prices rise and found it more and more difficult to get any goods at all, their resentment became great.[329] It became evident that with the possession of the vast territory west of the mountains, imperial control of the Indian trade based on an act of Parliament was the only solution. Though Gage, as a good politician, wrote home, "Let the savages enjoy their desarts in quiet," yet privately, he told Croghan that things would never be rightly managed until imperial control was restored.[330] He did not foresee that central management was to be secured through national action under the Articles of Confederation and the Constitution of a new nation.

The decline of the Indian department enabled the imperial government to reduce Indian expenditures and with one exception this was drastically enforced. Normal annual expenditures in the Northern District were to be limited to £5,000 and in the Southern District to £4,000. Extraordinary expenditures which were not provided for in the budget had to be recommended by the commander-in-chief and sanctioned by the home government before being incurred. Indian officials and military commanders who violated these rules were to be personally responsible for expenses

---

[329] M. Gratz to B. Gratz, Aug. 9, 1769, in Byars, *B. and M. Gratz,* 97.

[330] Gage to Hillsborough, Nov. 10, 1770, in C. O., 5: 88; *Doc. Hist. of N.Y.,* IV, 420.

they incurred. Johnson had asked for an increase in salaries for his four deputies from £200 to £300 and also an increase for himself. His own salary was now increased from £600 to £1,000. Stuart's salary was raised to £800 and he was made an ex-officio member of the councils of all the colonies in his district. In return, these men were asked to see that the new system worked out successfully. In the Northern District scarcely £3,000 remained for presents, traveling expenses and all other expenditures after salaries were paid to the superintendent, his deputies, an assistant, a surgeon, a clerk, a storekeeper, two smiths, and three interpreters.[331]

Croghan's salary and the salaries of all other officials were not increased. He still found it necessary to advance his own money to pay minor officials under him, and then found it difficult to secure reimbursement. Gage refused to pay any of Croghan's bills except through Johnson and the latter had to urge Croghan to practice the strictest frugality. Croghan called attention to the expenses entailed by his position and stated that he could not continue in his office unless they were allowed. He wrote to his son-in-law, Prevost, that he and Gage "coald nott agree in our sentiments, which was a prensaple Cause of my going out of the service".[332]

Various dates from 1771 to 1776 are given for Croghan's resignation. The evidence discovered proves that it was early in 1772.[333] Various causes were re-

[331] Gage to Johnson, Mar. 13, 1769 in the library of the Hist. Soc. of Pa.; Ill. Hist. Coll., XII, 568; N.Y. Col. Docs., VIII, 203, 211; Bd. of Tr. Pap., Plantations General, XXIX, U42; C. O., 5: 84 and 86.

[332] Johnson MSS., XIX, 57, 183; XX, 83; XXI, 41, 68; Croghan to Prevost, Jan. 27, 1773, in Haldimand Coll., B70: 104.

[333] Croghan's deed to John Kelly, in Deed Bk., XL, 163, Sec. of State, Albany.

sponsible for his resignation. The decline of the Indian department no longer challenged his interests and powers. There were no difficult and important duties in prospect and therefore Johnson no longer opposed Croghan's wish to resign. Should occasion demand it, Croghan agreed to return. Croghan's increasing age and ill health were not compatible with the strenuous life of an Indian agent. Beginning with the year 1769, Croghan suffered severely with the gout and rheumatism and was confined to his bed for weeks at a time. In the spring of 1770 he planned to go to Warm Springs in Virginia for relief. Croghan also yearned to retire from public life.[334] His landed interests were of absorbing importance, especially in 1772, when the establishment of Vandalia promised to demand his services as an official in the new colony. He also felt that the reversion to Amherst's policy of neglect of Indian affairs and the new encroachments upon the Indian's lands were only a part of the sinister policy of Lord Hillsborough and other enemies of Vandalia; this he thought aimed at bringing on an Indian war to thwart the establishment of the new colony. By resigning, Croghan would be able to combat this policy.[335]

As soon as it was rumored that Croghan had resigned, place hunters applied for his position. The selection of his successor was made upon merit, however. Johnson recommended Alexander McKee who had been Croghan's chief assistant at Fort Pitt for over a decade and who had often taken charge of affairs when Croghan was absent.[336] Croghan continued to give Johnson and McKee the benefit of his advice and,

[334] Johnson MSS., XVII to XX, *passim*.

[335] Croghan to B. and M. Gratz, Jan. 4, 1772, in Ohio Co. MSS., I, 93; Croghan to Wharton, Oct. 15, 1773, in *Pa. Mag. of Hist. and Biog.*, XV, 435.

[336] Johnson to Gage, May 20, 1772, in Johnson MSS., XXI, 189.

at critical times, of his services also. Sir William Johnson served until his death two years later, on July 11, 1774. Croghan was grief-stricken when the news came to him. Sir William Johnson was succeeded by Guy Johnson and later by John Johnson. To these men and to McKee fell the odious duty while in the service of their King to incite the Iroquois and western Indians to raid the frontiers during the Revolution.

Next to Sir William Johnson, Croghan was the most prominent English Indian agent of his generation. His journals and official correspondence give an epitome of the history of Indian affairs in the Northern District. He rendered eminent services to the colonies and to the empire by conciliating the Indians and securing their friendly support. Few white men were more welcome in Indian villages than he. He helped to turn the tide of French aggression, to secure the occupation of the West by the English, and to maintain peaceful relations between the red man and the white man in spite of their clashing interests in trade and in land. In 1775, James Adair, one of the most prominent and respectable traders with the Southern Indians, dedicated his famous *History of the American Indians* "To the Honorable Colonel George Croghan, George Galphin and Lachlan McGilwray, Esquires." [337] He summarized the work of these men thus: "To you with the greatest propriety the following sheets are addressed. Your distinguished abilities – your thorough acquaintance with the North American Indians' language, rites, and customs – your long application and services in the dangerous sphere of an Indian life, and your successful management of the savage natives, are well known over all the continent of America".

[337] Johnson had consented to have his name in the list, but his death in 1774 caused it to be omitted.

Land Speculation: Individual Purchases, 1746-1770

In 1760, the interests of the English colonies were largely agricultural. Less than four percent of the population lived in towns of more than 8,000 inhabitants. Free capital found the most promising investments in lands about to be settled. The treaty of Paris in 1763 had thrown open to the investor the magnificent forest-clad kingdom that stretched from the Appalachians to the Mississippi. The beautiful Ohio valley, the Lake Plains, and the Illinois prairies were rich with incalculable possibilities to tempt him. The psychological effect of a victory resulting in the winning of such an empire encouraged him to exploit it. Immigration and the natural increase of population were counted on to double and triple land values frequently. The royal proclamation of 1763 and other legal handicaps did not remove the temptation. Washington, a leading land speculator, wrote: "I can never look upon that proclamation in any other light (but this I say between ourselves), than as a temporary expedient to quiet the minds of the Indians. . . Any person, therefore, who neglects the present opportunity of hunting out good lands, and in some measure marking and distinguishing them for his own, (in order to keep others from settling them), will never regain it." [338]

The leadership in this movement was taken by Vir-

---

[338] Washington to Crawford, Sept. 21, 1767, in *Writings*, II, 220.

ginia planters, who were always land hungry, by Pennsylvania merchants, who had surplus capital to invest,
and by New Englanders, who sought to relieve the
pressure of population upon their available supply of
desirable land. New York lacked expansive power
until after the Revolution. The movement centered
in Philadelphia; this city had long been interested
in the *hinterland*. Colonial leaders, however, were
wise enough to interest influential Englishmen and
thus secure their political support and the use of the
capital of an old country. Croghan expressed the
intense interest of England in her new territories as
follows: "one half of England is Now Land mad and
Every body there has thire Eys fixt on this
Cuntry. . ."[339]

The spirit of land speculation found expression in
individual land operations, in the organization of
numerous land companies, and in the planning of new
colonies. Plans for colonies located around Detroit,
Pittsburg, Boonesborough, Kaskaskia, and Natchez
were drawn up and seriously considered. Companies
were also organized to develop silver, gold, and copper
mines on Lake Superior, and gold and silver mines in
the Pennsylvania mountains.[340]

Most of the public men of the east were interested
in this movement. Washington, Franklin, Johnson,
and Patrick Henry all held shares in such companies.
Henry wrote in 1774: "the west'rn world is my Hobby
horse".[341] Such connections were considered honor-

[339] Croghan to Johnson, Mar. 3, 1766, in *Ill. Hist. Coll.*, XI, 206.

[340] Croghan and Johnson were both offered shares in this company.
Forty miners were sent to Lake Superior with Alexander Henry as a
guide. – Henry: , *Travels and Adventures*, 223ff.; Johnson MSS., XVII, 105 and
VIII, 212; Ohio Co. MSS., I, 49.

[341] Wharton to Thomas Walpole, Sept. 23, 1774, in Thomas Wharton's
Letter Bk., 1773-1784.

able until after the Revolution when scandals and failures such as those of Nicholson, Morris, and of the Yazoo Company made them odious in the public eye. "Patriotic" historians long over looked or concealed this phase of American history and gave their attention to political and military affairs. Benjamin Franklin and his associates were representative Americans with human motives – one of which is the amassing of wealth. He did not conceal this, but expressed it in Poor Richard's maxims. When this motive found expression in land operations in the West, it had far-reaching social and political results which were of the highest significance for the future of their country.

To carry out their schemes, these colonial leaders had to secure the consent of the English cabinet. The policy of the cabinet was one of indecision and obstruction which these leaders labored to overcome. In trying to accomplish this they handicapped themselves by dividing into two hostile groups. One group, led by Virginians, had a vision of a West composed of innumerable additional Virginia counties for it to exploit and of a Virginia of preponderant size and power. The other group led by Pennsylvanians, Franklin and Croghan included, had a vision of a West composed of a considerable number of new colonies, or states, coördinate in every way with those along the seaboard. The fact that Pennsylvania was prevented by its charter from incorporating much of the West was largely responsible for their attitude. Their policy was first expressed by Franklin at the Albany Congress in 1754. In 1756, he drew up a well-matured plan for the establishment of such colonies. In the development of the map of the United States during the generation before 1787, this plan occupies a highly significant place.

Croghan was one of the most influential leaders of the Pennsylvania group. Few others devoted themselves so thoroughly to western land matters. "I find they preferr thire Ease and plesher to busness . . .", he wrote in disgust when some of his associates refused to make a journey to discuss land matters.[342] No other leader of any group had a better first hand knowledge of the most fertile and strategically located lands towards which the frontier was rapidly moving, nor did any other leader surpass Croghan in his faith in the rapid development of the West. This so inspired him that he was able to exert a dynamic influence upon eastern leaders. He won their gratitude by frequently helping them to secure choice tracts of land for private investments. Among those whom he served in this manner were Generals Bouquet, Bradstreet,[343] and Armstrong, Rev. William Smith, the Whartons, David Franks, Barnard and Michael Gratz, Richard Hockley, Richard and William Peters, and the Franklins. Croghan's official position brought him into intimate contact with them. He was thus enabled to interest them in organizing companies to develop western lands.

Croghan was also individually interested in western lands. He secured legal title to thousands of acres in Pennsylvania and New York, and he attempted to secure sole title to 200,000 acres near Pittsburg. It was in Pennsylvania that he secured his first lands. Penn's excellent land system, unlike that of Virginia, favored the settler with small means and this encouraged immigration and a phenomenal prosperity.

[342] Croghan to Trent, Jan. 18, 1769, in Lamberton Scotch-Irish MSS., I, 86.
[343] At the treaty of Fort Stanwix Croghan assisted Bradstreet to secure 20,000 acres in New York. – Am. Antiq. Soc., Transactions, XI, 104; Hanna: Wilderness Trail, II, 66.

"What the world has imputed to the happiness of our Constitution, is with more justice to be ascribed to the happy management of the Land offices", wrote Lewis Evans in 1753.[344]

Theoretically, a settler would secure his lands from the Penns through their officials in Philadelphia, they having extinguished all Indian claims. The settler applied to the secretary of the land office for a certain tract of unoccupied land, usually limited to 300 acres. If he were the first applicant, the surveyor-general would then have the tract surveyed. A warrant would then be issued by the secretary to the surveyor-general to accept the survey and certify it to the secretary. On payment of the purchase price, usually about £5 to £9 sterling per 100 acres, the secretary would issue a patent. Thereafter, a quit rent of from ½d. to 1d. per 100 acres was payable annually and the settler could enter into possession.

In actual practice, however, many lands were not granted in this manner because the prospective settler often did not have the capital it required. He therefore went to the frontier, squatted on a piece of land, and made a living for himself and his family. The tract upon which he settled became known as an "improvement" which the law soon came to recognize as his personal property which he could sell. The Penns gave to the squatter the first opportunity to secure a regular legal title to such a tract of land. It soon became established that if another person patented such a tract he must first pay for the improvement. The squatter who desired a legal title applied for a warrant of survey which would be issued upon his paying down part of the purchase money. After the

[344] Evans: Brief Account of Pennsylvania, in Du Simitiere Coll.

survey was made and registered it was practically as
good as a patent; consequently, many settlers never
secured patents for their lands. However, all land
in Pennsylvania was not immediately thrown open to
settlement by the Penns. Some was reserved in order
to secure the unearned increment. The "Manor of
Pittsburg", for example, was thus reserved to be sold
at higher rates.[345]

The first lands which Croghan secured after coming
to America were located in the fertile Cumberland
valley. Here he patented in 1746, 1748, and 1749,
three tracts of land totaling 474 acres. Nearby were
354 acres which had been patented in 1744 and then
conveyed to Trent and Croghan; of this tract Croghan
became sole owner in 1746. In 1747, he added 210
acres, patented in 1742. In the same year he purchased 172 acres in Paxtang Township, east of the
Susquehanna; this tract had only been patented since
1738 and yet Croghan was its fourth owner. In 1751,
Richard Hockley, receiver-general of quit-rents for
the Penns, Trent, and Croghan took out a warrant for
300 acres in this region. Croghan also purchased lots
and built several houses in Shippensburg which was
just being laid out. Altogether, within four years,
Croghan had acquired over 1,400 acres within a short
distance of Harris's Ferry and along the important
road leading to Virginia.

The frequent changes in the ownership of these
tracts are indicative of the spirit of land speculation
prevalent among these early pioneers. Croghan early
caught this spirit. At the same time that he was ac-

---

[345] Gov. Penn to Lord Shelburne, Apr. 24, 1767, in King's Manuscript,
No. 206, p. 208, Br. Museum; Huston, Charles: *History and Original
Titles to Land in Pennsylvania*.

quiring new lands he was mortgaging to Philadel-
phians, who had surplus capital to invest, those lands
which he had only recently acquired. In 1747, he
mortgaged two tracts to Jeremiah Warder for £500,
which he paid off in 1749. In 1748, he mortgaged
two other tracts to Mary Plumsted for £300. In 1749,
he mortgaged four tracts to Richard Peters, secretary
of the provincial council and of the land office, for
£1,000. In 1751, after Croghan had held six tracts for
only five years or less, he conveyed them to Peters,
thereby cancelling all his mortgages and receiving
£1,000 besides. His business relations with Peters and
Hockley, two influential officials, are significant.[346]
Land operations practically ceased during the decade from 1750 to 1760 as a result of the French and
Indian War. When they were resumed in 1760, the
frontier moved rapidly from the Cumberland valley
to the region around Bedford and Huntingdon. Near
these places Croghan secured legal title to many tracts
of land. On the upper Juniata Croghan secured more
than fifteen tracts of land, varying in size from 100
to 800 acres. One tract included the land at Aughwick where he had settled in 1754. Another was the
famous "Standing Stone Improvement" of 400 acres
which he purchased in 1760 for £100 and which he
sold for £300 in 1766 to Dr. William Smith, Provost
of the College of Philadelphia. Upon it Smith laid
out the city of Huntingdon.[347] Along Raystown
Branch of the Juniata, along Dunnings Creek, and
near Bedford, Croghan secured upwards of twenty
tracts of land. Some rivaled in excellence those which

[346] Deed Bk., A, I, p. 19, Register of Deeds, Carlisle, Pa.; Peters MSS., II,
86, 113, 114, 120 and VI, 87; Pa. Arch., 3rd. ser., II, 120; Shippen Corresp. I,
73.
[347] Deed Bk., B, I, 13, Register of Deeds, Carlisle, Pa.

the Penns reserved in the Manor of Bedford. One tract close to Fort Bedford was laid out into town lots. By 1763, Bedford had fifty houses and was surrounded by clearings with log cabins nestled among the mountains. This frontier community first became aware of Pontiac's uprising when fifteen mowers, busily engaged on one of Croghan's fields about a mile from the Fort, were attacked on June 30, 1763.[348]

In 1767, when it was evident that the Penns would soon open the lands as far west as the Ohio, Croghan applied to them for a special order for 40,000 acres. In spite of their close friendly relations with Croghan, the Penns remained true to their excellent land policy and refused to make such large grants.[349] Some concessions were, however, made to influential frontiersmen. When the purchase made at Fort Stanwix was thrown open to settlement on April 3, 1769, there was a great rush to get choice lands. A regular application was limited to 300 acres. Forty-six special applications for warrants to survey were granted before April 3; some called for tracts of 5,000 acres.[350] They were granted to provincial soldiers and to influential frontiersmen. Croghan filed eight applications for 4,700 acres lying near Fort Pitt. One called for 1,500 acres to include his plantation upon which he had erected "Croghan Hall". This actually surveyed 1,352 acres and is today within the city limits of Pittsburg. Of the 4,700 acres applied for, Croghan was granted only 3,100 acres because the Penns gave the first opportunity to persons who had secured military permits to occupy lands and the second to those who had made

[348] Penn Physick MSS., IV, 47 and VII, 5; Pa. Arch., 3rd. ser., IV, No. 5; Official Corresp., IX, 188, Penn MSS.; Pa. Gazette, July 7, 1763.

[349] Thomas Penn to Croghan, Sept. 12, 1767, in Penn Letter Bk., IX, 188.

[350] New Purchase Applications, 4-7; Warantee Atlas of Allegheny County.

improvements without such permits. Croghan also had a half interest in five applications of David Franks which gave them 3,000 acres on Sewickly Creek.[351]

Meanwhile, Croghan also purchased a tract of 18 acres which today lies within the limits of Philadelphia. It had a brick house upon it and was valued at £2,000. Here he planned to erect a fine country seat, "Monckton Hall," where he could live during his numerous visits in the east.[352]

Croghan's name is a familiar one to the experts of title companies of Pennsylvania because of the frequency with which his name occurs in important land records. Altogether, he patented only about 2,500 acres and many of the lands which he once owned are still on the state lien list. His titles to about 10,000 acres were based on warrants of survey which he took out. He purchased "improvements", and lands to which others had partial or complete legal titles; these also totaled about 10,000 acres.

Some colonists, like Washington and Johnson, planned to build up vast landed estates and therefore granted long-term leases; in contrast to these, Croghan planned to develop his lands slightly and then to sell them in small tracts. He seldom held a tract of land longer than five years. Many of his lands were sold to influential easterners; some were used to pay debts or to raise funds for his journey to England and for his contribution to the expenses of land companies. He invested all of his surplus funds in lands and when necessary, he used them as security for loans. He had a keen eye for choice, bottom lands located on a main line of communication. In four cases he took up

[351] McAllister Coll., Yi 2, 7311, F43.
[352] *Pa. Gazette*, Aug. 26, 1772.

tracts of lands on the future sites of cities.   He almost
always purchased lands on the frontier and shifted the
scene of his operations as the frontier moved westward.[353]

Croghan was also interested in lands on the frontier
in New York.   The land policy of this colony offered
great contrasts to the excellent land policy of Pennsylvania.   The latter served the welfare of the pioneer
settler, while the former served the interests of the
land speculator and the great landowner.   The great
landowners of New York usually aimed to build up
vast, semi-feudal estates; they offered settlers leases
instead of titles in fee simple and planned to exploit
their labor.   This system was in part inherited by the
English from the patroon system of the Dutch.   It
was at its heighth during the period from 1690 to 1710;
throughout the remainder of the colonial period efforts
were made to throw off the control of the great landowners, but with discouraging results.

The land system of New York was intrically inter-
woven with politics.   The great landowners through
their membership in the provincial council and
through their influence with the governor and the
assembly were able to control the granting of lands.
Large grants of from 10,000 to 200,000 acres were frequently made to members of the council or to their
friends.   Among the estates built up in this manner
were those of the Schuylers, the Livingstons, and the

[353] Besides the sources indicated in the preceding six notes, the following sources were used for the above account: Ohio Co. MSS.; Deed Box,
1760-1801, Penn MSS.; *Pa. Arch., 3rd. ser.*, I-V and XXII; Deed Bk., A, I and
II, B, I, and D, LXVIII, Register of Deeds, Carlisle, Pa.; Deed Bk., H, I and
F, I, Huntingdon, Pa.; Deed Bk., I, Nos. 2, 5, 6, and 10; Deed Bk., D,
1777-1800, No. 10, and Mortgage Bk., X, Philadelphia; New Purchase Applications, West Side Applications, Copied Surveys, Warrant Registers, and
Patent Books, on file in the Department of Internal Affairs, Harrisburg, Pa.

Johnsons. All vacant lands in New York belonged
to the crown, but in granting them it had to make use
of local provincial officials. The few loyal officials
like Colden were unable to check the prodigal waste
of the crown's resources.

Thus New York was handicapped in her competition with New England, Pennsylvania, and New
Jersey for settlers. As a result of her land system and
of the necessity until 1763 to avoid offending the Iroquois, New York lacked expansive power. This it did
not acquire until the American Revolution broke the
power of the Iroquois and overthrew the landed
oligarchy. When this was done, especially after the
Erie Canal was opened, New York City supplanted
Philadelphia as the metropolis of the American Continent, and New York took its place among the leading
states of the union.

The British imperial government came early to
view the operations of the New York land speculators
with disfavor. It aimed to encourage the growth of
the empire by enabling the poor immigrant to secure
his land from the state instead of from land speculators. It sought to curb the speculators and large land
owners through royal instructions to the governors.
Those issued in 1708, to Governor Lovelace are a landmark and differed but little from those under which
Governors Colden and Moore awarded grants to Croghan. The instructions sent to Colden and Moore forbade the granting of tracts larger than 1,000 acres to
one individual, or the surveying of tracts so as to include none but the most fertile lands or lands along
navigable rivers. They declared a grant null and void
unless a certain proportion of the land was cultivated
and settled within a reasonable period of time. They

also required the governor in person to make all purchases of land from the Indians.[354] How these benevolent imperial regulations were overcome by large land speculators is well illustrated by Croghan's land operations in New York.

In 1765, Croghan sent a memorial to the Board of Trade asking for a grant of 20,000 acres in New York as a bounty for his services during the French and Indian War. By the proclamation of 1763, a land bounty was offered to the soldiers who had served in this war; the highest amount offered to any officer was 5,000 acres. General Gage, Sir William Johnson, John Stuart, and others petitioned for such grants. Croghan's memorial was considered along with thirty-eight others, each asking for either 10,000 or 20,000 acres. The Board of Trade recommended that half the amount asked for be granted to each petitioner. Croghan was one of the four who were recommended for 10,000 acres. On September 6, 1765, an order in council was issued granting him 10,000 acres in New York without the payment of any fees or purchase money and free from quit-rents for ten years. The Board of Trade had recommended, however, that no applications for land should be considered in the future unless they related to the new colonies or offered special reasons to induce deviation from the ordinary method of granting lands.[355]

Croghan did not forget the additional 10,000 acres for which he had unsuccessfully petitioned. While

[354] Instructions to Gov. Monckton, 1762, in N.Y. Council Minutes, VI, 391; Instructions to Gov. Moore, 1767, in C. O., 5: 201; Spencer, C. W.: "The Land System of Colonial New York," in *N.Y. State Hist. Ass'n Proc.,* XVI, 150-164.

[355] Croghan's Memorial, in C. O., 5: 1071 p. 403; Bd. of Tr. Journal, LXXIII, 165-168 and LXXVI, 143, 144, 151, 153; Bd. of Tr. Pap., Plantations General, XXVI, A20; *Acts of the Privy Council,* IV, 819 and V, 596.

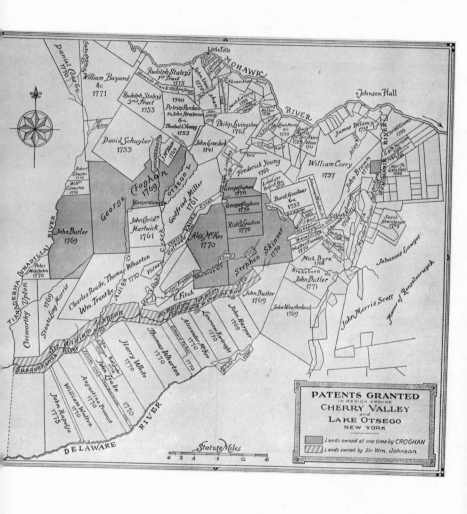

PATENTS GRANTED
IN REGION AROUND
CHERRY VALLEY
and
LAKE OTSEGO
NEW YORK

Lands owned at one time by CROGHAN
Lands owned by Sir Wm. Johnson

Statute Miles
0 2 4 8 12 16

his memorial had been under consideration in London, he was again risking his life in the hostile western wilderness in the service of his king. For such services Croghan was paid but £200 a year. The heavy war debts would not allow England to raise salaries at this time, but it was feasible to reward her loyal officials with land grants. It was under such conditions that Croghan, in 1768, prepared a memorial to the King in Council asking for the 10,000 acres for which he had asked in vain in 1765. John and Thomas Penn helped to present his case. On August 12, 1768, "because of the special merits of the Petitioner", Croghan's petition was granted.[356]

It now remained for Croghan to find 20,000 acres of ungranted lands to which the Indian title had been extinguished and to patent it. On February 14, 1770, he petitioned the governor and council of New York that he be granted a patent for two adjacent tracts of 9,000 acres each in Cherry valley and that they be organized into a township named "Belvedere", and that it might have popular election of its officials. Evidently Croghan intended to attract settlers by insuring them greater self-government than the average New York landlord permitted. His petition was granted.[357]

Croghan's success in obtaining these grants and the desire to be near his intimate friend, Johnson, caused him to change his residence from Pennsylvania to New

---

[356] C. O., 5: 1073 f. 209 and 1080, f. 287; C. O., 5: 1130, f. 424; Penn MSS., II, 62; Thomas Penn to Croghan, Apr. 11, 1767, in Penn Letter Bk., IX, 107.

[357] N.Y. Council Minutes, XXIX, 357; Land Pap., XXVI, 122; Bk. of Patents, XV, 256-263. Unless otherwise specified, the Land Papers, Books of Patents, and Books of Deeds referred to in connection with New York lands are to be found in the office of the Secretary of State. Cockburn, W.: A Map of the Province of N.Y., 1774; Sauthier, C. J.: Chorographical Map of N.Y., 1779. The Council Minutes show that such grants were common during this period.

York. Many legal documents of the time speak of Croghan as "formerly of the Province of Pennsylvania, now of the Province of New York." Doubtless he desired to be on the ground to take advantage of the rapid extension of the frontier line in central New York which was being made at this time. This movement was accelerated by the fact that nearly every patent issued included thousands of acres of land. The lands in the upper Mohawk valley were being patented by the aristocrats of New York, but those around the headwaters of the Susquehanna were largely taken up by a group of land speculators from Pennsylvania and New Jersey. Governor Franklin, Richard Smith, and Charles Reade – all from Burlington, New Jersey – together with Lieutenant Augustine Prevost, William Trent, Alexander McKee, and Samuel, Joseph and Thomas Wharton were the most prominent members of this group. Most of these were either relatives or close associates of Croghan. He made an Indian purchase for Governor Franklin, Trent, and Samuel Wharton, which was supposed to contain 130,000 acres. This became known as the "Otego," or "New Burlington" tract.

Though the first patent in the famous Cherry valley region had been issued in 1738, the region had developed so slowly that at this time contemporary maps showed nothing here except the names of the larger streams and lakes. The name "Croghan's Forest",[358] which like "Mt. Vernon" or "Johnson Hall" came to denote the residence of a large landowner, is eloquent testimony of the nature of the country and also of Croghan's important relation to it. Eight years after

---

[358] Day: *Calendar of Sir William Johnson* MSS., 495; Misc. MSS., I, 141, Etting Coll.

his death, when the first United States census was taken, the frontier line showed a distinct inland curve south and west of the Otsego and Cherry valley region; for this Croghan was largely responsible.

Croghan and his friends enlisted the influence of Johnson, who was a member of the Council and a close personal friend of Governor Colden. On one occasion Johnson wrote to Colden introducing Croghan as one who has "some Land matters to Settle and Patents to take out at NYork In which he hopes for your Countenance . . . as he is a Gent that is Well known, and one for whom I have always had a great regard, I persuade myself he will meet with your notice." [359] On June 27, 1767, Croghan and thirty-nine nominal associates, petitioned the governor and council for a license to purchase from the Iroquois 40,000 acres of land west of Lake Otsego. This was to be deeded by the Indians to George III in trust "for the sole use and benefit of the petitioners". On the same day another group, which included Lieutenant Augustine Prevost, Croghan's son-in-law, filed a similar petition for 260,000 acres around the headwaters of the Delaware. In both petitions there occurs the following stereotyped reference to the proclamation of 1763: the petitioners "humbly conceive that the Royal intention in said Proclamation was solely to prevent the defrauding the Indians in purchases made by Private Persons, and not to Inhibit Purchases made for the Benefit of Private Persons if made in his Majesty's Name with the Intervention of his Governors or Commanders in chief and at the Expense of such Private Persons. . . That your Petitioners are willing and beg leave to offer to attend the said Indians . . . to this City,

[359] *Doc. Hist. of N.Y.*, II, 956.

to defray the Expenses of their Journey, to take care of them during their Residence here, and to pay the Consideration money which your Excellency may agree to give for such Purchase." Croghan had previously used his friendship with the Indians to persuade them to sell. His petition ended by asking the governor to meet the Indians and make the purchase, and that the petitioners be granted a patent for the lands thus purchased. It was signed "George Croghan fer himself and associates." This petition was granted on July 6, 1767, and Governor Moore made the purchase at Croghan's expense at a meeting with the Indians at Johnson's residence on June 10, 1768.[360]

Such was the method used in New York to circumvent the proclamation of 1763. It could hardly be used by the poor pioneer, but the influential land speculators used it so successfully that a rapid extension of the frontier was in progress in New York before 1768. The treaty of Fort Stanwix made in that year, instead of aiding the expansion, as is usually stated, hindered it, for it set up a definite Indian boundary line as a barrier. For a few years, however, the surveyor with his rod and chain was a common sight in the forests around Lake Otsego and the upper Mohawk River. The method used in New York to circumvent the proclamation of 1763 is significant also because it served as a precedent at the treaty of Fort Stanwix for Croghan's Ohio grant and for the grant to the Indiana Company.

It is interesting to note that the purchase made for Croghan west of Lake Otsego, contained when sur-

[360] Land Pap., XXIII, 159; N.Y. Council Minutes, XXIX, 244, 245, 255, 286, 305.

veyed, not 40,000 acres, but 100,000 acres. Such a large tract could not be patented in the name of one individual. Croghan therefore followed the method which had been discovered by the "big interests" of the day to attain their ends. He associated himself with ninety-nine of his friends whose names were made use of for his particular and sole benefit. As prospective "tenants in common and not joint tenants", on March 15, 1769, they petitioned for a patent granting each one 1,000 acres. On November 30, after the survey had been returned, the patent was issued to George Croghan and his associates. The crown reserved forever all gold and silver mines and required a yearly quit-rent of 2s. 6d. sterling per one hundred acres. Pine trees suitable for masts for the royal navy were not to be cut down. Within three years three acres out of every fifty acres were to be cultivated and one family settled for every one thousand acres. If these conditions were not complied with, or if the patent was not registered within six months, it was to be void. Two days after the patent had been issued, his ninety-nine associates conveyed to Croghan the lands which they had just received. Each individual according to the deeds was paid £50 by Croghan, but probably received nothing.[361]

Thus by 1770, Croghan had patented in New York, Belvedere Township of 18,000 acres and the Otsego tract of 100,000 acres. He at once proceeded to purchase adjacent lands until he had acquired over 250,-000 acres around Lake Otsego and Cherry valley.[362] These included the Skinner patent of 40,000 acres lying

[361] Croghan's petition for a warrant to survey, in Land Pap., XXIV, 73; idem, XXVI, 39; Croghan's patent, Nov. 30, 1769, in Bk. of Patents, XIV, 466-472; Bk. of Deeds, XVIII, 257-260.

[362] Bk. of Deeds, XVIII, 260-275; Gratz-Croghan Deeds; Gratz-Croghan

southeast of Belvedere; the McKee patent of 40,000 acres lying southwest of Belvedere; and the Butler or "Tunaderry" patent of 47,000 acres lying southwest of his Otsego patent. He also purchased 1,893 acres of the Bowen patent on Schoharie Creek. Most of these patents were less than a year old when Croghan purchased them. These lands were well selected. When Washington, who had a keen eye for good lands, visited Lake Otsego on his western tour in 1783, he was impressed with their excellent location.[363]

When Croghan decided to settle in New York, he selected as the site for his future home, a delightful location at the foot of Lake Otsego. Here was the source of the Susquehanna which at this place was a swift little stream twelve yards wide. In the lake near its source lay "Council Rock", later made famous by James Fenimore Cooper. Towering white pines formed the background, while a natural strawberry patch and some copper ore invited exploitation. Fish and game abounded. "A very pleasant place" was the comment of an officer in General Sullivan's expedition who camped here in 1779. Hartwick had planned to include it in his patent, but his survey had left it outside.[364]

Croghan came to Otsego in 1769 to supervise its development in person. The ensuing year and a half constituted one of the happiest periods of his life. It was the period of great activity in the Otsego region. Croghan, with his indentured servants, carpenters, and

MSS., I, 19; The Butler patent had been patented for Croghan by John Butler, the notorious tory colonel during the Revolution.

[363] Washington: *Writings*, x, 325.

[364] Halsey, Francis W.: *The Old New York Frontier*, 125; Lt. Beatty's Journal, in Cook, Frederick: *Journals of the Expedition of Gen. Sullivan*, 20. Croghan's house was used as a magazine by Beatty's detachment.

other free laborers, and such Indians as could be employed, engaged in the work of transforming his visions into realities. Two dwelling houses and eight other buildings were soon erected. Around these, four fields were cleared and fenced. A large batteau was built for use on the lake and a bridge was erected over the Susquehanna. A millwright came to view the best site for the erection of a sawmill and a gristmill. Work was begun to make the Susquehanna navigable for canoes by hiring Indians to remove the logs from within it. There was a wagon road which led northward into the Mohawk valley, but Croghan planned to open a road which would run east and connect with the road which ran from the Schoharie settlements through the Catskill Mountains to the Hudson River. So well supplied was Croghan with skilled indentured servants from Dublin, Ireland, that he loaned to Johnson a bricklayer, a mason, and a gardener at different times. In return Johnson gave him some fine sheep. Croghan already had cattle which successfully wintered in the woods without hay; they furnished Croghan and his guests with butter which tasted like wild garlic. Hogs and poultry were soon added and four wagons were employed to bring in crockery, glass, and other goods. In the meantime, surveyors were preparing part of his land for sale and Croghan was advertising in Connecticut for settlers. "Croghan had several elegant improvements at this place and exceedingly well situated for trade", wrote a surgeon in 1779.[365]

Croghan's house soon became a landmark. Travel-

[365] Surveyor Pitkin's sketch, 1774, in Bk. of Deeds, xx, 315; Johnson MSS., XVII, 126, 185, 225, XVIII, 35, and XIX, 15; Journal of Dr. C. McArthur 1779, in Du Simitiere Coll.

ers made it their headquarters and Indians visited it
so that Croghan seldom had an hour to himself. He
wrote to Johnson on March 17,1770: "Ever since I
gott here to my Hutt we have been as full of visitors as
possible." [366]   Richard Smith, who visited Croghan in
1769, noted in his journal on May 26: "Last Night
a drunken Indian came and kissed Col. Croghan and
me very joyously; here are natives of different Nations
almost continually; they visit the Deputy Superintendent as Dogs to the Bone for what they can get." [367]   It
ought to be added that it was probably for the same
reason that Smith, himself, partook of Croghan's hos-
pitality.   Croghan's prospects for enjoying life at
Otsego were increased when his only white child,
Susannah, and her family settled at the opposite end
of Lake Otsego on 6,061 acres which Croghan had sold
to her husband, Lieutenant Augustine Prevost. Life
looked so attractive to them here that Susannah's husband sold his commission in the British army to build
a home on the frontier.

Besides securing lands in Pennsylvania and New York
in the 1760's, Croghan also tried to secure 200,000 acres
at the forks of the Ohio.   He stated that at the Logstown conference in August, 1749, three Ohio Iroquois
chiefs, Johonerissa, Scaroyadia, and Cosswentanicea, in
return for a large assortment of Indian goods, sold to
him three tracts of land; one of 40,000 acres just east
of the site of Fort Pitt, one of 60,000 acres located on
both sides of the Youghiogheny at the mouth of
Sewickly Creek, and one of 100,000 acres west of the
lower Monongahela. [368]   About 1760, Croghan began

---

[366] Johnson MSS., XVIII, 238.

[367] Halsey, Francis W.: *A Tour of Four Great Rivers*, etc., 47; cf.
also 29, 34, 36, 37, and 81.

[368] The earliest documents found which refer to this purchase are

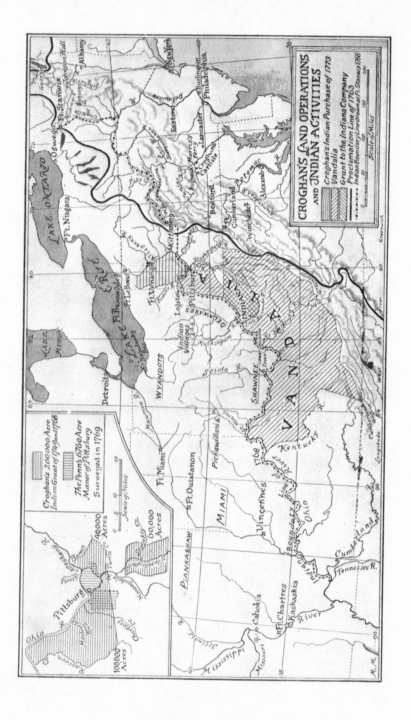

CROGHAN'S LAND OPERATIONS
AND INDIAN ACTIVITIES

Croghan's Indian Purchase of 1773
Vandalia
Grant to the Indiana Company
Proclamation Line of 1763
Indian Boundary Line drawn at Ft.Stanwix 1768

Scale of Miles

Croghan's 200,000 Acre
Indian Grant of 1749 and 1768
The Penn's 6760 Acre
Manor of Pittsburg
Surveyed in 1769

40,000

60,000
Acres

100,000
Acres

Scale of Miles

Pittsburg

to develop the Youghiogheny tract in association with Clapham and on the tract east of Fort Pitt he built Croghan Hall. He strengthened his claims by securing military licenses for these improvements.

When he was in England in 1764, he sought to secure royal confirmation of his grant. He presented a memorial to the Board of Trade which referred to his past services, described the grant, admitted the wisdom and legal necessity for securing royal confirmation, and then requested permission to locate the grant in New York and to have the governor of New York instructed to issue patents for it. After due consideration, the Board decided that it could not "with propriety and Policy either in respect to the largeness of the quantity, or the terms of the Proclamation of October 7, 1763," grant the petition.[369]

Croghan's claims needed immediate strengthening in 1768 when all three tracts were included in the Indian purchase made at Fort Stanwix. Johnson supported Croghan in securing the insertion of clauses renewing Croghan's grant in the deed for this purchase. The

dated 1762. The deed was dated Aug 2. Croghan did not arrive at Logstown till after August 12, when Céloron left, but the deed may have been drawn up beforehand. It might be that he used part of the provincial present to make the purchase. No copy of the deed dated 1749 was found, but the deed made out in 1768 quotes it at length. This deed was recorded in Philadelphia in 1769. (Register of Deeds, Bk. D, v, 239-242), in Augusta Co., Va., in 1775, at Pittsburg in 1775, and at Staunton, Va., in 1777.

This Indian purchase is frequently, but erroneously associated with Croghan's purchase of the Indian title to the Otsego patent in New York. The latter was made four months before the treaty at Fort Stanwix. This error is made in Halsey: *The Old New York Frontier*, 103; Halsey: *A Tour of Four Great Rivers*, etc., 36; *N.Y. Col. Docs.*, VII, 983n.; Craig, "George Croghan" in *Egle's Notes and Querries*, 3rd. ser., II, 348; Hanna: *Wilderness Trail*, II, 59; Byars: *B. and M. Gratz*, 90; and in *Ill. Hist. Coll.*, X, 221n.

[369] Croghan's Memorial, in C. O., 5: 1070, p. 531; Bd. of Tr. Journal, LXXII, 258, 278.

Iroquois included it in their cession to the King of England in trust "to and for the only Use, Benefit and Behoof of the said George Croghan" and stipulated that if any of the three tracts should fall within the limits of Pennsylvania that Croghan should be permitted to locate a corresponding amount elsewhere within the purchase. Croghan's grant was thus recognized by all the chiefs and colonial officials who signed the treaty.

Before Croghan's claim should become incontestable, however, this reservation and the entire treaty had to be confirmed by the crown. The treaty was first sent to the Board of Trade for study and recommendation. Delays now ensued. Lord Hillsborough referred in part to Croghan's grant when he criticized Johnson for "the improper conditions with which he has suffered the Cession from the Six Nations to be clogged. . ."[370] He also stated that Croghan's grant was too large for any subject in America. Gage felt that Croghan deserved consideration, but that to confirm his grant would set a precedent which would lead to endless difficulties. Finally, on May 13, 1769, Johnson was informed that the treaty was ratified, but that Croghan's grant was not included, but reserved for further consideration when he should make formal application. This Gage advised Croghan to do. The latter felt that he had made his purchase honestly and openly and that his services for twenty years deserved consideration. He therefore ignored the opinion of Hillsborough.[371]

After 1768, however, he acknowledged the fact that

---

[370] Hillsborough to Gage, March 24, 1769, in *Doc. Hist. of N.Y.*, II, 513.
[371] *Doc. Hist. of N.Y.*, II, 517, 938 and IV, 420; Johnson MSS., XVIII, 2, 268; Plan of the Manor of Pittsburg, *Pa. Arch.*, 3rd. ser., IV, No. 50.

the tract east of Pittsburg and the one on the Youghiogheny fell within Pennsylvania. The Penns laid
out the Manor of Pittsburg which respected one
of his tracts, but overlapped another, and they proceeded to sell two of his tracts. He applied to them
for title in fee simple to 4,700 acres falling within the
two easternmost tracts. Though he now tacitly
dropped his claims to these, he asserted his claim to the
third and largest tract. This he felt assured fell outside of Penn's grant and hence, as part of Virginia, it
belonged to the King who had not denied, but only
postponed consideration of Croghan's claims. But
above all, he relied on the establishment of a new
colony southwest of Pennsylvania to give him an incontestable title to it. His hopes now centered upon
the outcome of the struggle to secure the establishment
of a new colony along the upper Ohio.

Relations to Great Land Companies,
1763-1773

Croghan became a member of three important land companies – the Illinois Company, the Indiana Company, and the Grand Ohio Company. Eastern capitalists valued his membership highly because of his expert knowledge of western lands and because of his great influence with the Indians. His initiative and his inspiring faith in the West had an important bearing on the formation of these companies. He was responsible for the organization of the Illinois Company;[372] he was one of the two or three leaders who organized the Indiana Company, though he wisely kept in the background in this case; the Grand Ohio Company owed its rise largely to the influence of the Illinois and Indiana projects and its chief organizer, Samuel Wharton, owed much of his interest in the West to his past associations with Croghan.

The establishment of a colony in the northwest had been advocated in England as early as 1763. In 1764, while in London, Croghan's opinion on the project of some Englishmen to establish a colony in the Illinois country was sought by Lord Halifax and the former supported it before the Board of Trade.[373] The chief arguments advanced were that it would serve as an outpost on the furthest frontier against the French and

---

[372] William Franklin to Benjamin Franklin, Apr. 30, 1766, in *Ill. Hist. Coll.*, XI, 222.

[373] *Ill. Hist. Coll.*, X, 222, 260.

Spaniards, assist in controlling the Indians and in securing their trade, and provide provisions for the English garrison and for export. In opposition, it was argued at this and at later times that such a colony would lead to Indian wars, to troubles with the French and Spaniards, and draw settlers away from the seaboard into the interior. Here they could not buy English manufactured goods nor raise products England needed and they would be hard to govern.

When Croghan returned to America, he probably discussed the matter with Johnson and with his friends in Philadelphia. Little was known about the Illinois country when Croghan left on his first journey thither in 1765. He therefore kept a separate journal wherein he described minutely the nature of the country. The following are typical entries: "the Country [around Vincennes] is level and clear and the Soil very rich producing Wheat and Tobacco   I think the latter preferable to that of Maryland or Virginia." "we traveled thro a prodigious large Meadow [near the Wabash River] . . . here is no wood to be seen and the Country appears like an ocean the ground is exceedingly rich. . . The Land well watered and full of Buffuloes Deer Bears and all Kind of Wild Game. . . It is surprising what False information we have respecting this Country some mention this Spacious and Beautiful Meadows as large and Barren Savannahs I apprehend it has been the Artifice of the French to Keep us ignorant of the Country These Meadows bear fine Wild Grass and wild Hemp 10 or 12 Feet High which if properly Manufactured would prove as good and answer the Same purposes of the Hemp we cultivate." At the close of his journey he wrote to Benjamin Franklin that "The Illinois Country, far exceeds any other part of America, that I have seen – both as to Soil and Climate", and to Johnson he wrote that the colony would depend on Great Britain for clothing, but it would "soon be able, exclusive of provision, to raise readily indigo, sugar, cotton, oil, tobacco, rice, hemp and hops (the two latter of which grow spontaneously in many parts) and in time raw silk as the country abounds with immense quantities of white mulberry Trees." [374]

On his return from the Illinois country early in 1766, Croghan stopped at Johnson Hall and persuaded Johnson, who had been lukewarm, to write to the Board of Trade and in carefully chosen general terms, to recommend the establishment of a colony in Illinois. Croghan then went to New York to report to Gage; shortly afterwards, the latter was writing to Conway, the Secretary of War, concerning the military value of a colony in the Illinois country. Croghan and Johnson tried to interest Gage in their plan, but he always declined to participate in a colonizing project. Meantime, Croghan wrote a long letter to Benjamin Franklin who was in London and enclosed a copy of his journal and of his long explanatory letter to Johnson. From New York, Croghan went to Philadelphia to prepare for his second mission to the Illinois country.

Before leaving Philadelphia, he conferred with Governor Franklin, John Baynton, Samuel Wharton, George Morgan, Joseph Wharton, Joseph Wharton, Jr., John Hughes, and Joseph Galloway. As a result, on March 29, 1766, the "Articles of Agreement" [375] for the first Illinois Company were drawn up and signed

[374] Croghan's Journal, in *Ill. Hist. Coll.*, XI, 25, 32, 33, 34; Croghan to Franklin, Feb. 25, 1766, in C. O., 5: 66, p. 80; Croghan to Johnson, Dec. 27, 1765, in C. O., 5: 66, p. 76.

[375] Found in the Manuscript Division, Hist. Soc. of Pa.

by all of these men. Croghan also signed for Johnson. Benjamin Franklin, who had great influence in London, was invited to become a member and was given the right to add the names of two or three influential Englishmen. The original purpose was to apply for a royal grant of 1,200,000 acres in the Illinois country, but the establishment of a colony here of which these men should be proprietors was also considered. The fact that Johnson and Benjamin Franklin were members was kept secret.

All the members whose names had been made public now drew up a memorial to Johnson requesting his approbation. This gave him the opportunity to write Conway and to support the project with his great influence. Benjamin Franklin at once heartily supported the scheme. He saw Lord Shelburne and left with him Croghan's two long letters and his journal, together with two letters from William Franklin and a copy of Evan's *Map of the Middle Colonies* with the proposed colony marked off in red. It extended from the Wisconsin to the Ohio and from the Wabash to the Mississippi. Much depended upon Johnson's recommendation and upon Croghan's second mission. Franklin later dined with Conway and Shelburne and had the opportunity of presenting the matter in detail. Conway and Shelburne favored the project, but the Board of Trade could not be brought to recommend it. Factional politics in England in 1767 and 1768 caused such rapid changes in the ministry that Franklin's efforts were fruitless. By 1768, the project had to be given up because the ministry had definitely decided against the establishment of detached colonies in the interior, and in favor of moving the Indian boundary line westward. Croghan and his associates now shifted their main interest to the upper Ohio valley.[376]

Here the losses of the "Suff'ring Traders" provided a convenient basis for seeking a land grant. When Pontiac's uprising broke out, many traders who were scattered throughout the woods were massacred or taken captive and their goods seized. These goods had often been furnished on credit by eastern merchants. The two largest losers were the firms, Baynton and Wharton and Simon, Trent, Levy, and Franks. It was therefore natural that Samuel Wharton and William Trent should assume leadership in trying to secure restitution. Croghan, because of his intimate relations with these men and because of the desire to recoup his own losses of £4,500 in the uprising, assisted them as the third leader. Wharton and Trent at once presented a memorial to Amherst in New York. His sympathetic attitude encouraged them to attempt to secure payment of their claims by England.[377]

In December, 1763, Croghan, Trent, Wharton, Robert Callender, Jeremiah Warder, Thomas McKee, David Franks, and five other traders and merchants met at Indian Queen Tavern, Philadelphia, to form plans for securing restitution from England. These plans were made at this time because Croghan was about to leave for London. After many meetings and committee reports a majority agreed to engage Croghan and Moses Franks, a merchant in London, as agents; £210 sterling was raised for their expenses and they were guaranteed ten per cent of all money or land which might be secured. They were to present

---

[376] Franklin's *Works* (ed. Smyth), v, 45. The above account of Croghan's relation to the Illinois Company is based largely upon the documents found in the *Ill. Hist. Coll.*, XI, 198-574, *passim*.

[377] Prov. Pap., XXX, 90-110, *passim*.

a memorial in person to the Board of Trade in behalf of the traders and merchants who had incurred losses in 1754 or in 1763.   They sought the aid of Generals Amherst, Gage and Monckton, Colonel Bouquet, the governor, assembly and London agent of Pennsylvania, the Penns, Lord Halifax, and of all their correspondents in England, particularly those merchants who had extended credits for the goods lost and who might bring pressure to bear upon the Board of Trade or the Privy Council.   In spite of all efforts, the attempt to secure restitution in money failed.[378]

Upon Croghan's return, it was decided as a last resort to try to secure restitution through a land grant from the Six Nations.   Johnson, however, refused to demand from these tribes a grant for depredations committed by the French and their Indian allies in 1754, and thus forced a separation of the two groups. The plans for the organization of the "Suff'ring Traders" of 1763 were drawn up before Croghan left for the Illinois country in 1765.   The grant they sought became known as "Indiana" and those who sought it as the "Indiana Company".   This company was finally composed of twenty-three merchants and traders [379] with total claims amounting to £85,916, 16s. 8d.   Each

---

[378] The Minutes of the Philadelphia meeting, Instructions to Croghan and Franks, and the Memorial are found in the Johnson MSS., XXIV, 190-191. See also Bd. of Tr. Journal, LXXII, 259. The following incident is illuminating: Dartmouth, President of the Board of Trade, was a religious man influenced by the evangelistic movement of Wesley and Whitfield. Wharton sent a copy of the memorial to Whitfield, referred him to Franklin, and asked for his intercession with Dartmouth. — *Hist MSS. Commission of Gt. Br., Fourteenth Report, Appendix X*, II, 21, 74.

[379] They were Robert Callender, David Franks, Joseph Simon, William Trent, Levi A. Levy, Philip Boyle, John Baynton, George Morgan, Joseph Spear, Thomas Smallman, Samuel Wharton, John Welsh, Edmund Moran, Evan Shelby, Samuel Postlethwait, John Gibson, Richard Winston, Dennis Crohon, William Thompson, Abraham Mitchell, James Dundass, Thomas Dundass, and John Ormsby.

member's interest in the company was proportionate to his claim. The Jewish firm of Simon, Trent, Levy, and Franks and the Quaker firm of Baynton, Wharton, and Morgan controlled a majority of the shares. In 1765 and 1766, Trent, assisted by Wharton and Callender, secured from each member a detailed affidavit of his losses and the power of attorney to act for him.[380]

Croghan and Governor Franklin were also members of the Indiana Company from the very beginning, but this fact was kept secret. Croghan held 1,125 shares in his own name and 774 shares which Thomas Smallman had assigned to him. Croghan astutely kept in the background and worked through Trent. At various times from 1766 to 1769, he loaned Trent £1,319, 16s. to meet necessary expenses and to assist Trent personally, he made him a further loan of £1,500 secured by mortgages on Trent's Pennsylvania lands.[381]

Meanwhile, Croghan and Johnson were laboring with the Indians in private and in public conferences. At Johnson Hall in 1765, the Delawares, Shawnee, and Mingoes agreed to make restitution in lands to the traders whom they had attacked. Johnson reported this to the Board of Trade and Croghan informed Benjamin Franklin and asked his support.[382]

In 1768, when the news came that Johnson had re-

---

[380] *Lancaster Co. Hist. Soc. Papers*, IX, 10ff.; Ohio Co. MSS., I, 15, 16, 40-43, 51.

[381] Thomas Wharton's Indiana Co. MSS.; Croghan-Trent Accounts, in McAllister Coll., 7309, F10; Croghan-Trent Accounts, Dec. 26, 1772, in the library of the Hist. Soc. of Pa.

[382] *N.Y. Col. Docs.*, VII, 724ff.; Croghan to Franklin, Feb. 25, 1766, in C. O., 5: 66 p. 80. It is self-evident that Franklin was not thinking solely of the Stamp Act affair in 1765 and 1766. A somewhat similar scheme worked out successfully in the Southern District. Here traders and land speculators persuaded the Creeks and Cherokees at a conference at Augusta in 1773, to cede a tract of land to the King to be sold by him to pay their debts to the traders. – Wharton: *Plain Facts*, 64.

ceived orders to negotiate a new Indian boundary line, Wharton and Trent at once acted. June found Johnson at the seaside in Connecticut for his health and thither they went.[383] Croghan was also there and together they laid plans for securing a land grant. Much of the summer and autumn was spent by these men among the Iroquois in New York. Later, Governor Franklin came as the official representative of New Jersey and doubtless assisted them. Presents were effectively used with the chiefs. As a result, two days before the treaty at Fort Stanwix, a deed was drawn up ceding to the King, but in trust for the "Suff'ring Traders", about 2,500,000 acres bounded by the parallel marking the southern boundary of Pennsylvania, by the Ohio, the Little Kanawha and the Monongahela, and by a somewhat indefinite line on the southeast. The tract was favorably located for navigation and for early settlement.

The Indiana grant, like Croghan's grant, was incorporated into the final treaty. The protest of the Virginia commissioners went unheeded, but augured ill for the future. After the treaty, Trent wrote to a friend: "We are all greatly indebted to the uncommon kindness of Sir Wm Johnson and Mr. Croghan." [384]

[383] Wharton to Franklin, Dec. 2, 1768, in Franklin MSS., XLIX, 77, Samuel Wharton to Thomas Wharton, June 23, 1768, in Thomas Wharton MSS. Samuel Wharton wrote to his brother: "I have not had Leisure enough to scarcely write to my wife. . . I ardently sigh for *Home*:–But if the Revolution of Our Affairs, depended On a Seven Year Banishment I would relinquish all the Endearments of the Hymenial State–And acquiesce patiently to it.–This However, I am thoroughly convinced, There will be no Occasion for,– as I have a moral Certainty of suceeding in an object– not of a very trivial Nature." Little did Wharton and Trent realize that "years of banishment" were ahead of them.

[384] Ohio Co. MSS., I, 53. Johnson in his official report stated that he believed the grant was freely made without any influence being brought to bear, certainly none through him. Some shares belonging to the firm of Baynton and Wharton were entrusted to Croghan for use at Fort Stan-

As in the case of Croghan's grant, Hillsborough was successful in preventing royal confirmation when the treaty was ratified.   The hope of future confirmation, however, remained and it was soon decided that Wharton and Trent should proceed to London to attempt to secure such confirmation.   A small inner circle of five, Croghan being one, signed an agreement to contribute a large sum for their expenses.   Croghan's share for the first year was over £300.[385]   The efforts of a few unfortunate traders and merchants to secure restitution were thus involving ever widening circles of interests; individual fortunes were becoming inextricably involved; none foresaw the far-reaching political results that were entailed.

Not all claimants were satisfied with the plans of Wharton and Trent.   Some of the wealthy merchants had purchased the claims of traders at speculative prices, much as Washington was buying up the land bounty claims of Virginia soldiers.   There were of course many persons who had suffered losses who were not included in the Indiana Company.   One of the heaviest losers who was not included was Alexander

wix. He offered some to Guy Johnson, but the latter thought it wise not to accept them. Croghan returned them to Wharton in order that he might do "the needful" with them in England. Wharton, however, took them over in his own name. Baynton, disgusted with the whole matter wrote to Croghan: "I want all these Matters to be buried in total Oblivion." After Baynton's death George Morgan tried to secure an accounting of these shares from Croghan and Wharton. – Baynton to Croghan, Feb. 4, 1770 and to Abel James, Jan. 3, 1770, in Baynton's Private Letter Bk.; Morgan to Croghan Aug. 7, 1773, and to Wharton, Dec. 1, 1773, in Baynton, Wharton, and Morgan's Letter Bk. A.

385 Ohio Co. MSS., I, 56. For the subsequent activities of all claimants see pages 51-97, *passim*, and II, 20. While Trent was in England his wife and five children lived in penury in Trenton, New Jersey. Croghan and the Whartons assisted her at times. In the Ohio Co. MSS., I, 104, there is a list of Wharton and Trent's expenses totaling £8,600, but Croghan's name is not given among the contributors.

Lowrey. When he threatened to make trouble, Croghan, Trent, and Wharton quietly agreed to purchase his claim, payment to be made after royal confirmation. Others, who were not placated, referred to Trent and his associates as "a certain Junto who . . . have lately pursued such Indirect, Fraudulent, and Selfish Schemes, and have so embarrassed and confounded the whole matter. . ."[386] Some of these determined to oppose with all their strength the plans of the Indiana Company. They sent a memorial to the King in Council asking that no lands be granted unless all claims for losses incurred from 1750 to 1763 be carefully examined and, if found worthy, included; it also asked that the interests of prospective settlers be protected from scheming speculators.

Wharton and Trent finally arranged to make some concessions to the claimants of 1754. Trent secured a renewal of his power of attorney from a select group in which Croghan was included. Funds were again raised and Moses Franks of New York was sent to present a memorial to the Board of Trade. This memorial did not oppose the Indiana grant, but asked for a similiar grant. Franks presented the memorial in 1771, but failed to secure action upon it.[387]

After their arrival in London, Wharton and Trent also encountered competition from groups and companies from Virginia seeking grants in which influential Englishmen were financially interested. Wharton and Trent soon realized that if they followed their original plans failure was foreordained. To overcome

[386] Adam Hoops and William Buchanan to General Monckton, Feb. 22, 1769, in *Mass. Hist. Coll.*, *4th ser.*, X, 605.

[387] Frank's Memorial, in C. O., 5: 114, p. 236; *Acts of the Privy Council, Colonial Ser.*, 1766-1783, 601; Acts of the Privy Council, June 9, 1769, II, 114, p. 44.

their competitors and the opposition of the anti-expansionists they organized the "Walpole Company" to buy 2,500,000 acres on the Ohio. Benjamin Franklin actively assisted them and many Englishmen of wealth and official position were included as members. On December 27, 1769, this company was reorganized as the Grand Ohio Company.[388] It petitioned for the establishment of a new colony, later known as Vandalia. It was bounded on the north by the Ohio and by the southern and western boundaries of Pennsylvania, on the east by an irregular line in the Appalachians, on the south by North Carolina, and on the west by the Kentucky River. All the lands in this colony were to be purchased from the government. The establishment of such a colony would thus sever Virginia's direct contact with the West and the plans of the planters of Virginia to exploit this vast region would be wrecked.

Most of the seventy-two shares of the company were distributed among Englishmen, but Croghan, Johnson, the two Franklin's, the four Wharton's, and Trent were among the Americans included.[389] Croghan was

[388] For a detailed account of this company and its project for the establishment of Vandalia during the years 1769 to 1774, see Alvord: *Mississippi Valley in British Politics.*

[389] Wharton's old partners, Baynton and Morgan, were bitterly disappointed because he did not include them. A feud resulted which was to divide the Indiana Company into hostile groups. Both tried to secure Croghan's support. Morgan felt that it was unjust for Wharton to be enjoying the festivities of London society, while he exposed his life on dismal ventures in the Illinois country. He blamed Croghan for advising the firm to enter Illinois and wrote to him asking whether he did not deem himself responsible for one-fourth of their losses. Morgan also wrote: "With regard to that contemptible *Wretch Trent,* my Treatment of him will depend on your Conduct; for of himself he is not worth giving a Kick in the Breech to, or a Pull by the Nose." Later, Morgan challenged Trent to a duel. To Wharton he wrote: "Mr. Baynton lies at the point of Death and attributes the Cause to your ill Usage of him". He also

allotted two shares and it was agreed that the Indian grants made at Fort Stanwix to him and to the "Suff'ring Traders" should be located within the new colony. In order to placate opposition, provision was also made for the Ohio Company of Virginia, for Virginia soldiers who had been promised land bounties in 1754 by Governor Dinwiddie, and for pioneers already settled within the proposed colony. Croghan became enthusiastic as news kept coming from London; in a letter to Johnson he said: "By the best accounts I can larn the limits of the new grant will contain thirty od millians of ac^{rs} and the offise will open att £10 Sterling per hundred and a half penny per a^r quit-rent which will make a handsome division to the 72." [390]

After the new company's plans were formulated an enormous amount of influence was brought to bear upon the ministry and court under the skillful general-ship of Wharton. This cost the members approxi-mately £20,000. The opposition of men who favored the Virginia group, particularly Lord Hillsborough, president of the Board of Trade, delayed action in 1770 and 1771, but finally Wharton's manoeuvers forced Hillsborough's resignation in 1772. On Aug-ust 14, his successor, Lord Dartmouth, was ordered by the Privy Council to prepare detailed plans for the establishment of the new colony. On September 2, orders were dispatched to Johnson and Stuart to notify and prepare the Indians for its establishment. Further ominous delays ensued, but in 1773 the Privy Council decisively ordered the attorney-general and the solici-

accused Wharton of sacrificing his firm to become governor of Vandalia so that his enemies would "fall down and worship the rising Sun". — Entries for 1772-1774 in Baynton, Wharton, and Morgan's Letter Bk. A.

[390] Croghan to Johnson, Dec. 24, 1772, in Johnson MSS., XXV, 188.

tor-general to draw up the charter to be passed under the great seal of Great Britain.

During the years 1769 to 1773, many Americans manifested as much interest in the developments associated with Vandalia as in the Townshend Acts or the Boston Massacre. In spite of friction between England and America few dreamed of separation. Hence, to those whose interests were concerned, the establishment of a new colony over-shadowed other portending events. Both reliable news and all rumors from London concerning Vandalia were received with the utmost avidity. Perhaps no individual had relatively more at stake than did Croghan. To raise his share of the expenses involved he had mortgaged much of his property; success would insure to him a legal title to his 200,000 acre Indian grant near Pittsburg and to his share of the trader's grant, as well as a further interest in all the lands included in the new colony and the probability of a lucrative office in its government. Of the Virginia group probably none followed developments with a keener interest than George Washington. His plans to secure thousands of acres of new lands within the proposed limits of Vandalia were in jeopardy. He wrote Governor Botetourt on October 5, 1770, that the granting of a charter for Vandalia "will give a fatal blow, in my humble opinion, to the interests of this country." Such were some of the reactions in America of the conflict over Vandalia in London during these years.

The prospects for the establishment of the new colony increased year by year from 1770 to 1773. Soon there promised to be available all the offices needed in a colony and place hunters began to plan to secure them. "I flatter myself you will not forget us among your old friends if anything should offer", wrote Barnard Gratz to Croghan.[391] Washington sought Croghan's influence to secure a position as surveyor for William Crawford, his land agent on the Ohio.[392] Croghan, himself, expected a major office. Washington also began negotiations to purchase Croghan's two shares in the Grand Ohio Company. "My last Leters from England was the 5th of June w^h Leves No Doubt butt the New Charter Government wold be Confirm^d in Some Days after", wrote Croghan to Washington on August 18, 1771. On December 6, in a letter to Crawford, Washington said: "I believe, from what I have lately heard, that there is no doubt now of the charter government taking place on the Ohio; but upon what terms, or how lands will be granted to the people, I have not been able to learn." [393] Making the best of the situation he instructed his agent, Captain Bullitt, to locate and survey 10,000 acres as near to the western boundary of Vandalia as possible, and in advertising for sale 20,000 acres on the Great Kanawha, Washington took pains to point out that they were near the probable location of the capital of Vandalia.[394]

On May 15, 1773, William Murray wrote to the Gratzs from Pittsburg: "I was yesterday at Mr. Croghan's who inform'd me That the New Colony was

[391] Byars: B. and M. Gratz, 134.

[392] Washington to Croghan, Nov. 24, 1770, in Washington MSS., XII, 1469; Croghan to Washington, Aug. 18, 1771, in idem, 1558. Robert L. Hooper, employed by Croghan as surveyor, enlisted the influence of Croghan, Johnson, and Franklin for securing the office of Surveyor-General. – Johnson MSS., XX, 91. Lord Dartmouth had various applicants for the governorship, but offered it to Major Legge, his relative, at £1,000 salary. – Hist. MSS. Commission of Gt. Br., Eleventh Report, Appendix v, 335, and Fourteenth Report, Appendix x, vol. II, 94, 95, 188.

[393] Croghan to Washington, Aug. 18, 1771, in Hamilton: Letters to Washington, IV, 79; Washington to Crawford, Dec. 6, 1771, in Writings, II, 347.

[394] Maryland Journal and Baltimore Advertiser, Aug. 20, 1773.

fixed, Trent immediately expected and the Governor to be over in June." [395]   A few months later, Croghan was assured in the strongest terms by the promoters in London that everything was settled and that the charter would pass the seals in a few days.[396]   Croghan made arrangements to grant lands, which he expected would sell at £10 per 100 acres as fast as they could be surveyed, and he planned to erect houses for the governor, chief-justice, and other officials at Pittsburg, which was claimed to lie 12¾ miles outside of Pennsylvania. He also arranged to plant seeds imported from China – two kinds of indigo, white hemp, two kinds of Bohea tea, etc. – to see whether they could profitably be grown in Vandalia.

In the Spring of 1773, Samuel Wharton and several other associates instructed Croghan to invite the Indians to meet the new governor at a conference to be held in the fall.   Croghan was informed that presents would be forwarded from England for the occasion. In response to his invitation, chiefs from seven different nations began to assemble at Pittsburg in October, and by December four hundred Indians were present.   But Croghan found himself in a predicament when neither governor nor presents appeared.   There was a possibility that the success of the infant colony would be prejudiced and that Croghan's personal influence with the Indians would be seriously undermined.   Moreover, the general Indian situation was unfavorable because Virginians were going down the Ohio and settling lands which the Indians had been promised would not be settled; Gage and Johnson were distributing almost no presents; the Quaker province

---

[395] Ohio Co. MSS., I, 102.

[396] Croghan to Thomas Wharton, Dec. 9, 1773, in *Pa. Mag. of Hist. and Biog.*, XV, 437.

was giving scarcely any attention to the Indians; and finally, the frontiersmen were still murdering Indians.

Croghan decided to act, as he had so frequently acted before under similar circumstances, trusting that the proprietors of the new colony would not let him suffer personal loss. He supplied provisions out of his own private stock; on October 15, he observed that the Indians "are Eating up everything I had provided for the use of my family this Winter." The inhabitants of Pittsburg became alarmed and held Croghan responsible for the situation which they tried to ease by donating provisions and clothing. Croghan secured some goods for presents from Joseph Simon; and finally, he pawned his plate and other valuables to purchase additional provisions. As a result of his efforts, the Indians left much better satisfied than anyone had expected. Croghan was partially reimbursed, but as late as 1775 he was still trying to secure repayment from Trent, Wharton, and the English noblemen.[397]

The year 1773 thus saw Croghan's fortunes at their zenith. Throughout the years 1768 to 1773 he had brilliant prospects for becoming as great a landowner as Sir William Johnson, Lord Fairfax, or George Washington. He possessed houses and lots in Philadelphia, Bedford, and Pittsburg. He had legal title to thousands of acres of choice lands in Pennsylvania and New York on the settler's frontier where the westward migration was causing land values to rise rapidly. He had excellent prospects for securing a legal title to

---

[397] *Pa. Mag. of Hist. and Biog.*, XV, 433-439, and XXXIII, 320-322; Craig, *Ye Olden Time*, II, 9; Gratz-Croghan MSS., I, 33; Ohio Co. MSS., II, 6; Thomas Wharton's Letter Bk., 1773-1784. Thomas Walpole sent to Lord Dartmouth a polished and somewhat garbled copy of one of Croghan's letters describing the Indian situation and urging action. – *Hist. MSS. Commission of Gt. Br., Eleventh Report, Appendix* V, 360.

his 200,000 acre Indian grant on the Ohio, as well as to his share of the Indiana grant of 2,500,000 acres. Most promising of all, however, was the apparent certainty of the establishment of the new colony of Vandalia containing over 20,000,000 acres in which Croghan had a proprietary share and where, as the western representative of the Grand Ohio Company, he was certain to have large political influence.

Business Activities; Sale of New York and Ohio Lands

The belief in the certainty of the establishment of Vandalia was of fundamental importance in Croghan's business activities. His land projects all required a large amount of liquid capital. He had his share of the heavy expenses entailed in organizing the Indiana Company, in securing the grant of "Indiana" from the Indians, and in seeking a charter for Vandalia. Patenting his Pennsylvania lands required money. Purchasing the Indian title to his Otsego tract in New York cost about £6 per 1,000 acres; surveying and patenting it cost about £30 per 1,000 acres – a total of £3,600. His improvements upon it and his adjacent purchases caused the initial cost of his New York lands to approximate £10,000. To market these lands required additional capital.

The fact that Croghan had no money and that he was deeply in debt did not deter him in the least. His implicit faith in the future greatness of the West convinced him that he was making fortunes both for himself and for all those concerned with him. Part of this enthusiastic conviction he imparted to his creditors. He practiced a system of finance very much like that which was used to build railroads in the West after the Civil War; he "bonded" his great ideas when he could and mortgaged any property which represented them, in order to secure capital for further "development".

To illustrate: on December 12, 1768, he paid the £500 mortgage held by Thomas Wharton on three houses and four acres of land in Philadelphia; the next day he purchased fourteen acres of adjacent land and on the same day he mortgaged the entire property for £1,200 to Governor Franklin.[398] At the same time that many of his lands were being sold by sheriffs to pay his debts, he was pawning personal property at Pittsburg in order to further the interests of Vandalia and using some of his own ready money and borrowing in Virginia to make an Indian purchase of 6,000,000 acres on the Ohio, and only regretted that he did not have more capital at his command so that he could purchase more land. ". . . could I get Money on Interest at Ten p cent I should make thirty p cent by keeping my Lands but three years", he wrote to Thomas Wharton on June 21, 1769.[399] Croghan was not dishonest. He usually met all his just debts, but he did so very tardily. Creditors learned to watch the times when he received money in order to collect before he could invest it again in lands.

Before 1768, Croghan's eastern factors had been Baynton, Wharton, and Morgan. Later, his eastern factors were Barnard and Michael Gratz, Jewish merchants in Lancaster and Philadelphia; they were to remain his trusted bankers, faithful legal agents, and intimate friends till his death. They drew up and kept his legal documents; through them his bills and debts were paid; they made long journeys and spent much time in serving as his land agents; they loaned him money at a reasonable rate of interest when he needed

---

[398] Legal Memorandum, in McAllister Coll., 7309, FIO.

[399] *Pa. Mag. of Hist. and Biog.*, XV, 431. Compare Byars, William V.: "The Proprietors of Indiana as Pioneers of the Continental United States," in Gratz Pap., 1st ser., VII, 106-136.

it and as a result, he was nearly always in debt to them for several thousand pounds; from 1768 to 1773, the total of their loans amounted to £16,000; they also received and forwarded much of his mail; to satisfy his personal wants on the frontier they shipped to him salt, sugar, spices, salt fish, fine liquors, clothing, hats, bridles, paper, and glass; and finally, they continually filled his orders for Indian goods. In return for these services, Croghan aided them in their land operations and in their trading relations with the Indians; he usually paid them by conveying to them large tracts of his lands.[400]

Croghan secured his capital in such centers as New York, Albany, Philadelphia, Lancaster, and Burlington. His old friends and associates, such as Joseph, Thomas and Charles Wharton, Governor Franklin, Richard Peters, and the Gratzs, advanced him large sums. The Coldens and Goldsborrow Banyer of New York, William Peters, John Morton, and Dr. John Morgan of Philadelphia, and a group of eight investors from Burlington known as the "Burlington Company", were more exacting in their loans. Governor Franklin, in 1768, aided Croghan to secure from this company a loan of £3,000 for three years to enable him to patent his Otsego tract in New York; in return, Croghan sold at cost to Franklin and some associates his Indian purchase, "Otego", located southwest of the Otsego tract. When this proved to be too small to give Franklin the amount guaranteed to him, Croghan conveyed to him 51,000 acres out of his adjacent Otsego and Butler holdings. The Burlington Company refused to deal with Croghan except through Franklin.

---

[400] These generalizations concerning the relations of Croghan to the Gratzs are based chiefly upon documents in the Gratz-Croghan MSS., Ohio Co. MSS., and in Michael Gratz's Letter Book.

On December 13, 1768, Croghan therefore temporarily mortgaged his Otsego Indian purchase to Franklin and then took out his patent to it. After this was done he mortgaged to Franklin his houses and eighteen acres of land near Philadelphia and also 40,000 acres of his Otsego tract. Franklin then assigned these mortgages to the company and, as additional security, he gave his personal bond to cover the loan. This was to cost him dearly in later years. Richard Peters, who had long been trying to secure from Croghan the payment of a debt, was quietly informed by one of the members of the company when the money was paid and so secured part of the £3,000 which Croghan had planned to use in New York. Croghan's various loans from 1767 to 1770 totaled approximately £15,000 and were secured by bonds and mortgages based chiefly upon his New York lands. Unfortunately, nearly all of these debts fell due within from one to three years, during which period he expected that the Indiana and Vandalia projects would materialize.[401]

The wide extent of Croghan's investments in 1769 and 1770, the failure of some expected funds to come in, particularly certain large sums owed by John and

---

[401] Information from R. Wells, etc. and Franklin's Affidavit, 1811, in the Wm. Temple Franklin MSS.; Mortgage Bk., III, 66ff., Clerk's Office, Albany Co.; N.Y. Council Minutes, XXIX, 13, 343; N.Y. Land Pap., XXV, 97. The 10 shares of the Burlington Company were originally distributed as follows:

Richard Wells	3 shares	£900
Dr. Moore	1 share	300
Henry Hill	1 share	300
James Veree	1 share	300
Joseph Fox	1 share	300
Abigail Smith (Mrs. Geo. Browne)	1 share	300
Joseph Smith	1 share	300
Richard Smith	1 share	300

The name "Burlington Company" was also applied to the owners of the Otego patent of 69,000 acres.

Thomas Shipboy, merchants in New York, together
with the slow progress of the Indiana and Vandalia projects in London, soon showed how Croghan was strain-
ing his resources. On November 30, 1769, he wrote
to his old partner, William Trent: ". . . the only
Method [which] is Left to Save my Estate hear and
yr own [which] is Morgidgd to the Burlington Company is to Sell my Grants or mortgidge them in England . . ." At this time Croghan intended to sell
all his lands in Pennsylvania together with his interests
in the Indiana and Vandalia projects, keeping his New
York lands to the last. ". . . if this Cant be Don",
continued Croghan, "all that you and I have in this
part of the World is Intierly gon and our Ruin Completely finished . . ." [402] On February 20, 1770,
John Baynton wrote to his partner, Samuel Wharton
concerning Croghan: ". . . his present Embar-
rassments, are as great and pressing as they have been
for many years past. [1754-1756] I heartily wish he
may retain as many of them as may in a few years
hence, sell for as much as may enable him, to live according to the Elegance of his Desires and the Noble-
ness of his disposition." [403]

During the year 1770, Croghan sold approximately
152,000 acres out of his 250,000 acres in New York.
He sold the Skinner patent of 40,000 acres, the Butler
patent of 47,000 acres, and 65,000 acres out of his Otsego tract. For these he received nearly £10,000.
His purchasers were usually his creditors or his
friends; Governor Franklin, Governor Colden, David
Colden, Stephen Skinner, Prevost, Michael Gratz, V.
P. Dow, L. Moore, and the Whartons were the chief

[402] Gratz-Croghan MSS., I, 18; Johnson MSS., XVIII, 231.
[403] Baynton's Private Letter Bk.

purchasers. Although Croghan had held these lands
less than a year and had sold them under unfavorable
circumstances, he nevertheless realized a large profit.
Though he was still heavily in debt, he hoped to postpone foreclosure on his remaining 100,000 acres in
New York until Vandalia was established. To it he
pinned all his hopes, for its establishment would enable
him to pay off all his debts and mortgages. So promising was the outlook for Vandalia that most of his
creditors were willing to wait until 1772; some, like
Dr. John Morgan, demanded payment of their bonds
on the exact day when they were due and a few, like
the Burlington Company, desired to take advantage of
his plight in order to secure his lands at a low price at
a forced sale. Those who held second mortgages
favored postponement, at least until the lands could be
sold privately.[404]

To meet this situation, Croghan, in 1772, gave Barnard Gratz full power of attorney to act as his agent.
He wrote to Gratz: "I am anxious to pay Every
person as Soon as I can. . ."[405] "I am Determined
to Sell all the Lands I have in New York Government
and rely on you to Do itt."[406] Gratz met the chief
creditors and they agreed to postpone foreclosure until
September 1, 1773, to enable him to sell Croghan's
lands privately. Gratz advertised them and then
journeyed to Albany, Schenectady, Johnstown, and
Kinderhook to meet prospective purchasers. Croghan

[404] Bk. of Deeds (Sec. of State, Albany), XVIII, 281-285, 293-297, 371-381;
XIX, 20-31; XXX, 353-355; Deed Bk. (Clerk's Office, Albany Co.), VIII, 182-
189, 459-461; Ohio Co. MSS., I, 83; II, 100; Baynton to Croghan, Jan. 20
and Feb. 4, 1770, in Baynton's Private Letter Bk.; George Morgan to
Croghan, Aug. 5, 1772, in Letter Bk. A, of Baynton, Wharton, and Morgan.
[405] Croghan to B. Gratz, July 7, 1772, in Gratz-Croghan MSS., I, 29;
idem, 32.
[406] Croghan to B. Gratz, Aug. 26, 1772, in Simon Gratz Coll.

eagerly awaited the outcome. "I hope he will be able
to make Some Sals if Not all, to Liten my Burden",
Croghan wrote to Michael Gratz on July 29, 1773.[407]
No purchasers appeared, however, to offer the mini-
mum price agreed upon.

When Gratz returned he met the creditors and asked
for another year in which to advertise and sell the
lands, but was refused. It was, however, agreed that
the lands should first be surveyed into 1,000 acre tracts
before being offered for sale by the sheriff.[408]   Croghan
felt happy when he heard of this and he instructed
Gratz to delay matters as long as the New York law
would allow, for the prospects for Vandalia were so
bright that he felt sure that it would be established
before the sale could be arranged. On September 8,
1773, he wrote to Gratz: ". . . for if Mr. Wharton should sail from England in July as I have the
Greatest assurance he was, . . . I am Certain in
a mounth after his ariveal I shall be able to pay peters
of, the Mordiges Likewise, and protected bills as he
and Trent is fully prepair^d to Do itt, this with what I
can sell hear, on the Govern^ts being Establish^d will
before Crismas Make me a free man. . ."[409] Soon
this feeling of assurance was changed to such a strong
feeling of anxiety among those most interested that
Thomas Wharton stated in a letter to a friend in England: "I hope the Vandalia Affairs are settled, and
that a Matter of so great Consequence is no longer
hanging by the Eyelids."[410]

[407] Croghan to M. Gratz, July 29, 1773, in Simon Gratz Coll. See also,
Ohio Co. MSS., I, 87, 93, 103.

[408] B. Gratz to Croghan, Aug. 1, 1773, in McAllister Coll.

[409] Croghan to B. Gratz, Sept. 8, 1773, in Gratz-Croghan MSS., I, 33.

[410] Wharton to Thomas Walpole, Jan. 31, 1774, in Thomas Wharton's
Letter Bk., 1773-1784.

The turning point soon came, however. The prospects for Vandalia had reached their zenith in 1773 and declined so rapidly that by the end of that year it was reported even at Pittsburg that the new colony would not be established. In a letter written at Pittsburg on June 7, 1774, to Washington, Dr. John Connolly said: ". . . the great Government Scheme is blown over; which like the Mountain in labor has bro't forth a Mouse." [411] To Washington and his fellow Virginia land speculators it meant fortunes won; but to a large group of men including Benjamin Franklin, Governor Franklin, Samuel Wharton, William Trent, and George Croghan, it meant the loss of fortunes, almost won. By 1774, Croghan therefore ceased all efforts to delay the foreclosure of his New York lands and gave up his plan of spending his last years upon the shores of Lake Otsego. One can imagine his feelings when, on September 24, 1774, he wrote to Gratz: "I main to Sell the ottsego Tract and gett Don with that part of the Country." [412] "He is so Exceedingly Embarrassed", wrote Thomas Wharton to Samuel Wharton, "that any step you can take to throw matters fairly in his way will be useful to him."

Gratz again journeyed to New York in November, 1774, to attend the sheriff's sale. He hoped to save Croghan's remaining Otsego lands and to protect the titles of the lands which Croghan had conveyed to others. Unfortunately, the news of Sir William Johnson's death came just the day before the sale and this had a depressing effect upon the price of frontier lands.

[411] Hamilton: *Letters to Washington*, v, 9.

[412] Gratz-Croghan MSS., I, 38. Prevost wrote Gratz from Jamaica on November 22, 1774, of "those Confounded matters to the Northward" and prepared to be ready to buy his 6,061 acres should it be placed on sale, even if it meant selling his commission in the army.

McKee's patent of 40,000 acres, one half of Belvedere
consisting of 9,000 acres, and the 1,893 acres on the
Schoharie were sold in tracts of approximately 1,000
acres each.   These 50,893 acres brought £4,840 which
was sufficient to pay William Peters's judgment of
£2,000 with interest, Banyer's mortgage of £840, and
still leave £1,000 for other creditors.   Croghan paid
Gratz £242 for his services and thanked him.   Gratz
felt elated over the outcome, for he had saved not only
Croghan's remaining Otsego lands and 9,000 acres in
Belvedere, but also the 9,050 acres in Butler's patent
which Croghan had conveyed to him.   In 1774, Croghan had his remaining Otsego lands surveyed into
twenty-nine tracts of approximately one thousand acres
each.[413]

In April, 1775, Croghan entered into an agreement
whereby his Otsego lands were to be sold to meet Governor Franklin's judgment of £3,000, Morton's judgment of £5,000, and Thomas Wharton's mortgage of
£2,000.   He again instructed Barnard Gratz to sell
these lands either privately or through a sheriff.   Before this could be done, events which Croghan had not
foreseen, were taking place at Lexington, Concord, and
Bunker Hill which saved these lands for a few more
years and which were to render frontier lands in New
York almost unmarketable for a number of years.
The border warfare with the Iroquois during the Revolution postponed the rise in land values around Lake

---

[413] B. Gratz to M. Gratz, June 3, 1774 in McAllister Coll.; Bk. of Deeds
(Sec. of State, Albany), L, 163-168; Peters MSS., VI, 86, 89; Ohio Co. MSS., I,
103, 110, 111, 113, and II, 1, 26, 100; Sheriff White's deed to Duryee in the
library of the N.Y. Hist. Soc.   White proved to be corrupt and was later
imprisoned.   M. Gratz wrote to his brother on May 3, 1776: ". . . [I]
would, at present, not Say anything about it to Col. Croghan as Can do
him no good, but Frett him for he Can have no Satisfaction by Law. . ."
– Ohio Co. MSS., II, 21.

Otsego and Cherry valley until after 1783. Many of the New York patriots, who were massacred in Cherry valley or who helped drive back the Indians and tories, had settled on the frontier largely through the direct or indirect influence of Croghan.[414]

In addition to selling most of his New York lands, Croghan mortgaged Croghan Hall to Joseph Simon and sold some of his Pennsylvania lands. He also sold 1,125 shares in the Indiana Company to Joseph Galloway, keeping only 774 shares. Of the lands to which these 774 shares purported to give title, Croghan placed on sale 20,000 acres.

The other large, potential asset upon which Croghan tried to realize during the critical years, 1769 to 1775, consisted of his 200,000 acre Indian grant on the Ohio. Until royal confirmation should be specifically refused, or Vandalia's establishment rejected, or Pennsylvania's western boundary definitely marked, Croghan's claim to the land southwest of Pittsburg could not be overthrown. His Indian title and his improvements gave him a strong occupying claimant's preëmptive right. Until 1774, the strong probability of the establishment of Vandalia made the purchase of these lands a good speculative investment, though both Pennsylvania and Virginia were also disposing of the same lands.

Before offering these lands for sale, Croghan had them surveyed into townships and then into rectilinear tracts, 1,000 acres in extent. He refused to accomodate purchasers by surveying irregular tracts to include only good land, as was the custom in many colonies. His chief surveyors during the period 1770 to 1775

---

[414] Cooper, James Fenimore: *Chronicles of Cooperstown*, Chapter 1; *Pa. Gazette*, May 3, 1786; Brant MSS., 13 F 103, 1 F 24.

were William Thompson, John Campbell, Robert Lettis Hooper, and Dorsey Pentecost.

Disputes soon arose as to the location of the southwestern boundary line of Croghan's grant. His Indian deed stated it to be a straight line running from a point ten miles up Racoon Creek to the mouth of Thompson's run on the Monongahela opposite Turtle Creek. Did this mean ten miles as a bird flies or as indicated by the meanders of Racoon Creek? What was to be done if the line included more or less than the 100,000 acres called for in the deed? The Indians at Fort Stanwix had stipulated that if any portion of their grant fell within the limits of Pennsylvania, Croghan should be permitted to locate an equal quantity elsewhere in their cession. Two tracts totaling 100,000 acres fell within Pennsylvania. Should the boundary line of the third tract be shifted to compensate for this loss?

The legality of the line troubled Croghan but little. His first surveyor, Captain Thompson, ran the line in accordance with the deed, but when Croghan saw the survey he said it was not run right and employed Campbell to run it. When Campbell brought in his survey, Croghan remonstrated that they should have allowed him ten degrees for the variation of the compass. He then instructed Hooper to run the line. Hooper's line took in four times the amount called for by the deed. Finally, Croghan had his surveyors at work as far west as Wheeling Creek where others stopped their work. If he saw some excellent land he would push out his boundary to include it. Captain William Crawford reported to Washington for whom he was laying out claims in the same region:

"I have not told him where the Land Lys and I am
Afraid to tell him till he Runs the Line for I think if
he new of it he would run it in one purpose to have the
Seling of it to you. . ." [415]

The land which Croghan had surveyed was hilly,
but the soil was rich and mill sites were plentiful. His
surveys were soon cut up by surveyors laying out warrants issued by the Penns; and both of these sets of surveys were cut up by Virginia surveyors. To add to
the confusion squatters were so active that Crawford
reported to Washington in 1772: "There will be [no]
Posability of taking up such a Quantity as you want
near Fort pitt as there is such numbers of People out
now Looking for Land and one taking Each other"
Land from him as soon as a man" back is turn" an other
is on his Land the man that is strong and able to make
Other" Afraid of him Seem" to have the best Chance as
tim" go now." "I do not find I can get you the Quantity of Land . . . without I cold stay all Summer
and be on the spot as People Crowd out in such numbers the Like never was seen." [416]

In spite of this situation, Croghan opened a land
office at Pittsburg in 1770 and began selling his lands
to anyone who would buy. He offered to sell at £10
sterling per 100 acres, to be paid when Croghan could
give a good title, plus the cost of surveying to be paid
in cash; this cost amounted to £6 per 1,000 acres. If,
however, the purchaser would waive the guarantee,
Croghan offered to sell at £5 cash per 100 acres. He
soon took in several thousand pounds cash. Within
a year sixty families were settled on his lands. Repre-

[415] Crawford to Washington, Apr. 20, 1771, in Hamilton: *Letters to Washington*, IV, 57; *idem*, 56, 76, 117, 121, 294; *Pa. Arch.*, IV, 425; William Wilkins to Simon Gratz, July 16, 1810, Administration III, 88, Etting Coll.
[416] Hamilton: *Letters to Washington*, IV, 119, 121.

sentatives of some German settlers came to negotiate for 20,000 acres. Plumsted and Franks contracted for 30,000 acres. Thomas Lawrence, Edward Shippen, John Morgan, and others accepted deeds to more than 20,000 acres as security for their loans to Croghan. Alexander Ross, Croghan's old attorney, purchased 5,000 acres. As security or payment for debts, Croghan conveyed to Edward Ward 7,097 acres; to Joseph Simon 10,580 acres; and to Barnard Gratz 55,627 acres.[417]

One large sale Croghan was very anxious to make above all others; this was a sale to George Washington. Such a sale would give confidence in Croghan's ability to complete his legal title and it would insure influential support should it become necessary to seek a title from Virginia. Washington was interested in Ohio lands. In 1767, he instructed Crawford while ostensibly engaged on a hunting trip to spy out the choicest lands near Fort Pitt.[418] Crawford selected a tract of about 2,500 acres on Chartiers Creek about twenty-five miles from Fort Pitt. He surveyed it and reported to Washington on January 7, 1769: "[I] have done it

[417] Hooper to Johnson, Feb. 9, 1771, Johnson MSS., XX, 91; Wade to Johnson, Apr. 20, 1774, in *idem*, XXII, 247; Hooper to Gov. Franklin, May 22, 1771, in *Pa. Mag. of Hist. and Biog.*, XXXV, 450. Numerous accounts, deeds, bonds, and letters relating to Croghan's sales are found in the Gratz-Croghan Deeds, Gratz-Croghan MSS., and Ohio Co. MSS.; see also Crumrine, Boyd: "Records of Deeds for the District of West Augusta, Va"., in *Annals of the Carnegie Museum of Pittsburgh*, III, 237ff.

[418] *Writings*, II, 219. The following quotation describes the kind of lands Washington desired: "Ist If the Land is very hilly and broken, I shou'd not choose to be concern'd with it . . . unless those hills were of the richest kind; the growth of which shall be walnut, cherry, and such other sorts of timber, as denote the most luxuriant Soil. 2nd If, on the other hand, the Land shou'd be level, or at least wavy, that is, in little risings, sufficient to lay it dry and fit for the Plough, I wou'd put up with a soil less fertile, but in either case I shou'd expect the Tract to be well watered, and well timbered with a sufficiency of meadow ground upon it." – Instructions to Crawford, Nov. 24, 1770, in Washington MSS., XII, 1469.

as if for my self, taking all the good Land, and Leveing all that was sory, only some Joyning the Mill Seat." [419]

In 1770, Washington made a tour to the Ohio River and on October 19, he dined at Croghan Hall. Croghan took advantage of the opportunity to offer Washington 10,000 acres around the headwaters of Racoon and Chartiers Creeks.[420] After his return, Washington wrote Croghan that he wanted 15,000 acres in one tract and that Crawford would view the lands he had for sale and survey them providing Croghan would sell them at £5 per 100 acres, subject to a quit-rent after twenty years of 2 shillings sterling per 100 acres, and payment to be made when a legal title was established.[421] Croghan was elated and reported to Michael Gratz on February 20, 1771, that he had sold a parcel of lands to Colonel Washington and some other Virginia gentlemen and that he was engaged in surveying them.

Croghan offered Washington a township of 27,500 acres, but asked for immediate payment. To this Washington replied politely that this was more than he wanted and he assumed that Croghan would not want to sell part of a township; that he would, however, try to get some other gentleman to buy the portion he did not want; and that in the meantime, Croghan should feel free to sell the lands to anyone he could.[422] Had Croghan not asked for cash Washington would have made the purchase, but the latter was too shrewd

[419] Hamilton: *Letters to Washington*, III, 330.
[420] Washington's "Journal of a Tour to the Ohio River", in *Writings*, II, 290-292.
[421] Washington to Croghan, Nov. 24, 1770, in Washington MSS., XII, 1468.
[422] Croghan to Washington, Aug. 18, 1771 (with survey enclosed), in Washington MSS., XII, 1558; Washington to Croghan, Oct. 21, 1771, in *idem*, 1472.

a business man to engage in wild land speculation. As the months went by, Crawford and Washington manifested the keenest interest in Croghan's activities and in news concerning royal confirmation of Croghan's grant and of Vandalia.   In 1773, Lord Dunmore, while on a tour to the Ohio, told Crawford that unless news came from London that Vandalia was established by the time he returned east, he would grant Crawford patents for his surveys and appoint him surveyor of one of the new counties to be laid out by Virginia on the Ohio.   By the close of the year Crawford and Washington felt assured that they could soon secure patents for the surveys which they had been making in the region south of the Ohio.[423]

Croghan felt bitterly disappointed, but put forth every effort to hold his lands and to prevent Washington from winning them.   Squatter rights would be certain to be an important factor in the final outcome. Crawford therefore employed frontiersmen to build good log cabins on Washington's surveys and to clear an acre of ground around each cabin.   Croghan's brother and agent, Major Ward, encouraged persons to go and settle upon the same lands, telling them that they did not belong to Virginia officers and soldiers nor did Crawford have any orders from the governor of Virginia to survey them.   Crawford reported to Washington on December 29, 1773, that they "took your Land and say the will Keep it, I cold Drive them away but they will com back Emedetly as soon as my back is turn⁴, They man I put on the Land they have drove away and Built a house so Close to his dore he cannot

---

[423] Washington: *Writings*, II, 347; Hamilton: *Letters to Washington*, IV, 56, 118, 121, 275, 296, 311.

get into the house at the dore . . . there is no getting them of without by Force of Arms. . ." [424]

During this struggle, Washington's initial claims were based upon the land bounties which Governor Dinwiddie in 1754 had promised to Virginians who would enlist to fight the French; Croghan's initial claims rested upon his Indian purchase of 1749 and 1768. Both invested capital and tried to hold their lands by surveying them and by placing squatters upon them. Washington looked to Williamsburg where he would be able to secure a title in fee simple if the Vandalia project should be defeated. Croghan looked to London where the success of the Vandalia project would insure him a title in fee simple. This rivalry of Washington and Croghan represented the frontier phase of the great struggle going on in London over the proposed establishment of Vandalia.

---

[424] Hamilton: *Letters to Washington*, IV, 293. The squatters clung stubbornly to their improvements throughout the turmoil of succeeding years. Washington finally secured possession after the Revolution by lawsuits. Altogether, Washington secured title to nearly 40,000 acres in the Ohio region.

Obstruction in London and Williamsburg, 1773-1793

By the close of 1773, the opposition to Vandalia was so successful in London in its tactics of obstruction that the leaders of the westward movement who sought to satisfy their craving for western lands through Vandalia began to seek other ways of gaining their ends. The new imperial land policy announced in 1773 and 1774 strengthened their resolution. By this policy western lands in royal provinces were to be surveyed into tracts of from 100 to 1,000 acres, advertised for sale for four months, and then sold at auction to the highest bidder subject to a quit-rent of one half pence sterling per acre. The only exception made was for military grants under the proclamation of 1763. This policy promised to yield the imperial revenue which the Stamp Act had failed to produce and to make it difficult for one to secure an estate of thousands of acres. Revolutionary protests to this plan soon appeared.

To surmount these barriers the land speculators utilized first the famous legal opinion given by Lords Camden and Yorke, two eminent lawyers, both of whom held the position of Lord Chancellor. According to this opinion, a title to land granted by the natives was a full and sufficient title and rendered unnecessary the securing of a royal patent. Though announced as early as 1757 in connection with land disputes in

India,[425] and though it was stated that Lords Camden and Yorke personally confirmed the opinion to Croghan when he was in England in 1764,[426] land speculators in America made no use of it till 1773. Its existence was known to but a few and they kept it secret. Wharton and Trent knew of it shortly after they reached England in 1769; Gage and Haldimand did not seem to know of it till 1773.

The opinion was first utilized in America in 1773, by the Illinois Land Company. This company was organized by Croghan's close associates, David Franks, John Campbell, Barnard and Michael Gratz for the purpose of making a large Indian purchase in Illinois. The Gratzs furnished the necessary Indian goods and William Murray was sent to make the purchase. On his way to Illinois he stopped at Pittsburg for a conference with Croghan. The entire scheme was kept secret till Murray appeared in Illinois.[427]

The Camden-Yorke opinion offered another possible way for Croghan to complete legal titles in his 200,000 acre Indian grant. This opinion also encouraged him to secure other Indian grants. With great caution and prudence, Croghan, in 1773, purchased 1,500,000 acres lying north of the Ohio near Pittsburg for $6,000 from some chiefs of the Six Nations. He agreed that it was not to be settled for fifteen years unless the Indians around Pittsburg should move to hunting grounds

---

[425] Wharton: *Plain Facts*, 9.

[426] William Murray to B. and M. Gratz, May 15, 1773, in Ohio Co. MSS., I, 102.

[427] In 1775, Murray made another purchase for the Wabash Company. These two companies were united in 1779, under the chairmanship of George Ross, who had been prosecuting attorney for Cumberland County, Pennsylvania and also Croghan's attorney for a number of years. Croghan's influence with these men was probably an important factor in the rise and development of these companies.

farther down the Ohio. To secure money for this purchase Croghan borrowed $4,000 in Virginia. In 1775,
in order to pay this debt, Croghan offered 1,000,000
acres to Trent and the Wharton's at $4,000 cash before
his Virginia creditors should take it.[428]

On July 10, 1775, Croghan made another purchase
at Pittsburg on similar terms from five chiefs of the Six
Nations for $12,000, paid mostly in Indian goods. It
consisted of 6,000,000 acres and included most of the
land between the Allegheny River and Big Beaver
Creek. Two years later he sold to Thomas Walker
and his sons, John and Thomas Jr., and six other Virginians 1,200,000 acres thereof for $5,000.[429]

In 1772, Samuel Wharton, Trent, Johnson, and some
wealthy Englishmen organized a company to make a
similar purchase north of the Ohio. Wharton asked
Croghan to ascertain the attitude of the Indians towards it. The scheme was dropped till 1774 when
with the greatest secrecy the necessary Indian goods,
valued at £1,871, were shipped from England to Virginia. For an entire year Samuel Wharton kept even
his brother, Thomas, in Philadelphia thinking that the
goods were intended as a present for the Indians when
the governor of Vandalia should arrive at Pittsburg.
They were stored at Georgetown and to Samuel Wharton's chagrin, the gunpowder and lead were seized or
had to be sold to the Sons of Liberty in 1775.

The purchase was to have been made during the
summer of 1775. The continental congress was meet-

---

[428] Croghan to Trent, July 15, 1775, in Ohio Co. MSS., II, 6; "Minute
book of the Virginia Court held at Fort Dunmore", in *Annals of the Carnegie Museum of Pittsburgh*, I, 554.

[429] Croghan's original deed is in the possession of Thomas Walker
Page of Washington, D.C. It is printed in Page, R. C. M.: *Genealogy of
the Page Family*, etc., 188; cf. also 186.

ing in Philadelphia by this time and Samuel Wharton wrote to his brother and asked him to cultivate friendly relations with the Virginia delegates, particularly with Patrick Henry, and, if necessary, to concern some of them in the purchase.   He also asked that his brother and Benjamin Franklin use all their influence to get the congress to pass a resolution or declaration "expressive of the Validity and Sufficiency of a Title to Lands, fairly bought of the Aborigines and held under Grants (Only) from Them."   To make his task easier, Samuel Wharton authorized his brother to make a present of half a share apiece to eight delegates and he sent him four pamphlets discussing the Camden-Yorke opinion.   He asked that these be shown to but few persons and that Thomas write him in cipher.[430]

The Camden-Yorke opinion also led to a burst of renewed activity by the Indiana Company with the scene of action shifting back to America when Trent returned from London early in 1775.   From 1769 to 1775, this company had merged its claim in the larger project of Vandalia, but after this had failed to materialize, the Indiana Company, in 1775, resumed its independent position.   Before leaving England, Trent had secured from Henry Dagge and John Glynn, two of the most eminent lawyers in London, written opinions which stated in essence that the Camden-Yorke

---

[430] Thomas Wharton to Croghan, July 25 and Sept. 30, 1774; T. Wharton to Richardson, Jan. 17, May 13, and June 28, 1775; S. Wharton to T. Wharton, Jan. 31 and Aug. 7, 1775; and T. Wharton to Thomas Walpole, Sept. 23, 1774. – all found in Thomas Wharton's Letter Bk., 1773-1784 or in the Wharton Loose MSS. Of Franklin, Samuel Wharton wrote: "Dr. F. is grown old, and is not so active as He was Twenty Years ago, and however well disposed, as I know He is, To establish in America, the Rights of the Six Nations etc. to their Territories, and all fair Grants obtained from Them, Yet will be necessary for you and Major Trent, with *his* Concurrence, To take an active Part with the other Members of the Congress."

opinion was applicable to the Indiana grant. After he reached Philadelphia, Trent secured the written endorsement of Patrick Henry and Benjamin Franklin to these opinions.[431] He also sought to get similar statements from other delegates of the continental congress and through pamphlets and newspapers to create a favorable attitude toward the principle involved.

Trent then visited Croghan at Pittsburg and assumed the authority to call a meeting of the company at that place on September 21, 1775. Besides Croghan and Trent, six other members were present. Trent stated to them that on his arrival in England in 1769, Lord Camden, Franklin, and others advised him that it was not necessary to seek royal confirmation, but only to take possession of their grant and knowing that Hillsborough opposed confirmation he did not apply for it. The eight members then decided to ask Samuel Wharton in London to return the original deed of 1768 in order that it might be registered at Williamsburg and the sale of lands begun. The company adjourned to meet at Carlisle in November.[432] Trent and many others could not attend and the second meeting adjourned to Lancaster and then to Philadelphia.

By this time dissention was rampant in the company. The interests of Baynton, Wharton, and Morgan were now in the hands of their creditors; those members who had contributed time and money to the cause demanded a redistribution of shares; one group, to which Cro-

---

[431] *Pa. Mag. of Hist. and Biog.*, XXVII, 151. Trent apparently started to keep a book in which these opinions were written under the title "Opinions Regarding the Grant to Wm. Trent, 1775." It is found in the library of the Hist. Soc. of Pa.

[432] Minutes of the meeting at Pittsburg, in Ohio Co. MSS., II, 9. Many other documents relating to the company's history after 1775 are found in this volume and in the entries for the years 1775 and 1776 in Thomas Wharton's Letter Bk., 1773-1784.

ghan belonged, wished to recognize Virginia's authority, but to this the Whartons, Franklin, and Morgan
objected; George Morgan was bitterly hostile to the
Whartons and to Trent whom he finally challenged to
a duel.   However, when the company met at Indian
Queen Tavern, Philadelphia, on March 20, 1776, all
differences were conciliated under the influence of
Franklin.   Practically all members were present either
in person or by proxy.   Trent and Morgan represented
Croghan.   By unanimous votes, the company was reor-
ganized.   Joseph Galloway was elected President,
George Morgan, Secretary of the Land Office and also
Receiver-General, and Robert L. Hooper, Surveyor-
General.

It was also decided to open immediately a land office
at Pittsburg.   All settlers who had intruded upon the
lands and who had made improvements before 1776
were given the right to apply for not more than 400
acres at the price of $50 per 100 acres.   After 1777, all
remaining lands were to be surveyed and sold.[433]
When Morgan advertised these terms, the Virginia
delegates in Philadelphia went into conference with
the leaders of the company and indicated that they
would be able to support the company's claims if it
would recognize Virginia's authority over the region.
This it declined to do.   As a result of Virginia's opposition, settlers were encouraged to resist and deride the
company's claims.   This forced the relinquishment for
the time being of the plan to sell lands.

The impossibility of securing from frontiersmen and

[433] Thomas Wharton's Indiana Company MSS.; *Documents respecting the
claim of persons therein mentioned to a certain tract of land called Indiana.*
Morgan's major attention on his return to Pittsburg was given to his
work as Indian agent for the Middle Department for the continental
congress.

from the powerful colony of Virginia, recognition of a land title based upon the Camden-Yorke opinion caused the more practical land speculators to seek confirmation of their land claims at Williamsburg. With the failure of Vandalia to secure its charter in 1773, Virginia, under the leadership of Governor Dunmore, again asserted its authority in the West with a surprising decisiveness. Dunmore was welcomed by the Virginia land speculators as a patron who personally desired to increase his wealth by acquiring lands in the West.

Until the close of 1773, these persons had regarded the establishment of Vandalia as inevitable and had tried to save what they could for themselves. Recognition would probably be accorded to legally acquired titles to lands within its borders, but to secure such titles was difficult. One loop hole had been left in the imperial prohibitions on granting western lands: exceptions had been made so that bounties in land could be provided for the regular soldiers and perhaps also for the provincial soldiers of the French and Indian War. Surveyors were therefore sent out in all directions in the region south of the Ohio to survey such lands. Though rebuked by Lord Dartmouth, Dunmore and his council issued patents for these lands. Some were located as far west as the falls of the Ohio. Here, Dr. John Connolly, a nephew of Croghan and the representative of Dunmore in the West, John Campbell, and Edward Ward received grants and started to lay out a town on the present site of Louisville. Dunmore even recommended to London the recognition of the Illinois Land Company's purchase of 1773 and participated in a similar purchase by the Wabash Land Company in 1775.

Croghan was among those who sought favors from Lord Dunmore. He laid his Indian deed for 200,000 acres before Dunmore and the latter pronounced it legal. To secure a patent for it, Croghan planned a journey to Williamsburg in June, 1774. Crawford and Connolly, fearing that because of his diplomatic ability he might succeed, wrote to Washington and urged him to use his utmost power to defeat the attempt. Because of this opposition and because Croghan felt that his presence was needed at Pittsburg in the critical opening days of Lord Dunmore's Indian war, his proposed journey was abandoned.[434]

The rapid advance of the settler's frontier angered the Indians, particularly the Shawnee. Since 1768, when the Shawnee had been disregarded in the sale of the lands south of the Ohio, they had been discontented. Sporadic murders of both whites and Indians occurred. Because of the policy of economy followed in the Indian department, presents were not available to help the situation. War might have at least been postponed had Lord Dunmore followed a different policy. He was charged with bringing on war in order to halt the plans for the establishment of Vandalia and to secure a large Indian grant at the treaty of peace for himself. The rashness of his western agent, Connolly, served to start the war which later became known as Lord Dunmore's War. Shortly after April 16, 1774, when the Shawnee had attacked three traders, Connolly issued an open letter commanding the frontiersmen to hold themselves in readiness to repel an Indian attack. This served practically as a declaration of war. On the 27th, Cresap killed two

---

[434] Croghan to B. Gratz, Sept. 24, 1774, in Gratz-Croghan MSS., I, 38; Hamilton: *Letters to Washington*, IV, 311 and V, 8.

Shawnee who were quietly assisting white traders and on the 30th occurred the foul murder of nine kinsmen of the famous Mingo chief, Logan. Soon the Virginia frontier was again engaged in a bloody Indian war. Hundreds of frontiersmen abandoned their cabins and fled in panic to the east. Had the Delawares and the Six Nations on the Ohio joined the Shawnee, a formidable Indian war would have resulted which would probably have involved Pennsylvania as well as Virginia.

During this crisis, Croghan was called upon once more to take charge of Indian affairs. McKee, who held the office of deputy superintendent, and Connolly, who appeared to be appalled by the threatening storm, both looked to Croghan to stem the tide. The Whartons in Philadelphia in the interests of Vandalia, quickly forwarded 50,000 black and white wampum to Croghan.[435] May and June saw the frontier in feverish activity. Indian runners brought news to Croghan and took back with them his invitations to Indian chiefs whom he knew personally to come to his house for a conference. The Shawnee chiefs declined to come, but the leading Delaware and Six Nation chiefs came. Croghan, McKee, Connolly, and St. Clair, the western representative of Pennsylvania, met them in numerous conferences and were able to keep them from joining the Shawnee.[436] At times, bands of frontiersmen surrounded Croghan's house and tried to

[435] Thomas Wharton to Thomas Walpole, Sept. 3, 1774, in Thomas Wharton's Letter Bk., 1773-1784. Valuable material for Lord Dunmore's War is found in this Letter Book and also in the Croghan and Wharton letters printed in the *Pa. Mag. of Hist. and Biog.*, xv, 435ff.

[436] McKee's Journal of Transactions with the Indians at Pittsburg, May 1-June 10, 1774, in *N.Y. Col. Docs.*, VIII, 512ff.; Connolly's Journal and other documents are found in Letters and Documents Relating to the Indians, 1750-1775, Chalmers Coll.

kill such Indians as came. In order to prepare for
the worst, Croghan and the Pennsylvania officials
agreed to raise, provision, and pay a company of one
hundred rangers to patrol western Pennsylvania.
They hoped that this province would reimburse them.
"Whatever may be Mr. Croghan's real views, I am
certain he is hearty in promoting the general tranquil-
lity of the Country, indeed He is indefatigable in en-
deavouring to make up the Breaches . . .", reported St. Clair to Governor Penn on June 22, 1774.[437]
Croghan had been able to serve the interests of Vandalia, Pennsylvania, Virginia, the Delawares, and the
Six Nations, as well as his own personal interests.

While Pennsylvania, the Delawares, and Six Nations
were thus being kept neutral, the Virginia militia was
being mobilized under orders from Lord Dunmore.
It defeated the Shawnee in the bloody battle of Point
Pleasant. The Shawnee, abandoned by the other
tribes, met Lord Dunmore and agreed to a preliminary
peace. What terms Dunmore intended to exact in the
final treaty and therefore his motives in the war, can
only be surmised for he was soon compelled by the
outbreak of the Revolution to flee to an English war-
ship. Lord Dunmore's War resulted in keeping Kentucky open to settlement and gave peace to the frontier
during the first two years of the Revolution.

The aggressive western policy of Lord Dunmore in
1773 and 1774 was also reflected in the boundary controversy between Virginia and Pennsylvania. According to the charter granted to William Penn, the western
boundary of Pennsylvania was a very irregular line
located five degrees west of the Delaware River and
paralleling it. The Penns maintained that this line

---

[437] *Pa. Arch.*, IV, 524; see also 501, 509, 523, 527, 552ff., 574.

began at the 39th parallel and therefore gave them a large tract west of Maryland and reaching down towards Virginia. This line had never been surveyed. It so happened that Pittsburg lay only five miles east of the line and therefore, before accurate surveys were made, no one could tell whether it was in Pennsylvania or in Virginia. In deciding this question, the opinion rendered by Lord Chancellor Camden during the dispute between Pennsylvania and Connecticut over Wyoming was cited. He had stated that since the recognition of the "parchement" boundaries of all colonies would lead to endless disputes, many other factors must be taken into consideration in locating boundary lines; such factors as possession, acquiescence, agreement, or geography might result in the extension or contraction of charter boundaries.[438]

These conditions led the proprietors of Vandalia to hope that their proposed colony would include Pittsburg. The Penns, on the other hand, were led to maintain the impracticability of a line which should follow the windings of the Delaware River; they advocated a straight line for their western boundary and proceeded to grant lands and serve legal processes beyond their charter limits. And finally, Virginia also began to grant lands in southwestern Pennsylvania and seized Pittsburg.

In the bitter controversy which followed, Croghan took sides with Virginia because, if her jurisdiction were established, it would at least be possible for him

---

[438] Connolly to Washington, Feb. 1, 1774, in Hamilton: *Letters to Washington*, IV, 320; Dunmore – Dartmouth correspondence, 1774-1775, in C. O., 5: 1352; Crumrine, Boyd: "The Pennsylvania Boundary Controversy", in *Annals of the Carnegie Museum of Pittsburgh*, I, 514ff.; Craig, N. B.: *Lecture upon the boundary controversy between Va. and Pa.*; Petition of Thomas and John Penn to the King, 1773, in Bd. of Tr. Pap., Plantations General, XXIII, 303; *idem*, XXIV, 35.

to secure legal title to his various land claims; "real Friendship you must not expect, for by his Interest alone he is regulated", wrote St. Clair to Governor Penn concerning Croghan on June 22, 1774.[439] As early as 1771, Croghan had refused to pay taxes on some of his lands in Pennsylvania and his example had much influence on others. Armed mobs of settlers drove off tax collectors and prevented sheriffs from performing their duties.

In her conflict with Virginia, Pennsylvania was handicapped because she had no militia law and because her assembly during the years 1749 to 1755, had refused to erect a fort at the forks of the Ohio and had maintained that this place lay beyond her limits. Subsequent events had submerged the issue, but in 1774, the Pennsylvania authorities were rudely awakened when they heard that Dr. Connolly, a bold intriguer, had seized Fort Pitt, renamed it Fort Dunmore, and asserted the authority of Virginia over the surrounding region. He was arrested by Pennsylvania authorities, but released on his promise to return for trial. He returned, but at the head of 150 armed men. He now acted in a very high-handed manner; horses and sheep were seized; Pennsylvanians had their lands taken away and saw them given over to Virginians; Pennsylvania traders were stopped and forced to pay duties on their furs and skins; Pennsylvania officials were arrested and sent to Virginia. Counter arrests followed. Everyone who undertook to perform any official act was liable to be thrown into jail by partisans of the other side. Riots and broils were common and intense passions existed among the frontiersmen. Lord Dart-

---

[439] *Pa. Arch.,* IV, 525; cf. 424-612, *passim.*

mouth supported Dunmore's policy and attempts made by the Penns to settle the matter peaceably, failed.

Pennsylvania had established the new county of Westmoreland in 1773. It included Pittsburg and the surrounding region. On December 12, 1774, Governor Dunmore by proclamation organized the District of West Augusta; it included Pittsburg and much of southwestern Pennsylvania. As justices of the peace he appointed the old justices of Augusta County together with the leading Virginia adherents in the disputed area. These included Croghan and some of his relations and close associates. Attorneys, constables, deputy sheriffs, and militia officers were also appointed. When the first court was held at Pittsburg on February 21, 1775, Croghan "took the Usual Oaths to his Majesties Person and Government, Subscribed the Abjuration Oath and test, and also took the Oaths of Justices of the Peace and of Justices of the County Court in Chancery, and of Justices of Oyer and Terminer".[440] He then sat as the presiding justice. Among the justices who sat with him at this and later meetings were John Campbell, Dorsey Pentecost, Thomas Smallman, Edward Ward, and John Connolly. Among the cases decided by this court were cases involving land titles, mortgages, thefts, and murders.

The following extracts from its Minute Book show the nature of its other activities and also of some economic and social conditions around Pittsburg in 1775: "Ord[ered] that the Sheriff Imploy a Workman to build a Ducking Stool at the Confluence of the Ohio with the Monongohale. . .

[440] Crumrine: "The Minute Book of the Virginia court held at Fort Dunmore for the District of West Augusta", in *Annals of the Carnegie Museum of Pittsburgh*, I, 526; *ibid*, 525-540, *passim*.

"On the Motion of Henry Heath, leave is granted him to keep a ferry on the Monongohale River at his own Plantation and he provide a Boat for the sd ferry.

"On the Motion of John Gibson, It is Ord. that his Mark be a Slit in the right and a Crop in. the left Ear and brand I G.

"License to keep an ordinary [tavern] is Granted to John Ormsby, he hav'g compld with the Law.

"On the Complt of John MacNully ag'st his Master, Casper Reel, for beating and abuseing him, being Sum'd, appeared, and on hear'g the parties and the Wits the Court are of Opinion that the Complt is Groundless and be dismised, and It is Ord that the Sheriff take the Serv't and give him 25 Lashes well Laid on. . .

"Ord that Paul Froman, Thomas Cook, Josiah Crawford, Jacob Long and Rich'd Crooks, they being first sworn, View a road from Fort Dunmore to Paul Froman's and make a report of the Conveniences and Inconveniences thereof to the next Court.

"William Elliot, being bound over to this Court by Thomas Smallman, Gent., for disturbing the minds of his Majesties Good people of this County, by demanding in an arbitrary and Illegal Manner of sundry Persons what Personal Estate they are possessed of, that the same may be tax'd according to the Laws of Pennsylvania, being called, appeared and on hearing the argument of the attorneys the Court are of opinion that he be Committed to the Goal of this County, and there remain until he Enter into recog. in the sum of £100, with 2 Srtys in the sum of 50£ Each, for his good Behavior for the space of One Month. . ."

On November 3, 1776, Virginia created out of part of the District of West Augusta, the counties of Ohio,

Yohogania, and Monongalia. They took in what is today southwestern Pennsylvania and northern West Virginia. In the courts of these counties Croghan brought more than fifty suits against persons who had settled on the lands which he claimed.[441]

In return for the support which Croghan had given to Virginia, he expected Lord Dunmore and his adherents to grant recognition to his Indian grant. Dunmore was privately interested in seeing the principle of the Camden-Yorke opinion recognized by Virginia and therefore Croghan's prospects were good until the outbreak of the Revolution placed new leaders in control in Virginia. The brunt of the struggle over the principle involved was borne by the Indiana and Transylvania Companies.

Virginia threw down the gage of battle to the numerous companies and individuals who hoped to exploit her unoccupied lands when her famous convention of 1776 passed a resolution that no purchases of land within her chartered limits should be made from any Indian tribe without the consent of her legislature. The convention also provided for a commission to take evidence against all persons pretending to claim lands upon purchases made from the Indians before 1776. Until the legislature should act all settlers upon lands in dispute were encouraged to remain.

The Indiana Company now drew up a memorial to the legislature of Virginia, dated October 1, 1776, wherein it stated that to apply the resolutions of the convention to its grant was unjust. It maintained that the grant was solemnly made in public to the King in

---

[441] The records of deeds for the District of West Augusta and the Minute Books of the Virginia Courts held for Ohio and Yohogania counties are printed in *idem*, III, 237ff., 5ff. and II, 71ff., 205ff., respectively.

trust for its members, that it was based on principles of justice established in the law of nature and of nations; that the Indians had a right to make such a grant at the time; and that no law at the time forbade the acceptance of the grant or made royal confirmation necessary. To declare its title null and void was therefore an *ex post facto* action and a violation of private property. The memorial ended by stating that the company would never hesitate to defend its title before a proper court. It refused, however, to defend it before the commission which had been appointed.[442]

Croghan watched this case closely for he still held 774 shares in the Indiana Company; moreover, should the principle for which it was fighting be established, a legal title to his Indian grant would be assured. Many Virginians defended the principle involved; among these were Edmund Pendleton, speaker of the house of delegates, once a delegate to the continental congress and judge of the court of appeals, and James Mercer, also a delegate to congress. The matter came to a final issue in Virginia in 1779. The legislature of Virginia had invited all persons who claimed lands within the former charter limits of the colony based on Indian titles, to appear before it. Croghan and his associates agreed that the case of his Indian grant should be presented through a memorial of Barnard Gratz and others, asking for patents for the lands which they had purchased from him.[443] Barnard Gratz, himself, went to Williamsburg to present the memorial. The Indiana Company sent Trent to argue its case. The Ohio Company of Virginia and the Transylvania,

---

[442] *Documents relating to Indiana,* etc., 5-8; Wharton: *Plain Facts,* 101ff.

[443] Memorial of Barnard Gratz and others, in Large Misc. MSS., 98, Etting Coll.; Ohio Co. MSS., II, 33, 39.

Illinois, and Wabash Companies also presented their claims. The Indiana Company, whose claim was the strongest of all, secured a favorable vote in the house, but when it lost in the senate the fate of all similar petitioners was predetermined. Virginia did offer the members of the Indiana Company "consolation" grants in the West similar to the grant accepted by the Transylvania Company, but this offer was refused.

One petition involving the validity of Croghan's grant was, however, granted. Croghan had sold a tract of about 3,000 acres in his grant to Alexander Ross in 1772, and the latter in turn had sold it in 1775 to Colonel Charles Simms of Virginia. In 1779, Simms asked Washington for a furlough in order to go to Williamsburg to present a petition for a patent for this tract. Washington, who had laid aside all of his plans for speculating in western lands when the Revolution opened, denied the request, but congress granted it. Simms's petition was granted, but only because his being in the service of his country prevented him from making such improvements as would have secured for him a like quantity of land. So great was the opposition which his petition encountered that General William Croghan and others interested in Croghan's lands decided not to present similar petitions.[444]

Having disposed of claims to millions of acres of lands within her charter limits, Virginia now proceeded to outline a western land policy which would gather the fruits of her investment of blood and treasure in the military expeditions of George Rogers Clark and others. Resolutions were passed by its legislature in 1779, reaffirming those passed in 1776. They went

---

[444] William Croghan to B. Gratz, Aug. 22, 1779, Gratz-Croghan MSS., I, 65; Wharton: *Plain Facts*, 115; Byars: *B. and M. Gratz*, 188; Wm. Croghan to M. Gratz, Feb. 7, 1780, in N.Y. Public Library.

further and claimed for Virginia all lands within her limits which had belonged to the crown. The door was closed to all further petitions from Croghan and the land companies when the legislature declared "utterly void and of no effect" the deed for Indiana and all similar Indian deeds which had been or might be issued to or for the benefit of any private person or persons. New counties were now organized in the West and the legislature passed laws which provided for the sale and patenting of western lands in accordance with conditions laid down or with conditions previously recognized as legal in Virginia.

The last recourse left for Croghan, the Indiana Company, the United Illinois-Wabash Company, and for the American promoters of Vandalia was to appeal to the new central government as represented by the continental congress. The boundary dispute between Virginia and Pennsylvania was taken up in this body for settlement and the settlers along the upper Ohio, confronted by chaos and revolution, also appealed to it.

Croghan had incurred the ill-will of the settlers because of his large land claims, his associations with land companies, and his consideration for the Indians. He reciprocated their attitude for to him they were "the rabble" making him endless trouble in his land affairs.[445] Many of the settlers wished to enjoy the benefits of law and order, and to them it was of minor importance whether their land titles emanated from Croghan, the Indiana Company, Pennsylvania, or Virginia, or whether the laws under which they lived were made by Pennsylvania, Virginia, or Vandalia. As one way out of the difficulties, a number of the settlers sent

---

[445] Croghan to Haldimand, Oct. 4, 1773, in Haldimand Coll., ser. B, 70: 269; McClure: *Diary*, 101; *Pa. Arch.*, IV, 619.

a memorial to congress in 1776, asking for the erection
of a new state, Westsylvania. In their memorial they
stated that the Pennsylvania-Virginia boundary dispute
had resulted in "inumerable Frauds, Impositions,
Violences, Depredations, Feuds, Animosities, Divi-
sions, Litigations, Disorders", with civil war threatening. They feared that a bloody Indian war would
result from the land operations carried on by Virginians. "There are a number of private or other claims
to Lands within the Limits of this Country equally
embarrassing and perplexing", continued the memorial; "George Croghan Esquire in various Tracts,
claims Land . . . on which are Settled already
150 or 200 Families; Major William Trent on Behalf
of himself and the Traders, . . . claims another
large Tract containing at least 4,000,000 of acres
. . . on which 1500 or 2000 Families are already
settled . . . [Vandalia] rich fertile and healthy
even beyond Credibility is peopled by at least 25,000
Families." These persons came west amid great hardships and sacrifices in search of freedom, liberty, and a
livelihood and they objected to being "Enslaved by any
set of Proprietary or other Claimants, or arbitrarily
deprived and robbed of those Lands and that Country
to which by the Laws of Nature and of Nations they
are entitled as first Occupants." [446]

Partly as a result of such remonstrances, but more
largely because of the necessity of utilizing all their
strength in the Revolutionary War, congress urged
Pennsylvania and Virginia to settle their boundary
controversy. The dispute dragged on, however, and
when George Rogers Clark tried to enlist recruits for
his western expedition at Pittsburg he received but

---

[446] This Memorial is found in the Yeates MSS.

little support from the Pennsylvania adherents.   His
recruits were referred to as "armed banditti" in reports
to the supreme council of Pennsylvania.   Finally, in
1780, the present boundary line was agreed upon.
Great difficulty was encountered in settling land titles
for it was provided that they should be based on grants
made by either Pennsylvania or Virginia, depending
upon which grants were first made.   The extension of
the western boundary line of Pennsylvania beyond her
charter limits threw the whole of Croghan's Indian
grant within Pennsylvania.   After 1780, Croghan and
those to whom he had conveyed lands hoped to secure
recompense elsewhere in the West from congress.

Croghan, the Indiana Company, the Illinois-Wabash
Company, and the American promoters of Vandalia all
memorialized congress for recognition of their claims.
Should it not prove feasible to secure their original
land claims they hoped to secure substitute land grants
elsewhere in the West.   Their cause was still a hope-
ful one.   Shares in the Indiana Company were advertised for sale and brought when sold about twenty per
cent of their estimated face value; [447] Croghan's deeds
were still being drawn up and accepted in partial payment of his debts.

It was self-evident that these memorials would be of
no avail unless the rights of the crown to western lands
passed to congress as the central government instead of
to the individual states.   Hence the memorials were

[447] *Pa. Gazette,* July 7, 1779; Morgan to John Gibson, Jan. 5, 1779, in
George Morgan's Letter Bk.   Indiana also found a place on some contemporary maps.   A French edition of Hutchins: *Topographical description of Va., Pa., Md. and Car.,* dated 1781, included a map entitled "Carte
des Environs du Fort Pitt et de la Nouvelle Province Indiana" which
showed Indiana in colors.   Morse's *Universal Geography* (1793) and
Guthrie's *A New System of Modern Geography,* both described Indiana.

inevitably drawn into the great and bitter conflict going on in congress over the disposition of the West. In it, Maryland, Pennsylvania, and the other states that had no western land claims were arrayed against Virginia and those that had such claims. For a time it seemed that this struggle would wreck the plans for a union under the articles of confederation. The states with no western land claims welcomed the memorials of the land companies because they could be used to assist them in their struggle to force the states with such claims to cede them for the common benefit of all the states. The representatives of the land companies were men of political experience ready to use every means to secure their claims; they held out the opportunity for personal gain to influence members of congress.

The brunt of the attack again fell upon the Indiana Company. After its petition to the legislature of Virginia had been denied, it sent a memorial to congress dated September 11, 1779. This recited the claims of the union to western lands, pointed out that Virginia being an interested party could not pass judgment upon the questions involved, and asked congress to request Virginia to delay opening its land offices until Virginia and the Indiana Company could both be heard before congress. On October 30, congress passed a resolution earnestly requesting Virginia to reconsider her decision to open land offices and requesting all states having western land claims to forbear settling or issuing warrants for unappropriated lands until the war had ended. The legislature of Virginia remonstrated against such interference in her affairs and especially to the arrogation by congress of the right of adjudication in such disputes. The Indiana

Company soon sent a second memorial to congress inviting congress to decide its case and requesting it to appoint a time for hearing all parties interested.[448]   In the same year, 1780, congress requested the states having western land claims to surrender a liberal portion thereof to the confederacy for the common benefit of all of its members.

Virginia made such a cession in 1781, but attached to it so many conditions that it was not favorably received; one of these conditions stated that all purchases made within the cession by private persons from the Indians were to be null and void.   A committee of congress was appointed to consider the cessions made by Virginia, New York, and Connecticut; to it were also referred the petitions of the Indiana and the Illinois-Wabash Companies, of the Vandalia group, and of Croghan.   All felt that a crisis had now been reached and that not merely the interests of land companies, but that the union itself was at stake.   Decisions were about to be made which were to have far reaching influences upon the nature of the political union of the states and upon the western policy to be followed during the territorial expansion of the new nation.

Three important documents, all advocating the cause of the memorialists and of the nationalization of the West, appeared in 1780 and 1781.   Benjamin Franklin sent his *"Passy Memorial"* to Congress from Passy, France.   It was read in Congress on March 16, 1781. It recounted the history of the Vandalia project beginning with the year 1768 and made a calm, restrained plea for justice.[449]   In 1780, there appeared in Phila-

---

[448] *Documents relating to Indiana,* etc., 9-23.

[449] The Passy Memorial is found in the Papers of the Continental Congress, No. 77, folios 167-205.

delphia a pamphlet written by Thomas Paine, the most popular and influential pamphleteer of the Revolution, entitled *"Public Good: Being an Examination into the Claim of Virginia to the Vacant Western Territory, and of the Right of the United States to the Same; to Which is Added Proposals for Laying off a New State, to be Applied as a Fund for Carrying on the War or Redeeming the National Debt."* Interesting inferences can be drawn from the fact that Thomas Paine was soon listed as owning 300 shares in the Indiana Company.[450] Finally, there appeared an anonymous pamphlet entitled *Plain Facts* written by Samuel Wharton. It massed historical data beginning with the discovery of America in support of the petition of the Indiana Company and was written in a clear forceful style. A new committee of congress had been appointed to consider the problems involved. It held meetings with the delegates of New York, Connecticut, and Virginia and it also met with the agents of Croghan and the three companies and examined their deeds, vouchers, and other papers. The Virginia delegates were invited to attend the meetings of the committee, but refused to acknowledge the authority of congress in the matter. They demanded a roll call in congress in which every delegate would declare upon his honor whether or not he was personally interested in the claims of any company involved. They also fought to prevent congress from acting in the matter. Finally, on May 1, 1782, the committee made an important report. It recommended that congress accept the cession of New York, that it request Massachusetts and Connecticut to cede their western land claims, and

---

[450] Gratz Pap., 2nd ser., I, 105. "Public Good" is printed in the *Writings of Thomas Paine,* edited by Conway.

that the cession of Virginia be rejected and Virginia requested to make a more acceptable cession. One condition of Virginia's cession had stated that all purchases from the Indians by private persons should be deemed and declared absolutely void and of no effect.

The committee also reported that "the purchases of Colonel Croghan and the Indiana Company were made bona fide for a valuable consideration, according to the then usage and custom of purchasing lands from the Indians, with the knowledge, consent and approbation of the Crown of Great Britain, [and] the then governments of New York and Virginia. . ." No stronger recommendation for a land grant by congress could have been desired by these two parties. The case of Vandalia was complicated because both alien enemies and loyal citizens were affected and because the lands involved were so vast in extent; however, the committee recommended that all citizens be granted lands sufficient to cover the expenses they had incurred in connection with this project, on condition that those interested in Vandalia relinquish all their claims. The committee also recommended that the petition of the Illinois-Wabash Company be dismissed because of the irregular manner in which its purchases had been made from the Indians. The report closed by urging federal control of Indian affairs, especially in the purchasing of lands, and the creation of new states in the West.[451]

Finally, in 1784, Virginia made an acceptable cession of all her lands north of the Ohio River. This fact, together with her bitter hostility to the petitions of the land companies and Croghan, and the low estate

[451] *Journals of the Continental Congress* (Library of Congress ed.), XXII, 223-229; Rowland, Kate: *Life of George Mason.*

into which congress had fallen, made it impossible to secure favorable action upon the petitions. They were sacrificed in the interests of the union. Left in possession of Kentucky, Virginia was willing, however, to make large land grants to individuals like the Gratzs who had been among the petitioners. The Vandalia and Illinois-Wabash Companies appear to have given up further attempts to secure action by the continental congress, but the heirs of Croghan and the Indiana Company continued to send petitions and memorials to congress.[452]

The inauguration of a strong national government in 1789 provided a new method for seeking redress. George Mason, in opposing the ratification of the federal constitution in the Virginia convention, had pointed out that under it the large land companies would be able to reopen their cases and overthrow the security of western settlers. The Indiana Company once more took the initiative in fighting for a principle which, if established, would also be applicable to Croghan's case. The company first sent a memorial to the Virginia legislature in 1790 and asked it to reconsider the decision it had made in 1779. When Virginia refused, the company proceeded to bring its case before the supreme court of the United States as a matter of original jurisdiction in equity. The case became known as Grayson vs Virginia because William Grayson was the first of the shareholders named. A summons to appear as defendant was served on Virginia in 1792, but Virginia failed to respond. In 1796, the court therefore decided the important point that in

---

[452] Such memorials are found in the Papers of the Continental Congress, No. 32 f. 159; No. 41, Vol. 3, f. 493; No. 41, Vol. x, f. 87-90 and 99-105. Cf. Gratz Pap., 2nd ser., II 42; Ohio. Co. MSS., II, 71; and *Journals of the Continental Congress*, XXIV, 332.

such cases process should be served upon the governor and attorney-general and in case of no answer being received within sixty days, to proceed *ex parte*. The court was relieved of its difficulty when the eleventh amendment to the constitution, which deprived it of jurisdiction in cases where individuals sued a state, became law in 1798. The court ruled that it applied retroactively and on February 14, 1798 it ordered the case of Grayson *vs* Virginia dismissed for lack of jurisdiction. Accounts of the losses of the original members of the company and of the expenses incurred in seeking reimbursement, were still kept and the members bequeathed their shares to their heirs; after 1798, however, the name "Indiana" gradually disappeared south of the Ohio on contemporary maps, but it soon reappeared north of the Ohio.[453]

Thus Croghan and his associates had failed in their attempts to secure recognized legal titles to thousands of acres on the Ohio. They had failed to secure acquiescence in the principle of the Camden-Yorke opinion, or a grant from Virginia, or a grant from the continental congress, or a favorable decision from the newly created supreme court of the United States. With much forethought and energy they had followed in turn each of these possible ways of achieving their aims. They had labored long to enlist every available influence and had spent large sums of money for the fulfillment of their plans; but all the time and money invested failed to bring them personal returns. After 1775, western land problems became involved with the establishment of the new American nation and with

---

[453] *Documents relating to Indiana, etc.,* 10-24; Dallas, A. J.: *Reports of cases ruled and adjudged in the several courts of the United States, etc.,* III, 320; Docket of the Supreme Court of the U.S., A p. 14.

Spanish, French, and English diplomatic policies. As a result, they passed out of the hands of men like Croghan and Wharton, whose interests were primarily economic, and into the hands of diplomats and statesmen, whose interests were primarily political. Though suffering personal defeat, Croghan and his associates had exerted a permanent influence in the founding and the extension of the present map of the United States.

Last Years, 1775-1782

Croghan lived to see the end of the struggle for American independence. He displayed but little interest in the revolutionary movement from 1763 to 1775. During this period it was confined chiefly to the eastern seaboard, whereas Croghan spent most of this period in the West. During the Stamp Act agitation, for example, he was engaged in his mission to the far off Illinois country. References to revolutionary disturbances were rarely made by him in his correspondence; if he did comment on them, it was only as a bystander. To him the Boston Massacre was a "fray in Boston" which manifested a popular dislike of the imperial army and a troublesome outlook.[454]

During these years the idea of independence was to Croghan unthinkable, just as it was to practically all Americans. His long and loyal service to his king and his close associations with other royal officials made it difficult for him to take any other attitude. He regarded the revolutionary disturbances as only temporary and as unfortunate. Non-importation agreements meant chaos in the Indian trade and therefore in Indian affairs; beyond this Croghan did not appear to have foreseen. The disruption of much of his life work by the attempt of both the English and the Americans after 1775 to enlist the active support of the Indians was still hidden in the future. Moreover, all of Croghan's extensive land operations were based upon the premise of continued dependence upon England.

---

[454] Croghan to Johnson, Apr. 8, 1770, in Johnson MSS., XVIII, 268.

When the break came in 1775, many of Croghan's closest relatives and associates became ardent tories. Guy and John Johnson, the successors to Sir William Johnson, with Joseph Brant, the Mohawk chief who had married Croghan's Indian daughter, were to lead many a bloody raid on the New York and Pennsylvania frontiers. Alexander McKee, Croghan's chief assistant and successor, changed his base from Pittsburg to Detroit and from there he sent forth or led Indian war parties that brought fire and slaughter to the Kentucky, Virginia, and Pennsylvania frontiers. Alexander Ross and David Franks, Croghan's close business associates, both sought refuge within the British lines. Dr. John Connolly, Croghan's nephew, was captured while proceeding in disguise to Detroit. He bore messages from Gage to Dunmore which dealt with the sending of an expedition from Detroit to capture Pittsburg and then to move eastward to the coast, thus attempting to separate the northern from the southern colonies. Augustine Prevost, Croghan's son-in-law, had resumed his commission in the British army; he became a captain and served under his father, General Prevost, at the capture of Savannah and Charleston.[455] It was therefore natural that Croghan should be suspected of being a tory. His enemies fostered this belief. It was partly on this account that the continental congress, when it took charge of Indian affairs in 1775, disregarded Croghan when it appointed George Morgan as agent for the Middle Department and when it drew up plans affecting the western tribes.[456]

---

[455] Draper MSS., 16F76; Byars: *B. and M. Gratz*, 199-200.

[456] William Trent, Croghan's half brother and partner in many undertakings, was charged with receiving from Lord North £40,000 to be used

Croghan, however, cast his lot with the colonists. When the news of the battle of Lexington came to the settlers on the upper Ohio, the patriots at once arranged for public meetings. The Pennsylvania partisans met at Hanna's Town and the Virginia partisans at Pittsburg. The latter meeting took place on May 16, 1775, the day of the opening of the Virginia court. Resolutions were passed approving the conduct of Massachusetts in "resisting the invaders of American Rights and Privileges to the utmost extreme." A committee of correspondence of twenty-eight members was appointed with Croghan as chairman. John Campbell, Edward Ward, Dorsey Pentecost, Thomas Smallman, and William Crawford were among his associates.[457]

This committee, like the numerous similar committees scattered throughout the colonies, had charge of putting its community upon a war footing and of preserving law and order. It placed under surveillance persons suspected of being tories and confined some who were considered tories. Among these was Alexander McKee. Until his escape two years later, McKee was kept in confinement under the direction of Croghan as chairman of the committee.[458] General Carleton in Canada was sending emissaries among the Indians and Croghan feared that he would send a strong garrison to reoccupy Fort Pitt.[459] To combat this movement and to prepare for war, the committee coöperated with Morgan in holding treaties with the

---

to incite the Indians against the Americans.—Trent to Dr. E. Bancroft, Oct. 15, 1775, in C. O., 40 Cf. Siebert, William H.: "The Tory Proprietors of Kentucky Lands," in *O. Arch. and Hist. Pub.*, XXVIII, 48ff. and "The Tories of the Upper Ohio", in *Biennial Rep., Archives and Hist., W. Va., 1911-1914*, 38ff.

[457] *Pa. Arch., 6th ser.*, II, 3; Craig: *Hist. of Pittsburg*, 128.

[458] French Refugees, 66 and 69, Dreer Coll.

[459] Croghan to Trent July 15, 1775, in Ohio Co. MSS., II, 6.

Indians. It also secured supplies of arms and ammunition and raised money. In spite of the danger of attacks by the British and Indians, two regiments were raised and sent to the east. Provision was made for supporting dependents of men who enlisted. The last service rendered by Croghan as a member of this committee appears to have been in 1777. While at Williamsburg in that year he helped Governor Patrick Henry plan the defense of the frontier. Upon his return to Pittsburg he carried Henry's letters and dispatches to General Hand.[460]

Croghan's services to the patriot cause appear to have been terminated in 1777 because he fell under suspicion of being a tory. After 1776, in all the states, the lines between the tories and whigs were much more carefully drawn. Pennsylvania passed an act on February 11, 1777, defining treason. Another act, passed on June 13, 1777, required all adult white male inhabitants to take an oath renouncing all allegiance to King George III and pledging allegiance to the newly created state. On March 6, 1778, an act was passed which named certain prominent citizens as tories and commanded them to appear for trial. This act also authorized the supreme executive council to issue thereafter proclamations to the same effect. On May 29, agents were appointed in each county to take charge of confiscated estates.

On June 15, 1778, the supreme executive council, exercising its newly given power, issued a proclamation which named several hundred persons, George Croghan included, as having "knowingly and willingly

[460] Henry to Hand, Aug. 9, 1777, in Emmet Coll., 6144; Thwaites and Kellogg: *Frontier Defense of the Upper Ohio*, 30.

aided and assisted the Enemies of the State and of the
United States of America", and commanded them to
present themselves for trial before August 1. If they
failed to present themselves they were to "stand and be
attainted of High Treason, to all intents and purposes
and shall suffer such pains and penalties and undergo
all such forfeitures as persons attainted of High
Treason ought to do." [461] On June 28, 1779, Croghan
appeared for trial and was discharged.[462] In a confi-
dential letter to Barnard Gratz, William Trent said:
"I am sorry the People were so foolish as to use Col.
Croghan so ill, as, to force Him to go to Philadᵃ. I
am of Opinion He neither could be of any Injury to the
Country, nor would be if He had it in his Power." [463]

About the year 1778, while Croghan was suspected
of being a tory, he moved his place of residence from
Pittsburg to Lancaster. Here, in his old age, he lived
in poverty. He depended upon the Gratzs and William Powell to supply him with food, clothing, and
money. He purchased a house without a chimney for
his residence and therefore had to buy an English open
stove; he wrote Michael Gratz that this left him in
debt and "Not a Doller to pay itt with or go to Market
with till I hear from you." "The old Gentⁿ is much in
want", was the comment of a friend when he relieved
Croghan's anxiety by paying a debt amounting to but

[461] *Pa. Col. Rec.*, XI, 512-518; *Pa. Evening Post*, June 25, 1778. This
issue of the *Post* was taken up almost entirely by the proclamation.

[462] Records of the Courts of Oyer and Terminer, etc., *Pa. Arch.*, 6th ser.,
XIII, 475.

[463] Trent to Gratz, Nov. 10, 1777, in Revolutionary Pap., Colonial Wars,
12, Etting Coll. Kingsford (*History of Canada*, IV, 24) and William H.
English (*Conquest of the Country Northwest of the River Ohio, etc.*, II,
1003) both state that Croghan was a tory. Cf. Cook: *Journals of the
Expedition of Major General Sullivan, etc.*, 21.

ten dollars. In 1780, Croghan removed to Passyunk Township which today lies within the limits of Philadelphia.[464]

Until 1780, Croghan still owned thousands of acres of land; these included the estates known as Croghan Hall, Croghan's Forest, and Monckton Hall. Most of his property was, however, heavily mortgaged and he was heavily in debt besides. He held his lands as long as it was at all possible, because there was still a good possibility of favorable action upon his memorials that were pending before the continental congress and because, as long as the Revolution continued and continental currency was the chief medium of exchange, lands could be sold only at a sacrifice. However, such a business situation could not be maintained indefinitely. An old debt to Shippen and Lawrence dating from 1754 from which Croghan had been legally released, but which he still intended to pay, proved particularly annoying because they demanded immediate payment in gold or silver. Other creditors, refusing to wait longer, brought legal actions against Croghan.[465]

Croghan was anxious to settle his business affairs. "Time you know flys fast away and a Life of Suspence is the Most Disagreeable Life in the World to Me", he wrote to Barnard Gratz on October 3, 1780.[466] His indebtedness to the Gratzs during this period fluctuated around £4,000. He now offered them their choice of

[464] Croghan to Gratz, Nov. 22, 1779, in Gratz-Croghan MSS., I, 71; Ohio Co. MSS., II, 26, 49, 60; Byars: *B. and M. Gratz*, 185, 194; Powell's account with Croghan's estate, 1804, Register of Wills, Philadelphia.

[465] Croghan to B. Gratz, Mar. 15, 1779, in McAllister Coll., YI2, 7310 FI5; Croghan to B. Gratz, Dec. 21, 1778, MS. in N.Y. Public Library; Gratz-Croghan MSS., I, 100 and II, 3.

[466] Draper MSS., I N49.

everything he owned to settle his debt. They selected
Croghan's five tracts in western Pennsylvania on Sewickly Creek totaling 1,488 acres.[467] Monckton Hall
was advertised for sale in 1781 and foreclosed in 1783
by the Burlington Company.

In order to pay an old debt of £2,100 which he owed
to Joseph Wharton and to provide himself with food
and fuel for the winter, Croghan, in 1780, conveyed to
Wharton the remaining 26,634 acres of his Otsego
patent in New York. This included the site of Croghan's Forest which Croghan had selected for his permanent residence eleven years before and which he
had kept to the last. The title which Wharton had
received was beclouded by Croghan's mortgage to
Governor William Franklin which had been assigned
to the Burlington Company. As a result, Wharton
lost his purchase in 1786, four years after Croghan's
death.[468]

Governor Franklin also lost money as a result of his
relations to the Otsego lands. He held a mortgage on
these lands for £1,800 and, in 1772, he purchased five
of the ten shares of the Burlington Company, valued
at £1,500. When the Revolution came, he became a
loyalist and was imprisoned; later he moved to England. Because all of his papers were lost in a New
York fire and because he had been a tory, Franklin
gave up all thought of recovering his loans. In the
meantime, the remaining original members of the Burlington Company had sold their shares to Andrew
Craig and William Cooper, both of Burlington, New

[467] Ohio Co. MSS., II, 26, 48, 53.

[468] Joseph Wharton to Samuel Wharton, Jan. 31, 1775, in Thomas
Wharton's Letter Bk., 1773-1784; Croghan to M. Gratz, Nov. 22, 1779, in
Gratz-Croghan MSS., I, 71; M. Gratz to B. Gratz, Sept. 26, 1779, in Mc-
Allister Coll.; Bk. of Deeds, XX, 306-315 (Sec. of State, Albany).

Jersey. The latter was the father of James Fenimore Cooper, the novelist. To Cooper and Craig were assigned Franklin's mortgages on 40,000 acres of Croghan's Otsego tract and on his Philadelphia property, together with Croghan's bond and the judgment foreclosing the mortgages.

Cooper and Craig, taking advantage of Franklin's situation, hastily proceeded in January, 1786, to arrange for the sale of the Otsego lands under the judgment of 1773 without giving any notice to either Franklin or to Croghan's executors. Appreciating the value of the prize they sought, Cooper and Craig engaged as their attorney, Alexander Hamilton, who secured the writ of *fieri facias* to issue to the sheriff. The other creditors of Croghan, his heirs, and executors likewise realized what was at stake and to oppose Hamilton, they employed Aaron Burr. Burr obtained an injunction to stop the sale, but in spite of it the sale was held. It took place in the middle of winter in a remote locality. By questionable methods Cooper and Craig themselves purchased the Otsego lands for only £2,700. An attempt was made by other creditors of the Croghan estate to pay their claims and take over the lands, but this attempt was unsuccessful. Cooper and Craig found their title complicated because Croghan had conveyed 6,061 acres in their tract to his son-in-law, Prevost and 26,634 acres to Joseph Wharton. To quiet these claims, they paid Prevost $1,250 and Wharton $2,000.[469] Cooper played the leading part in developing the lands which he and Craig had acquired. Previous improvements had almost all disappeared as

[469] When Cooper and Craig advertised their lands, for sale in the *Pa. Gazette*, Apr. 5, 12 and 19, 1786, Barnard Gratz, as Croghan's executor, and Dr. John Morgan warned prospective purchasers that their titles

a result of the border warfare during the Revolution. Cooper brought in many New England settlers, as Croghan had planned to do. He laid out the town of Cooperstown on the site selected by Croghan for his residence and built there his famous mansion, Otsego Hall.[470] Here on the frontier, his son, Fenimore, laid the foundation for his success as a novelist. The lands soon rose twenty fold in value, and the elder Cooper made the fortune and reaped the profits which Croghan had the vision to forsee, but which he never realized.

The Prevost heirs and Franklin came to feel very bitter toward Cooper. Augustine Prevost, Jr., wrote Franklin on December 31, 1812: "We have lost an immense property from the infamous advantage taken by Cooper and others without your knowledge by a forced Sale under your Title." When the elder Prevost met Franklin in London in 1791, they agreed to attempt to recover Franklin's debts of £3,300 with interest amounting to over £8,000 and also the lands

would not be good. Morgan and Gratz's articles, with the replies by Cooper and Craig, in the *Pa. Gazette*, May 3, 17, and June 7, 1786, give much information concerning Croghan's New York lands.

The William Temple Franklin MSS. contain a large number of letters and legal papers dating from 1786 to 1815 and present Franklin's side of the case. Cooper's side is presented in James Fenimore Cooper's *Chronicles of Cooperstown*, written in 1838 from original documents in the possession of the Cooper family. Cooper omits, however, all reference to the Hamilton-Burr episode and to the attempts of Franklin and the Prevosts to have the sale of 1786 declared illegal. Instead, Cooper presents figures to show that the lands cost Cooper and Craig a fair price and that Croghan and his family received more than $40,000 for them, which was five times their value at Croghan's death. To reach this conclusion Joseph Wharton's loan of £2,100 is listed in Pennsylvania paper money of 1780 as £9,553. Moreover, the year 1782 was hardly a good year in which to value fairly New York frontier lands. Cf. Land Pap., XXXVIII, 34 and XLIX, 68.

[470] Judge William Cooper's long letter (*cir.* 1806) to William Sampson, an Englishman, was published under the title of *Guide in the Wilderness,* etc. It describes his land operations and also those of his contemporaries in central New York.

which had been lost to Prevost. Suits for ejectment were brought, but no judicial opinion upon the title to the entire tract could be secured because judgment was always entered by default against the settlers. Their frontier spirit and common interests made them stronger than the laws and courts and prevented eject- ment. Moreover, a dispute arose between Franklin and the Prevosts as to the proper division of risks, expenses, and possible returns. Though the best attor- neys were engaged, A. J. Dallas, later Secretary of the United States Treasury, being one, and though these believed that their clients had "an incontrovertible right to recover", all that the Prevosts and Franklin could do was to bequeath to their heirs their equity in Croghan's estate in New York. Of the 250,000 acres which Croghan had once owned, only one half of Bel- vedere consisting of 9,000 acres remained for his daughter and grandchildren. Croghan Hall, the val- uable plantation near the rising city of Pittsburg where Croghan had spent so much of his life, was also lost after Croghan's death through the foreclosure of mort- gage holders.

Croghan escaped seeing his estates crumble away. He kept his faith in the West to the last and lived long enough to hear of the favorable report which the com- mittee of the continental congress had made relative to his land claim near Pittsburg and to the claims of the Indiana and Vandalia interests. He died on August 31, 1782, at his residence in Passyunk. His funeral took place at the Episcopal Church of St. Peter's in Philadelphia. Of his last days and death, we have only the cold, bare, legal records to tell us the story.[471]

[471] Croghan's Will, along with the Deposition of Powell in 1804, Powell's Account of his Relations to Croghan's Estate, 1804, a List of Legal Papers

The inventory of his personal property taken after his death shows that he possessed few of the comforts of life. The total value of his personal property was placed at £50, 13s. 6d. Among the interesting items were the following:

	£	s.	d.
1 Feather bed and 1 pillow	2	10	0
1 pair coarse sheets	1	10	0
1 pair shoes	0	10	0
1 Coat, 2 Jackets, 1 pair of Breeches	2	0	0
1 pewter dish	0	5	0
9 ditto plates	1	0	0
1 Old Pinchbeck Watch	3	5	0
1 Old Antediluvian coach or Waggon with Harness	3	0	0

Croghan's will named Barnard and Michael Gratz, Thomas Smallman, William Powell, and James Innis as his executors with power to act only with the consent of Barnard Gratz. They were directed to sell sufficient lands to pay his funeral expenses and all debts. Bequests of from 1,000 to 5,000 acres located in his Indian grant near Pittsburg were made to those who had cared for him in his last years and to the Gratzs and some kinsmen. The residue of his estate was left to his daughter, Susannah Prevost. The task of the executors was most difficult. Many spurious claims were made against the estate. Croghan's heirs, executors, and creditors, and the occupants or claimants of his lands were involved in innumerable and compli-cated suits; many of these were not finally decided till

left by Croghan, and the Inventory of Croghan's Personal Estate, are preserved in the office of the Register of Wills, Philadelphia. Cf. Records of Wills, Bk. A, 29-35, Clerk of Court of Appeals, Albany Co., N.Y.; Ohio Co. MSS., II, 61, 115. Volume II of the Gratz-Croghan MSS. gives many documents concerning his estate after his death.

they reached the supreme courts of Pennsylvania and the United States in the nineteenth century.

The place of Croghan's burial remains unknown; no tombstone, tablet, or monument perpetuates his name. Historians have generally neglected his work entirely, or have barely mentioned his name. In contrast, Daniel Boone, a much less important figure in the history of the West, has been apotheosized. The average student of American history is acquainted with Braddock, Pontiac, and Boone, but not with Croghan. Judged by material standards he was a failure; yet he was one of the most persuasive, persistent, and influential of the great American pioneers of his period and he typified, not the abnormal, but the normal development of society.

Insofar as any one man can influence history, Croghan had much to do with laying the foundations upon which George Rogers Clark, the American diplomats at Paris in 1783, and the authors of the Ordinance of 1787 built. His dreams helped to inspire such younger men as Daniel Clark, John Campbell, Dorsey Pentecost, William Thompson, Barnard and Michael Gratz, and William Croghan to carry on similar work on more distant frontiers. He encountered two great forces; first, the desire of the white man for the profits of the Indian trade and the reciprocal desire of the Indian for the white man's goods, and second, the irresistible westward movement of the Anglo-Saxon settler. These forces were affected by the rivalry of England and France, by political troubles between England and her colonies, and by mutual jealousies between the colonies or states.

In his land operations Croghan touched the lives of

many prominent Americans and he influenced the lives of numerous unknown settlers. He helped to provide the settlers with land by helping to eliminate the claims of the Indians, by surveying the land, by patenting it, by beginning the clearing of forests, by laying out roads, by beginning the erection of houses, sawmills, and gristmills, by advertising and marketing the land, and by supplying the necessary capital and assuming great risks. His viewpoint, however, belonged to the past for he thought in terms of proprietary colonies with individualistic control over land; he was not yet socialistic enough in his viewpoint to see that the state would make a better landlord than an individual or a land company.

George Croghan, Sir William Johnson, Benjamin and William Franklin, George Washington, and others, in their great land operations, performed services for the small settler similar to those which after the Revolution were performed by the state and federal governments. They were representative Americans with human motives – one of which is for amassing wealth; but aside from this, in spite of it, and through it, their ideas and actions had a social significance and influence. They were not mere real estate dealers, but rather commonwealth builders who gave expression to the deep impulses of American life to seek homes by pushing westward. Their immediate purposes often failed, but their efforts prepared the way for their successors to enjoy the fruits of their labors.

Croghan and his associates dreamed of towns and cities and commonwealths teeming with people, rising where their chain carriers were running their lines. They were typical pioneers who encountered difficulties and made sacrifices because they saw far beyond their own generation and saw as certainties what could only be realized many years later. Croghan's visions of the future greatness of the western wilderness have been realized, but not in his generation.

Bibliography

I. GUIDES AND CALENDARS

(The more general wellknown guides such as that by Channing, Hart, and Turner are not included in this list).

AMERICAN Historical Association: Public Archives Commission of; Reports, in the annual reports of the Association for 1900, 1901, 1904 and 1905.

ANDREWS, Charles M. and Frances G. Davenport: Guide to the manuscript materials for the history of the United States to 1783, in the British Museum, in minor London archives, and in the libraries of Oxford and Cambridge. Carnegie Institution of Washington, Publication No. 90. Washington, 1908.

ANDREWS, Charles M.: Guide to the materials for American history to 1783 in the Public Record Office of Great Britain. Carnegie Institution of Washington, Publication No. 90 A 1. Washington, 1912.

BANCROFT, George and assistants, compilers: Chronological index to the American correspondence in the Bancroft Collection, 1748-1789. 22 vols. In manuscript in the New York Public Library.

[BRITISH] Royal Historical Manuscripts Commission: Fourteenth Report, Appendix X, Calendar of the manuscripts of the Earl of Dartmouth, II, American papers. London, 1895.

CANADIAN Archives, Reports, Ottawa, 1882-date. A calendar of the Bouquet manuscripts is found in the report for 1889; of the Haldimand manuscripts in the reports for the years 1884 to 1890; of many manuscripts in Paris archives in various reports.

CONGRESS, Library of: Handbook of manuscripts in the Library of Congress. Washington, 1918.

DAY, Richard E., compiler: Calendar of the Sir William Johnson manuscripts in the New York State Library. Albany, 1909.

DEPUY, Henry F.: A bibliography of the English colonial treaties with the American Indians including a synopsis of each treaty. New York, 1917.

FERNOW, Berthold, compiler: Calendar of the council minutes of New York, 1668-1783. New York State Library Bulletin 58, History 6, March 1902.

FITZPATRICK, John C., compiler: List of the Washington manuscripts from 1592 to 1775 . . . in the Library of Congress. Washington, 1919.

FORD, Worthington, C., compiler: List of the Benjamin Franklin papers in the Library of Congress. Washington, 1905.

FRIEDENWALD, Herbert, compiler: Calendar of Washington manuscripts in the Library of Congress. Washington, 1901.

HAYS, Isaac M., compiler: Calendar of the papers of Benjamin Franklin in the library of the American Philosophical Society. 5 vols. Philadelphia, 1908.

LINCOLN, Charles H., compiler: Calendar of Sir William Johnson manuscripts in the library of the American Antiquarian Society. Transactions of the Society, XI, Worcester, 1906.

NEW YORK Public Library: Manuscript collections in the New York Public Library. Bulletin of the New York Public Library, V, July, 1901.

O'CALLAGHAN, Edmund B., compiler: Calendar of historical manuscripts in the office of the secretary of state of New York. Albany, 1866.

O'CALLAGHAN, Edmund B., compiler: Calendar of New York colonial manuscripts indorsed land papers in the office of the secretary of state of New York, 1643-1803. Albany, 1864.

PALMER, William P., compiler: Calendar of Virginia state papers and other manuscripts . . . preserved at Richmond, I. Richmond, 1875.

STEVENS, Benjamin Franklin: Catalogue index of manuscripts in the archives of England, France, Holland, and Spain relating to America, 1763-1783. In manuscript in the Library of Congress. London, 1870-1902.

UNITED STATES, department of state: "Catalogue of the papers of the Continental Congress," in Bulletin of the Bureau of Rolls and Library, No. 1, September, 1918.

II. PRINTED SOURCES

(This list includes only those books which yielded material for this particular study. For a more complete bibliography for this period,

the reader is referred to the excellent one in C. W. Alvord's "Mississippi Valley in British Politics").

ADAIR, James: History of the American Indians. London, 1775.

ADAMS, Herbert Baxter: "Washington's interest in western lands", in Johns Hopkins University Studies in History and Political Science, III (1885), 55ff.

ALDEN, George H.: New governments west of the Allegheny mountains before 1780. In Bulletin of the University of Wisconsin, Series in Economics, Political Science, and History, II (1899).

ALVORD, Clarence W.: The Mississippi valley in British politics. 2 vols. Cleveland, 1917.

————: The Illinois country, 1673-1818. Volume I of the Centennial history of Illinois. Springfield, 1920.

AMERICAN Historical Association, Annual Reports. Washington, 1890-date. The "Intercepted letters to the Duc de Mirepoix, 1756" are printed in the Report for 1896, I, 660ff.

BOSSU, N.: Nouveaux voyages dans l'Amerique septentrionale. Amsterdam, 1777.

[BRITISH] Acts of the Privy Council of England, Colonial Series. Edited by Wm. Grant, Jas. Monro and A. W. Fitzroy. 6 vols. London, 1908-1912.

BURTON, Clarence M.: "John Connolly, a Tory of the Revolution," in the proceedings of the American Antiquarian Society, XX (1920), 70ff.

BUTTERFIELD, Consul W., editor: The Washington-Crawford letters, 1767-1781, concerning western lands. Cincinnati, 1877.

BYARS, William Vincent, editor: Barnard and Michael Gratz, merchants of Philadelphia, 1754-1798. Jefferson City, 1916.

CARTER, Clarence E.: Great Britain and the Illinois country, 1763-1774. Washington, 1910.

————: "British policy towards the American Indians in the South, 1763-1768", in English Historical Review, XXXIII (1918), 37ff.

CHALKLEY, Lyman, compiler: Chronicles of the Scotch-Irish settlement in Virginia extracted from the original court records of Augusta County, 1745-1800. 3 vols. Rosslyn, Va., 1912.

CLEMENTS, William L., editor: "Journal of Major Robert

Rogers", in the proceedings of the American Antiquarian Society, new series, XXVIII (1918), 228ff.

COLLINSON, Peter: "An account of some very large fossil teeth found in North America", in the Philosophical transactions of the Royal Society of London, LVII (1767), 464ff.

CONGRESS, Library of: Journals of the Continental Congress, 1774-1784. 22 vols. 1904-date.

COOK, Frederick, editor: Journals of the military expedition of Major General John Sullivan against the Six Nations of Indians in 1779. Auburn, N.Y., 1887.

COOPER, James Fenimore: Chronicles of Cooperstown. New York, 1838.

COOPER, William: Guide in the wilderness, or the history of the first settlements in the western counties of New York, etc. Dublin, 1810.

CRAIG, Neville B., editor: The olden time: a monthly publication, devoted to the preservation of documents and other authentic information in relation to . . . the country around the head of the Ohio. 2 vols. Pittsburgh, 1846-1848.

————: Lecture upon the controversy between Pennsylvania and Virginia about the boundary line. Pittsburgh, 1843.

————: The history of Pittsburgh. Pittsburgh, 1851.

CRANE, Verner W.: "The Tennessee River as the road to Carolina; the beginnings of exploration and trade," in the Mississippi Valley Historical Review, III (1916), 3ff.

————: "The southern frontier in Queen Anne's war", in the American Historical Review, XXIV (1919), 379ff.

CRUMRINE, Boyd, editor: "The records of deeds for the District of West Augusta, Virginia, for the court held at Fort Dunmore, [Pittsburgh]", in the Annals of the Carnegie Museum of Pittsburgh, III, 237ff.

————: "Minute book of the Virginia court held at Fort Dunmore for the District of West Augusta, 1775-1776," in idem, I, 524ff.

————: "Minute or order book of the Virginia court held for Yohogania County, first at Augusta Town and afterwards near West Elizabeth, 1776-1780," in idem, II, 71ff., and 205ff.

————: "Minute or order book of the Virginia court held for Ohio County, Virginia, at Black's cabin, 1777-1780," in idem, III, 5ff.

————: History of Washington County, Pennsylvania. Philadelphia, 1882.

DAHLINGER, Charles W.: Pittsburgh, a sketch of its early social life. New York, 1916.

DALLAS, A. J., compiler: Reports of cases ruled and adjudged in the several courts of the United States and of Pennsylvania held at the seat of the federal government. 4 vols. Philadelphia, 1790-1799.

DARLINGTON, Mary C.: Fort Pitt and letters from the frontier. Pittsburgh, 1892.

————: History of Colonel Henry Bouquet and the western frontiers of Pennsylvania, 1747-1764. Pittsburgh, 1920.

DARLINGTON, William M., editor: Christopher Gist's journals with historical, geographical, and ethnological notes and biographies of his contemporaries. Pittsburgh, 1893.

DIFFENDERFFER, Frank R.: "Indian traders' troubles – Joseph Simon and his associates in the Indiana or 'Suff'ring Traders' grant," in the papers of the Lancaster County Historical Society, IX, 10ff.

DINWIDDIE, Robert: The official records of Robert Dinwiddie, Lieutenant-Governor of Virginia, 1751-1758. Edited by R. A. Brock, Virginia Historical Collections, new series, III and IV. Richmond, 1883-1884.

DOCUMENTS respecting the claim of persons therein mentioned to a certain tract of land called Indiana [Ridgway Library, Philadelphia]. Philadelphia, cir. 1794.

EVANS, Lewis: An analysis of a general map of the middle British colonies in America, etc. Philadelphia, 1755.

FORCE, Peter, editor: American archives . . . a documentary history of . . . the North American colonies (1774-1776). 4th series, 6 vols.; 5th series, 3 vols. Washington, 1837-1853.

FRANKLIN, Benjamin: Writings. Edited by A. H. Smyth, 10 vols. New York, 1907.

GENTLEMAN'S magazine, 223 vols. London, 1731-1868.

GOLDER, Frank A.: Russian expansion on the Pacific, 1641-1850. Cleveland, 1914.

GOODMAN, Alfred T., editor: Journal of Captain William Trent from Logstown to Pickawillani, 1752, etc. Cincinnati, 1871.

HALSEY, Francis Whiting, editor: A tour of four great rivers: the Hudson, Mohawk, Susquehanna, and Delaware in 1769 –

being the journal of Richard Smith of Burlington, New Jersey. New York, 1906.

————: The old New York frontier, 1614-1800. New York, 1912.

HAMILTON, Stanislaus Murray, editor: Letters to George Washington and accompanying papers, 1752-1775. 5 vols. New York, 1898.

HANNA, Charles A.: The wilderness trail, etc, 2 vols. New York, 1911.

HASSLER, Edward W.: Old Westmoreland: a history of western Pennsylvania during the revolution. Pittsburgh, 1900.

HAZARD, Samuel, editor: Register of Pennsylvania, 16 vols. Philadelphia, 1828-1836.

HENDERSON, Archibald: The conquest of the old southwest. New York, 1920.

HODGE, Frederick W., editor: Handbook of American Indians north of Mexico. Bulletin 30, Bureau of Ethnology, Smithsonian Institution. Washington, 1907.

HOUGH, Franklin B., editor: Journal of Major Robert Rogers. Albany, 1883.

HULBERT, Archer B.: Historic highways of America. 16 vols. Cleveland, 1902-1905.

HUNTER, William: "Observations on the bones, commonly supposed to be elephants' bones, which have been found near the River Ohio in America," in the Philosophical transactions of the Royal Society of London, LVIII (1768), 34ff.

HUTCHINS, Thomas: A topographical description of Virginia, Pennsylvania, Maryland, and North Carolina, 1778. Edited by F. C. Hicks. Cleveland, 1904.

————: Description topographique de la Virginie, de la Pensylvanie, du Maryland et de la Caroline septentrionale, etc. Paris, 1781.

ILLINOIS Historical Collections: vol. x, The critical period, 1763-1765; vol. xi, The new regime, 1765-1767; vol. xii, trade and politics, 1767-1769 – all edited by C. W. Alvord, and C. E. Carter. Springfield, Ill., 1915-1923.

JACKSON, George B.: "John Stuart, superintendent of Indian affairs for the southern district, 1763-1779," in Tennessee Historical Magazine, III (1917), 165ff.

JONES, Rev. David: A journal of two visits made to some nations of Indians on the west side of the River Ohio in the years 1772 and 1773. Edited by H. G. Jones. New York, 1865.

JONES, U. J.: History of the early settlement of the Juniata valley. Philadelphia, 1856.

KELLOGG, Louise Phelps: The French regime in Wisconsin and the Northwest, Madison, 1925.

KEPPEL, Thomas R.: Life of Augustus Viscount Keppel. 2 vols. London, 1842.

KIMBALL, Gertrude S., editor: Correspondence of William Pitt with colonial governors and military and naval commissioners in America. 2 vols. New York, 1906.

KINGSFORD, William: History of Canada. 10 vols. Toronto, 1887-1898.

KLEIN, Joseph: Der Sibirische Peltzhandel und seine Bedeutung für die Eroberung Sibiriens. Bonn, 1906.

KOHLER, Max J.: "The Franks family as British army contractors," in American Jewish Historical Society publications, XI (1903), 181ff.

LYTLE, Milton S.: History of Huntingdon County, Pennsylvania. Lancaster, 1876.

McCLURE, Rev. David: Diary. Edited by F. B. Dexter. New York, 1899.

McILWAIN, Charles H., editor: Wraxall's abridgement of the New York Indian records, 1678-1751. Cambridge, 1915.

MARYLAND Historical Society: Archives. Baltimore, 1883-date. The correspondence of Governor Horatio Sharpe, 1750-1771, is printed in volumes VI, IX, and XIV.

MASSACHUSETTS Historical Society, Collections, fourth series, vols. IX and X (1871). These volumes contain the "Aspinwall papers".

MICHIGAN Pioneer and Historical Collections. Lansing, 1877-date. In volume XIX there are printed selections from the Bouquet manuscripts and the Haldimand manuscripts.

MITCHELL, J. T. and Henry Flanders, compilers: The statutes at large of Pennsylvania, 1682-1809. Vols. 2-18. Philadelphia, 1896-1915.

[MOREAU, Jacob Nicolas]: Mémoire contenant le précis des faits, avec leurs pièces justificatives, pour servir de réponse aux observations envoyées par les ministres d'Angleterre, dans les cours de l'Europe. Paris, 1756.

O'CALLAGHAN, Edmund B., editor: Documentary history of the state of New York. 4 vols. Albany, 1849-1851.

————: Documents relative to the colonial history of the state of New York. 15 vols. Albany, 1856. Cited as "N.Y. Col. Docs." in footnotes.

O'NEIL, James L.: "George Croghan and Aughwick, Huntingdon County, Pennsylvania," in American-Irish Historical Society, Journal, IX (1910), 348ff.

PAGE, Richard C. M.: Genealogy of the Page family in Virginia, etc. New York, 1883.

PAINE, Thomas: The writings of Thomas Paine. Edited by M. D. Conway. 4 vols. New York, 1894.

PARKMAN, Francis: The conspiracy of Pontiac and the Indian war after the conquest of Canada. 2 vols. Sixth Edition. Boston, 1870.

————: Montcalm and Wolfe. 2 vols. Boston, 1890.

————: A half century of conflict. 2 vols. Boston, 1892.

PENNSYLVANIA Archives; edited by Samuel Hazard. 12 vols. Philadelphia, 1852-1856. The later series, second to seventh, are less important than the volumes edited by Hazard.

PENNSYLVANIA Colonial Records. 16 vols. Edited by Samuel Hazard. Philadelphia, 1852. The minutes of the Provincial Council, 1683-1776, are given in volumes I-X; volumes X-XVI give the minutes of the Supreme Executive Council, 1776-1790.

PENNSYLVANIA, Department of Internal Affairs, Land Office; Warrantee atlas of Allegheny County, Pennsylvania. Harrisburg, 1914.

PENNSYLVANIA Gazette, 1728-1789.

PENNSYLVANIA Magazine of History and Biography. Philadelphia, 1877-date. In volume II, 303ff., and VI, 344ff., there are given the census reports for Pittsburgh in 1760 and 1761, respectively; in volume XXIV, 17ff., there is an article on "Old Mother Cumberland"; in volumes XXXIII, 319ff. and 432ff. and in volumes XXXIV, 41ff., there are printed selections from the letter books of Thomas Wharton; in volume XXXV, 415ff., there are printed letters from William Franklin to William Strahan, and on pages 429ff. letters of George Croghan; in volume XXXII, 1ff., 152ff. and 395ff. there is printed the Journal of James Kenny, 1761-1763.

[PENNSYLVANIA] Report of the Commission to locate the sites of the frontier forts of Pennsylvania. Second Edition. Harrisburg, 1916.

[PENNSYLVANIA] Votes and proceedings of the house of representatives [assembly] of the province of Pennsylvania, 1682-1776. 6 vols. Philadelphia, 1752-1776.

PERKINS, James H.: Annals of the west, etc. Cincinnati, 1846.

ROGERS, Robert: Ponteach or the savages of America, a tragedy. Edited by Allan Nevins. Chicago, 1914.

ROWLAND, Kate M.: The life of George Mason, 1725-1792. 2 vols. New York, 1892.

RUPP, Isaac D.: Early history of western Pennsylvania and the west, 1754-1833. Pittsburg, 1846.

SARGENT, Winthrop: The history of an expedition against Fort DuQuesne in 1755 under Major-General Edward Braddock. Philadelphia, 1856.

SEVERANCE, Frank H.: An old frontier of France – the Niagara region and adjacent lakes under French control. 2 vols. New York, 1917.

SIEBERT, William H.: "Tory proprietors of Kentucky lands", in Ohio Archæological and Historical Society, publications, XXVIII (1919), 48ff.

SMITH, William Henry: The life and public services of Arthur St. Clair with his correspondence and other papers. Cincinnati, 1882.

SPENCER, C. W.: "The Land System of Colonial New York," in New York State Historical Association proceedings, XVI, 150-164.'

STONE, William L.: The life and times of Sir William Johnson. 2 vols. Albany, 1865.

SULLIVAN, James, editor: The papers of Sir William Johnson. 3 vols. (to date). Albany, 1921.

SURREY, N. M. Miller: The commerce of Louisiana during the French regime, 1699-1763. In vol. LXXI, No. 1, of the Columbia University studies in history, economics and public law. New York, 1916.

[THOMSON, Charles]: An enquiry into the causes of the alienation of the Delaware and Shawanese Indians from the British interest and into the measures taken for recovering their friendship, etc. London, 1759.

THWAITES, Reuben Gold, editor: Early western travels, 32 vols.

Cleveland, 1904-1907. Volume I consists chiefly of Croghan's journals.

THWAITES, Reuben Gold and Louise P. Kellogg, editors: Documentary history of Lord Dunmore's war, 1774. Madison, 1905.

TURNER, Frederick Jackson: "Western state-making in the revolutionary era," in American Historical Review, I (1895), 70ff. and 251ff.

————: The frontier in American history. New York, 1920.

TURNER, Morris K.: The commercial relations of the Susquehanna valley during the colonial period. Manuscript Ph.D. thesis, University of Pennsylvania, 1916.

VILLIERS du Terrage, Marc de: Les dernières années de la Louisiane française. Paris, 1903.

VIRGINIA Magazine of History and Biography. Richmond, 1893-date. Documents concerning the treaty at Logstown in 1752 are printed in volume XIII (1905), 143ff.

WALKER, Mabel G.: "Sir John Johnson, Loyalist," in Mississippi Valley Historical Review, III (1916), 318ff.

WALPOLE, Horace, fourth Earl of Orford: Letters. Edited by Mrs. Pagot Toynbee, 16 vols. London, 1903.

WALTON, Joseph S.: Conrad Weiser and the Indian policy of colonial Pennsylvania. Philadelphia, 1900.

WASHINGTON, George: Writings, Edited by W. C. Ford. 14 vols. New York, 1889-1893.

[WHARTON, Samuel]: Plain facts: being an examination into the rights of the Indian nations of America to their respective countries; and a vindication of the grant from the Six Nations of Indians to the proprietors of Indiana against the decisions of the legislature of Virginia. Philadelphia, 1781.

WILLIAMS, Charles R.: "George Croghan, 1791-1849," in Ohio Archæological and Historical Society, Publications, XII (1903), 375ff.

WINSOR, Justin: The Mississippi basin — the struggle in America between England and France, 1697-1763. Boston, 1895.

WISCONSIN State Historical Society: Collections. Madison, 1888-date.

WITHERS, Alexander S.: Chronicles of border warfare (1831). Edited by R. G. Thwaites. Cincinnati, 1912.

III. MANUSCRIPT SOURCES

AMERICAN Antiquarian Society Library (Worcester, Mass.) The *Sir William Johnson MSS.* in this library proved useful for this study.

AMERICAN Philosophical Society Library (Philadelphia). Important material relating to this study was found in the *Papers of Benjamin Franklin,* 132 vols., preserved in this society's library.

BRITISH Museum (London). The miscellaneous set of transcripts secured from the library of the Museum are noted in the footnotes.

[BRITISH] Public Record Office (London). The miscellaneous set of transcripts secured from this depository are noted in the footnotes. Those most important came from the *Colonial Office Papers.*

CANADA, Public Archives of (Ottawa). Use was made of transcripts of the *Bouquet MSS.,* 17 vols., and of the *Haldimand MSS.,* 231 vols., in these archives.

CONGRESS, Library of (Washington, D.C.) Scattered documents useful for this study were found among the following: *Croghan MSS.,* in *Personal miscellany; Sir William Johnson MSS.,* 1 vol.; *Edw. and Jos. Shippen MSS.; Pennsylvania miscellaneous MSS.,* *Benjamin Franklin Papers; Papers of the Continental Congress,* 385 vols.; *Washington Papers,* upwards of 400 vols.; and the transcripts from the *Colonial Office Papers* in the Public Record Office, London.

CUMBERLAND County (Carlisle, Pa.) Croghan's earliest deeds and mortgages are on record here.

GRATZ (Anderson) Private Library (St. Louis, Mo.) Mr. Anderson Gratz very generously placed the twenty-six manuscript volumes of the *Gratz Papers, 1750-1850, collected with relating documents, maps and notes,* edited by William V. Byars in 1914, at the disposal of the writer. The other copy of this work is deposited with the Missouri Historical Society. The book, *Barnard and Michael Gratz, merchants in Philadelphia, 1754-1798,* also edited by Byars, contains the most important documents found in the *Gratz Papers.* These twenty-six volumes consist of transcripts of documents found in various libraries and private collections. They are arranged chronologically and are particularly valuable for the study of the westward movement and for the commerical life of Philadelphia.

GRATZ (Simon) Private Collection (Philadelphia). The courtesy of Mr. Gratz enabled the writer to make use of the Croghan and Trent letters in this collection.

ILLINOIS University Library (Urbana). Fortunately, this library had transcripts made of some of the *Sir William Johnson MSS.* before the Albany fire. Use was made of these important transcripts, marked (Ill.) in the footnotes, and also of the transcripts from the French *Archives nationales, colonies, series C 13*, consisting of letters and reports sent home by French officials in America, and *series B*, consisting of the correspondence of French ministers with colonial officials.

NEW YORK CITY Public Library. The section of the *Aaron Vanderpoel MSS.* entitled, *William Temple Franklin's estate*, throws much light on land speculation in New York and Pennsylvania during the latter half of the eighteenth century and describes Croghan's relations to Governor William Franklin. Use was also made of the *Virginia Papers* and the *Cadwallader Colden letters, etc.*, in the Bancroft Collection; of the *Papers relating to Canada, 1692-1792, Letters and documents relating to the Indians, 1750-1775, Virginia Papers, 1606-1775*, and the *Monckton Papers* – all in the George Chalmers Collection; and of the Emmett Collection. Several valuable contemporary maps and nine Croghan letters were found here.

NEW YORK Historical Society Library (New York City). A few deeds and other Croghan documents were found here.

NEW YORK, Office of the Secretary of State (Albany). Many original papers relating to the land history of New York and to its Indian affairs are preserved in this office. Those most useful for this study were the *Books of patents, 1664-1866*, 41 vols., the *Original Books of patents 1664-1774*, 13 vols., the *Books of deeds, 1659-1855*, 43 vols., and the *Indian deeds and treaties*, 2 vols.

NEW YORK State Library (Albany). Of the original 26 volumes of the important *Sir William Johnson MSS.* in this library, volumes 1, 2, 6, and 16 to 25 inclusive are left and are in only fair condition. Fortunately, a part of the material in the earlier volumes had been prepared for the press before the fire in 1911 and is now appearing in the *Papers of Sir William Johnson*, edited by Dr. James Sullivan. Here also were found the original *New York colonial council minutes* and some transcripts from the British Public Record Office.

PENNSYLVANIA, Department of Internal Affairs (Harrisburg). Use was made of the following land records of the State: *Patent books, Deed books, Letters of attorney, Copied surveys, New purchase (1768) applications* and *West side applications.* Besides these records, there are many miscellaneous documents which should be made more accessible to the historical investigator.

PENNSYLVANIA Historical Society Library (Philadelphia). Croghan's activities made it difficult for him to preserve his papers; most of those which he did preserve were legal, business, or official papers. Fortunately, his leading correspondents were in the habit of preserving incoming letters and making copies of outgoing letters in their letter books. Upon Croghan's death most of his papers passed into the hands of his executors, Barnard and Michael Gratz, and were kept with many Gratz papers above the Gratz store in Philadelphia. A small number of persons, including the grand-son and great-grandson of Michael Gratz, namely Colonel Frank M. Etting and Simon Gratz respectively, selected and preserved a few of the more important papers. The rest of this large collection has disappeared. Etting's and Gratz's collections are now in the library of the Historical Society of Pennsylvania. Of Etting's Collection, the *Ohio Company MSS.* in two volumes (covering the period 1754 to 1813 and dealing chiefly with the traders' losses in 1754 and 1763 and with the Vandalia project), the *Gratz-Croghan MSS.* in two volumes, and the *Gratz-Croghan Deeds* are especially rich in Croghan material. The *Revolutionary MSS., Miscellaneous MSS.* and *Large miscellaneous MSS.* of the Etting Collection were also useful. The Gratz papers in this and other libraries and in private collections have never been extensively used by historians. They deal particularly with inland commerce west from Philadelphia, with the sea-going trade of Philadelphia and with land speculation and colonizing projects in the West during the century from about 1750 to 1850.

PENNSYLVANIA State Library (Harrisburg). *The Provincial Papers, 1664-1783,* 85 volumes, are well catalogued; most of the important documents in this series, however, have been printed in the *Pennsylvania colonial records* or in the *Pennsylvania archives.* Baynton, Wharton, and Morgan's Letter book A and John Baynton's Private letter book contain some letters relating to Croghan.

PHILADELPHIA (Pa.) City Hall. Croghan's will with related

papers is still on file in the office of the Register of Wills; the records in the office of the Register of Deeds describe many of. Croghan's land transactions and incidently often give other information not directly related to his land transactions.

PHILADELPHIA, Library Company of, Ridgway Branch. The Du Simitiere Collection, dealing with American History before 1783, and the McAllister Collection contain many documents relating to the westward movement. The McAllister Collection consists chiefly of papers relating to business houses in Philadelphia from 1760 to about 1870.

WISCONSIN State Historical Society Library (Madison). Use was made of transcripts from Lyman C. Draper's *Life of Daniel Boone,* from other *Draper MSS.,* and from the *Croghan Papers.* The latter, however, deal chiefly with the Kentucky Croghans. Information concerning Croghan's relatives was secured from the *Brant Papers.*

Index

Index

by the English, 154-155; Indian conference in 1761 at, 155-156; Indian conference in 1765 at, 188; English colony proposed around, 234

Dieskau, Baron: 119

Dinwiddie, Gov. Robert: 43, 82, 137 *footnote*, 86-88, 94, 120, 272

District of West Augusta: 224, 307, 308

Dobson, Joseph: 168

Dunmore, Lord: on impossibility of checking westward movement, 211; attitude toward Croghan's land claims around Pittsburg, 293; aggressive western policy after 1773, 301; land speculators welcome, 302; his war with Shawnee, 302-304; boundary controversy with Pennsylvania, 304-309

DuQuesne, Gov. Le Cain: instructed to drive English from the Ohio, 78, 79

EASTON: Indian conference in 1757, 133-136; in 1758, 137-140, 210; in 1762, 157-158

Ecuyer, Capt. Simeon: 147; besieged in Fort Pitt, 164-170

Edmonstone, Capt. Charles: 215

Evans, Gov. John: 21

Evans, Lewis: 37, 112, 264

FAIRFAX, William: 81

Farmar, Major Robert: 264 *footnote*, 187, 188, 192

Fauquier, Gov. Francis: 210, 218

Filius Gallicae letters: 108-111

Fincastle Co., Va.; organized, 224

Finley, John: 39

Forbes, Gen. John: Indian department assists, 124; appreciates importance of Indian affairs, 136-137; captures Fort DuQuesne, 137-142

Forbes's Road: 28, 94, 143, 189; settlement along, 212-214

Fort Augusta: 133

Fort Bedford: 165, 212

Fort Cumberland: 92, 94, 95

Fort de Chartres: 175, 181, 184, 186, 188, 192, 195, 197, 198, 199, 226

Fort Dunmore: 306

Fort DuQuesne: 83, 102, 105, 106, 107, 124, 137, 213; Braddock's expedition against, 191-199; abandoned by French, 139-141

Fort Granville: destroyed by French, 105

Fort Johnson: 123

Fort Le Boeuf: 77, 156; French establish fort at, 82; Washington's mission to, 82-83

Fort Ligonier: 167, 212

Fort Loudoun (Pa.): 130, 180, 212

Fort Lyttleton: 158, 165

Fort Miami: 35, 143, 155, 156

Fort Michillimackinac: 143, 156, 188, 206, 226, 228; occupied by English, 154-155

Fort Necessity: 137 *footnote*, 85, 87; surrendered, 88

Fort Niagara: 156, 228; captured by Johnson, 119

Fort Ouiatenon: 20, 175, 185, 186; Indian conference at in 1765, 187

Fort Pitt: 156, 160, 177, 178; established, 140-142; importance, 143; Indian conferences in 1759 and 1760, 143-153; difficulty to provision and maintain, 146-148; Pennsylvania establishes trading house at, 150-152; in danger till 1760, 153; besieged in 1763, 164-166; base for occupation of Illinois country, 175 ff.; Indian conference in 1765 at, 181-182; Indian conference in 1766, 194-195, 219; Indian conference in 1768, 220-222; in state of war, 224; abandoned by English, 226, seized by Virginia, 306; see *Pittsburg*

Fort Presque Isle: 153, 154, 156; established by French, 82

Fort St. Joseph: 156

Illinois country: 21-22, 118; Bouquet
plans to occupy in 1763, 157;
French still controlled in 1765, 175;
difficult to occupy, 175-177, 183;
Croghan's mission to, 177-189; occupied by English, 188; English interest in its Indian trade, 189 ff.;
Croghan's second mission to, 191-
199; trade disappointing to English, 203-204; Croghan reports on
fine lands in, 262; organization of
Illinois Co. in 1766, 263-264
Illinois Indians: 175-204, *passim*;
restless under French control, 21-
22; placed in Northern District,
118
Illinois Land Co. (of 1773): 427
footnote, 301, 311; organization,
296; see *Illinois-Wabash Co.*
Illinois-Wabash Co: 314, 316-319
Indian boundary line: see *Proclamation line of 1763* and *Indian Land
Sales*
Indian department: reasons for establishment, 115-116; early organization, 116-118; Northern and
Southern Districts, 118; under control of military, 119-121; no funds
of its own, 120, 126, 174, 229; deputy superintendents in Northern
District, 121; nature of boundary
between the two Districts, 129-
131; difficulties with Pennsylvania,
133-135, 138; arranges Indian
treaties in Pennsylvania and assists Forbes, 131-142; services to
army at Fort Pitt, 143-153; attitude
of military officials to, 147, 148; assists in occupying French forts,
153-155; difficulty in securing
funds, 158-163; plan to strengthen
it, 166-170; proclamation of 1763,
170-172; plan of 1764, 172-173;
weakness of plan, 173-175; put into
effect, 192 ff.; expenditures and
powers limited after 1766, 201-
207; effect of revolutionary trou-

bles on, 205, 225; services rendered, 1758-1763, 208; turns attention
to land affairs after 1766, 209;
attempts to quiet Indian resentment
at settlements in West, 216 ff.;
treaty of Fort Stanwix, 221 ff.; decline after 1768, 225 ff.; regulation
of Indian trade abandoned, 227-
230; decrease in staff, 227; drastic
cut in budget, 229; relation to Lord
Dunmore's War, 302-304; see
Johnson, Sir William; Stuart, John
and *Croghan, George*
Indian land sales: to Pennsylvania
before 1755, 55, 59; proposed purchase by Pennsylvania of lands to
the Ohio, 68; Iroquois purchase of
1754 by Pennsylvania, 71, 210;
sale of Ohio lands in 1754 denied,
84; Penns retrocede southwestern
Pennsylvania, 138-139; around interior forts, 144; private purchases
forbidden, 171, 173; Croghan's
purchases on the Ohio, 214-225,
254 ff., 296-297; large regions sold
at Fort Stanwix, 221-225; method
of sale of part in Pennsylvania,
240-241; method of sale in New
York after 1763, 249-250; sale to
Illinois and Wabash Land companies, 296
Indian trade: demand for furs and
skins in Europe and China, 17;
economic basis, 18; rivalry of
England and France for, 18; their
conflict along the trader's frontier,
19; rapid westward movement of
Pennsylvania traders, 21-22, 27-
29; packhorses used, 29; articles
bartered, 30; how financed, 30;
relative advantages of English and
French, 42, 68; bad character of
white traders, 43; danger to life,
45; regulation in Pennsylvania before 1754, 55; rivalry of English
and French for trade in Ohio region, 59 ff.; regulation by Pennsyl-

DATE DUE

JUL 27			
MAY 2 '73			
E H			
MAR 30 76			
GAYLORD			PRINTED IN U.S.A.